Suddenly, I couldn't believe my eyes. First one, then three gooks appeared out of the jungle and started down the trail. I knew instantly they had no idea we were less than 100 meters above. I quietly passed word that we would all shoot at once, two with the bolt rifles and the other four with their M14s with iron sights.

What a deal! In all my time in Vietnam, I'd never had a chance like this one. As we waited, five more gooks appeared, bringing the total to nine—all wearing uniforms and carrying rifles and packs. They moved slowly but with confidence. We waited a few more minutes. I wanted to be sure the nine were not the point element for a whole company.

When I was sure the nine were alone, I whispered, "Now," and six shots cracked nearly as one. Six gooks dropped. We'd done it! We'd hit six for six. . . .

By Michael Lee Lanning

THE ONLY WAR WE HAD: *A Platoon Leader's Journal of Vietnam*
VIETNAM 1969–1970: *A Company Commander's Journal*
INSIDE THE LRRPS: *Rangers in Vietnam*
INSIDE FORCE RECON: *Recon Marines in Vietnam* (with Ray W. Stubbe)
THE BATTLES OF PEACE
INSIDE THE VC AND THE NVA: *The Real Story of North Vietnam's Armed Forces* (with Dan Cragg)
VIETNAM AT THE MOVIES
SENSELESS SECRETS: *The Failures of U.S. Military Intelligence*
THE MILITARY 100: *A Ranking of the Most Influential Military Leaders of All Time*
THE AFRICAN-AMERICAN SOLDIER: *From Crispus Attucks to Colin Powell*

INSIDE THE CROSSHAIRS

Snipers in Vietnam

Michael Lee Lanning

IVY BOOKS • NEW YORK

An Ivy Book
Published by The Ballantine Publishing Group
Copyright © 1998 by Michael Lee Lanning

All rights reserved under International and Pan-American Copyright Conventions. Published in the United States by The Ballantine Publishing Group, a division of Random House, Inc., New York, and simultaneously in Canada by Random House of Canada Limited, Toronto.

http://www.randomhouse.com

Library of Congress Catalog Card Number: 98-92560

ISBN 0-8041-1620-2

Manufactured in the United States of America

First Edition: September 1998

10 9 8 7 6

To
Gerald Hugh "Gerry" Corcoran

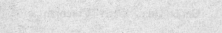

✳✳✳✳✳✳✳✳

Contents

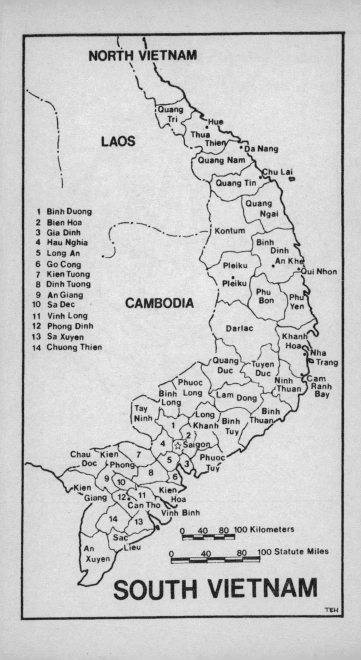

NORTH VIETNAM

LAOS

1 Binh Duong
2 Bien Hoa
3 Gia Dinh
4 Hau Nghia
5 Long An
6 Go Cong
7 Kien Tuong
8 Dinh Tuong
9 An Giang
10 Sa Dec
11 Vinh Long
12 Phong Dinh
13 Sa Xuyen
14 Chuong Thien

CAMBODIA

Quang
Tri
Hue
Thua
Thien
Da Nang
Quang Nam
Chu Lai
Quang Tin
Quang
Ngai
Kontum
Binh
Dinh
An Khe
Pleiku
Qui Nhon
Pleiku
Phu
Bon
Phu
Yen
Darlac
Khanh
Hoa
Nha
Trang
Quang
Duc
Tuyen
Duc
Ninh
Thuan
Cam
Ranh
Bay
Phuoc
Long
Lam Dong
Binh
Long
Long
Khanh
Binh
Tuy
Binh
Thuan
Tay
Ninh
1
2
Saigon
4
Chau
Doc
Kien
Phong
7
5
3
Phuoc
Tuy
9
8
6
10
Kien
Giang
11
12
Kien
Hoa
Can Tho
14
13
Vinh Binh
An
Xuyen
Sac
Lieu

0 40 80 100 Kilometers

0 40 80 100 Statute Miles

SOUTH VIETNAM

TEH

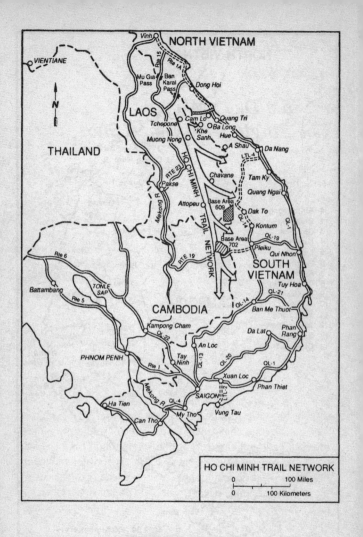

VIENTIANE

NORTH VIETNAM

Vinh

Rte 15 Rte 1A

Mu Gia
Pass

Ban
Karai
Pass

Dong Hoi

LAOS

Tchepone

Cam Lo

Quang Tri

Ba Long

Khe
Sanh

Hue

THAILAND

Muong Nong

A Shau

Da Nang

LTL-1

Chavane

Tam Ky

Quang Ngai

RTE 23

HO CHI MINH

Pakse

Attopeu

Base Area
609

Dak To

QL-1

Mekong R.

Se Kong R.

TRAIL NETWORK

Kontum

QL-19

Pleiku

Qui Nhon

Base Area
702

SOUTH
VIETNAM

RTE 19

Tuy Hoa

QL-21

CAMBODIA

QL-14

Ban Me Thuot

Rte 6

Kampong Cham

Da Lat

Phan
Rang

TONLE
SAP

Rte 5

QL-22

An Loc

QL-13

QL-20

QL-1

Battambang

Tay
Ninh

Xuan Loc

Phan Thiet

PHNOM PENH

Rte 1

Mekong R.

QL-4

SAIGON

QL-15

Ha Tien

My Tho

Vung Tau

Can Tho

HO CHI MINH TRAIL NETWORK

0   100 Miles

0   100 Kilometers

CHAPTER 1

✳✳✳✳✳✳✳✳

All in a Day's Work: The Single Well-Aimed Shot

As a "different" kind of war, Vietnam required tactics, operational procedures, and weapons uniquely adapted for the conflict. The U.S. Army and Marine Corps especially had to constantly adjust fighting concepts—revamping tried-and-true techniques and designing innovative methods—to counter an enemy whose operations varied from Vietcong hit-and-run guerrilla tactics to North Vietnamese Army multi-division offensives.

Of all these adjustments and changes during the war, one of the most effective, and certainly the most economical, was the use of individual marksmen known as snipers. While taking advantage of individual marksmanship skills was clearly not new to warfare, the way the U.S. military developed the expertise to new standards in Southeast Asia certainly was. In terms of the efficiency they achieved, army and Marine marksmen consistently engaged and killed enemy soldiers at ranges often exceeding 800 meters with a single round from special, telescope-equipped rifles. From the densely forested mountain highlands near the Demilitarized Zone to the open spaces of the watery Mekong River Delta, American snipers consistently downed enemy soldiers before their targets even heard the crack of their rifles.

In terms of economics, the innovative use of snipers in Vietnam meant that virtually every bullet produced a body count—a statistic drastically different from bullet-to-body ratios for other wars and other infantrymen in Vietnam. Studies of frontline combat during World War II reveal that U.S.

troops expended 25,000 small arms rounds for every enemy soldier they killed. In the Korean War the number doubled to 50,000 rounds per enemy death. By the time the United States went to war in Southeast Asia, technological advances in weapons had made it possible to place a fully automatic rifle in the hands of every American infantryman, and the firepower of fully automatic "rock and roll" resulted in the expenditure of 200,000 rounds of ammunition for every enemy body.

Army and Marine snipers, on the other hand, produced a dead enemy for nearly every round fired. U.S. snipers in Vietnam averaged one kill for every 1.3 to 1.7 rounds expended. According to Lieutenant General John H. Hay Jr., who commanded the army's 1st Infantry Division in 1967 and wrote *Tactical and Material Innovations* as a part of the Department of the Army's Vietnam Studies series in 1974, "The use of snipers was not new in Vietnam, but the systematic training and employment of an aggressive, offensive sniper team—a carefully designed 'weapon system'—was. A sniper was no longer just the man in the rifle squad who carried the sniper rifle; he was the product of an established school."

Yet, when the United States entered the Vietnam War, it had no trained snipers or sniper units. Although the military had organized, trained, and fielded snipers during earlier U.S. conflicts, sniper units had been quickly disbanded and the shooters discharged or returned to the ranks of the infantry when peace returned. Expert marksmen, who could fire with no warning and kill with a single shot, were necessities of war that, at times of peace, a "fair-minded" American society preferred to forget ever existed.

But at war again, both services recognized the need to renew sniper training. The Marines fielded their first sniper teams in Vietnam in October 1965; the army, a bit slower, did not begin in-country sniper training until the spring of 1968. In the meantime, a few expert Army riflemen secured sniper weapons left over from the Korean War and rifles used by marksmanship competition teams to unofficially begin adapting to the unique war zone.

Even though policy eventually caught up with practicality and snipers received official sanction and support, what became one of the war's most efficient "weapon systems" was ultimately the direct result of the individual men behind the scopes. These men met the established criteria for acceptance into training and most often exceeded the expectations of their commanders. In doing so, they used their native talents and acquired skills to eliminate the enemy and save American lives.

Lieutenant General Julian J. Ewell, who assumed command of the 9th Infantry Division in February 1968 and took the leadership role in establishing army snipers in Vietnam, recorded some of his experiences with snipers and their expertise in *Sharpening the Combat Edge*, another Vietnam Studies title, in 1974. Ewell wrote, "Our most successful sniper was Sergeant Adelbert F. Waldron III, who had 109 confirmed kills to his credit. One afternoon he was riding along the Mekong River on a Tango boat when an enemy sniper on shore pecked away at the boat. While everyone else on board strained to find the antagonist, who was firing from the shoreline over 900 meters away, Sergeant Waldron took up his sniper rifle and picked off the Vietcong out of the top of a coconut tree with one shot (this from a moving platform). Such was the capability of our best sniper. We had others, too, with his matchless vision and expert marksmanship."

The following individual accounts provide a look into the typical day's work of American snipers in Vietnam.

Gary M. White of Utica, New York, joined the Marine Corps in January 1969 and shortly thereafter reported to Parris Island for boot camp. The following September, White arrived in Vietnam, where he joined M Company, 3rd Battalion, 26th Regiment, 1st Marine Division. White recalls, "I had been in Vietnam for a couple of months when a sergeant with a sniper team temporarily attached to the company said they needed recruits for the regiment's scout-sniper platoon. I volunteered.

After an interview to confirm that I had shot expert* in basic, I went to Da Nang for sniper training.

"The sniper school issued me a Remington Model 700 rifle with a 3X9 variable-power scope that had an internal 600-meter range finder. I was already a good shot before the training but during the ten-day school I became even better. The 'bolt rifle,' as we called the Remington, was a great weapon. I never had any trouble with it.

"Upon graduation I reported to the 26th Marine Regiment Headquarters Company Scout-Sniper Platoon. It had a lieutenant platoon commander, a platoon sergeant, an armorer, and twenty-eight snipers organized into fourteen two-man teams. Most everyone was twenty years old like myself or a year or so younger or older. Me and one Marine from Connecticut and a surfer from California were the only ones not from the South or the western mountain states. Most had done a lot of game hunting before joining the corps.

"Like every newly assigned sniper, I began as the observer, searching for targets, spotting rounds, and providing security for the primary shooter. Due to lots of guys completing their tours, I moved up from observer to shooter after only a few weeks.

"My first mission as the senior team member came in November 1969. As soon as I got the order, I went to a makeshift firing range at the edge of the base and 'doped,' or zeroed, my weapon. I reconfirmed my zero with three or four shots and then packed up my rucksack for the mission. We snipers usually went pretty light in the field since we rarely stayed out more than five days to a week. I wore camouflage utilities made up of a pattern of shades of green, tan, and black along with a soft-brim boonie hat and the issue jungle boots.

"In addition to carrying my Remington 700, I strapped a

---

*The Marine Corps and the army trained recruits with M14s early in the war and with M16s later in the conflict. Although the ranges (50–500 meters), firing positions, and the number of rounds fired (40–80) varied with the service and the time period, generally, shooters whose hits totaled 90 percent qualified as expert; those who scored 75–89 percent qualified as sharpshooter; and those who scored 60–74 percent qualified as marksman.

.45-caliber Thompson submachine gun and extra magazines on my rucksack and had a standard M1911 .45-caliber pistol on my web gear. Some snipers carried only the pistol, but I liked the idea of having the Thompson if we got into any close-in fighting. We never planned on more than a few shots on each mission with the Remington, but I carried fifty of the 7.62-mm match-grade rounds—better too many than too few. Water, some C rations, weapons-cleaning gear, and a lightweight camouflage poncho liner rounded out my equipment load.

"My observer dressed the same and had about the same gear. Instead of a bolt rifle he carried an M14 or an M16 to provide more firepower. He also usually had a pair of binoculars and a Starlight scope* for night observation that could also be mounted on the M14 for sniping after dark.

"My observer and I joined a grunt company of the 3rd Battalion north of Da Nang at Hill 190. We reported to the company commander, who, like all the field commanders, treated us real well. They seemed to like having a sniper team along. Of course, they knew we were assigned to the regimental headquarters and would return there after the mission.

"After we joined the company, the commander assigned us a radio operator and a security team for times we might be separated from the main force, like doing a 'stay behind' to see if anyone was following after the unit moved on. During movement we usually walked with the company command post in the center of the formation. In addition to 'stay behinds' we occasionally set up on a hillside and provided an overwatch of the company's march.

"Since this was my first mission as a team leader, I really didn't expect much to happen. However, only a few hours into the march, as we were advancing into what we called Elephant Valley, I heard the company commander order, 'Sniper up!' My observer and I quickly moved to the front of the company on the side of a gentle slope, where the point man directed

---

*A Starlight scope is an electronic-image intensifier that uses reflected light from the stars or moon to identify targets. For additional information see Chapter 10 "Tools of the Trade: Arms and Equipment."

our attention to five figures moving away from us at a distance of about 500 meters along a trail in the valley below. The company commander turned to me and said, 'This is a free-fire zone. Those guys don't belong here. Shoot if you want to.'

"Through my scope I could see the five were carrying heavy packs and wore a mixture of uniforms and civilian dress. I braced my rifle and squeezed off a shot. By the time I regained the sight picture I could see my target going down. I swung around to try to get another shot but the other gooks quickly melted into the surrounding jungle.

"We moved down the hill and found the body and a pack full of medical supplies and rice. One shot, one kill. Man, I was excited, completely exhilarated. It was like hitting a home run.

"Over the next few months I went out on many more missions with the infantry as well as doing some tower duty at various fire bases. Before the 26th Regiment withdrew from Vietnam the following March, I got three more confirmed kills for a total of four. I had five more unconfirmed, but unless we put a foot on the body or an officer could visually verify it, we did not claim a confirmed kill—even if there was a heavy blood trail.

"I think the enemy knew the regiment was getting ready to pull out, so activity was not all that great in our area. Some of the other snipers in my platoon had more kills, some less. A couple got wounded, but we did not lose a single sniper in the six months I was there. They were a great bunch of guys—a whole different breed, real professionals."

Army and Marine snipers differed in their unit organization and in their individual weapons, but their general operational procedures were remarkably similar. Two-man sniper teams operated with infantry companies in the field or provided long-range firepower from various base camps and fire bases. Sniper teams also accompanied army long-range reconnaissance patrols (LRRPs) and Marine reconnaissance units. On occasion, with an infantry team of five to ten men to provide security and communications, they operated semi-independently. Still other snipers, especially in army units, returned to their companies after training, becoming unit snipers like their predecessors in World War II and the Korean conflict.*

Snipers in Vietnam, like other Americans in the war zone, did not remain static in their tactics and methods of operations. They changed, modified, or invented whatever was necessary to successfully engage and destroy the enemy.

Marine Sergeant Ed Kugler, who served as a sniper with the 4th Regiment of the 3rd Marine Division for two years after his arrival in-country in March 1966, performed all the usual missions, including a confirmed kill at 1,300 meters from a fire base at Con Thien in the fall of 1966.

Kugler, from Lock Seventeen, Ohio, enlisted in the corps on June 18, 1964, and was wounded on April 30, 1965, in the Dominican Republic campaign. Kugler arrived at the replacement center at Da Nang in March 1966. There, an NCO from the recently established 3rd Marine Division Scout-Sniper School spoke to the replacements, soliciting volunteers. "He did the great sales job," Kugler remembers, "and I bought it." After three weeks of training, Kugler and his Winchester Model 70 and telescopic sight joined the 4th Marine Regiment Scout-Sniper Platoon.

For the next year Kugler worked with Marine companies in his regiment, performed sniper duties from platforms and ground positions at fire bases, and spent several months attached to the division's Force Recon Company. By June 1967, Kugler, on a second-tour extension, was one of the most experienced snipers in his platoon. Tired of the typical sniper missions, Kugler had an idea for something different that he thought would produce better results.

Kugler and his chain of command convinced the regiment

*Motion pictures, novels, and even a few nonfiction books have portrayed Vietnam snipers routinely acting alone, without communications, and far from friendly lines. While good fiction, these stories are simply not true of actual sniper operations in Southeast Asia.

commander to permit the platoon to conduct semi-independent operations with teams composed entirely of snipers. Over the next six months, the special sniper teams, operating in groups as small as four and as large as eight, conducted missions organized around two shooters armed with scope-equipped bolt rifles. Other team members carried M14s in addition to at least one M79 grenade launcher and one M60 machine gun. They planned their missions carefully, coordinating with artillery and air support as well as with a regiment reaction company that stood ready to be airlifted to support the team or to secure its extraction.

Kugler's sniper team used the radio call sign Rogues. He recalls, "We worked mostly out of Camp Evans and Hill 51 into the Co Bi Than Tan Valley, between Laos and the Ashau Valley. We would move onto a hillside and camouflage ourselves and then watch the valley below. We saw lots of small groups of VC and NVA. Most were minus a man or two after we took them under fire.

"We usually traveled at night to our positions. We also had fallback locations to which we could vanish after we fired or if we were compromised. We'd generally hide all day. Most of our shooting took place during the first hour of daylight and the last hour before dark.

"We did do some day shooting. One afternoon six of us set up on a rise to observe an open area about 400 meters across a river. About two in the afternoon we saw a soldier carrying a rifle and a pack step out into the clearing. In a few minutes a couple more joined him. Soon I had counted 110 fully armed NVA. I called in artillery, and when it was in the air, me and the other sniper squeezed off a few rounds. We knocked down four before the artillery shells began to impact. We then called in an air strike. The forward air observer made a low pass over the clearing and counted thirty-five bodies.

"Not all of our shots were at long range. In the fall of 1967 we were operating at the northeast end of the valley. On day three of a five-day mission we were on a small hill overlooking some dense jungle vegetation now choking a deserted village. There was a trail running to right and left, somewhat toward us, connecting a trail that came by our hide position.

"We were all camouflaged into the grass and underbrush about four feet high. It was a seriously hot day and about to get hotter. We were aligned left to right, six of us. I was in the middle with my radioman to my left, close enough that I could gain eye contact with everyone.

"Suddenly, I couldn't believe my eyes. First one, then three gooks appeared out of the jungle and started down the trail. I knew instantly they had no idea we were less than 100 meters above. I quietly passed word that we would all shoot at once, two with the bolt rifles and the other four with their M14s with iron sights.

"What a deal! In all my time in Vietnam, I'd never had a chance like this one. As we waited, five more gooks appeared, bringing the total to nine—all wearing uniforms and carrying rifles and packs. They moved slowly but with confidence. We waited a few more minutes. I wanted to be sure the nine were not the point element for a whole company.

"When I was sure that the nine were alone, I whispered, 'Now,' and six shots cracked nearly as one. Six gooks dropped. We'd done it! We'd hit six for six. The other three really freaked and dashed for the jungle. We got one more but the other two disappeared like a streak of fire. They never returned a single round at us or even knew our position.

"We watched the bodies for about an hour to see if anyone came to retrieve them. Then with four guys providing cover, me and another Marine crept into the kill zone. All of the dead gooks were real young. Just kids. But, hell, so were we. We recovered two AK-47s, three carbines, and a bunch of grenades and papers. The team then quickly withdrew to another position. We'd had a successful day. Sniper Rogues 7, Gooks 0.

"During six months of action, the Rogue sniper team, never more than eight men, accounted for 105 confirmed enemy kills. We had several guys wounded but none killed."

Army snipers trained and operated quite like their Marine counterparts. Sergeant Ed W. Eaton of Walla Walla, Washington, entered active duty in October 1968 and arrived in Vietnam the following May as an infantryman in B Company, 3rd Battalion, 60th Infantry, 9th Infantry Division. Eaton recalls, "From the first time I heard that the division had a sniper school, I was interested. I immediately requested the opportunity to attend. I wanted to be a sniper worse than anything— well, not more than a bartender in Saigon or a general's aide, but if I had to be a grunt this is what I wanted."

Eaton attended one of the army's first formal sniper classes, those conducted by the 9th Infantry Division, and during his last six months in-country accounted for twenty-seven successful engagements of enemy personnel. "Like the other units in the 9th," Eaton remembers, "we had the usual forms of employment, including setting up with infantry companies to cover opportune fields of fire. We also conducted night hunter missions, where members of a two-man team would occupy each door of a Huey helicopter and cruise the rivers after dark. Using Starlight scopes, we would look for targets. When we spotted the bad guys, we shot a tracer round at them. Then two Cobra gunships would roll in and hose down the area."

Most of Eaton's kills were at ranges of 500 meters or more—but not all. On one occasion Eaton went on a company sweep operation during which the unit established a defensive position near an abandoned village shortly before sundown. According to Eaton, "The company commander asked me to set up just outside the perimeter to keep an eye on the village. After it got good and dark, I quietly moved out to my position to scan the area through the fuzzy green hue of my Starlight scope. Immediately to my front, only fifty meters away, I spotted a VC squatting near a hootch. He must have heard me moving, because he was cupping his hands to his ears to hear better. He may have *heard* me, but I *saw* him. I froze and then watched to see if he was alone or maybe part of a larger element. Nothing moved for several minutes; I decided it was time to do away with this guy and find myself a better location. I knocked him on his back with one shot—my shortest as a sniper."

Eaton, who turned twenty-one while in sniper school, also had success on the night hunter missions. "We were flying at 500 feet one evening. I lay on the chopper's floor looking out over the side through a Starlight scope mounted on my M21 rifle.* Suddenly I observed a sampan on a river with one person aboard. The waterway was closed to all but military navigation, and it was after curfew. I prepared to fire. It's hard to hit anything from a moving helicopter, especially since you are shooting downward through lots of turbulence, but all I had to do was get close.

"I shot a tracer to mark the target," Eaton continues, "and waited for the Cobras to fire up the area. They swept in, illuminated the sampan with their searchlights, and then broke off without firing. When we returned to base to refuel, I asked the Cobra pilots, 'Why didn't you guys fire? Was it a woman or a kid?' "

"The lead pilot laughed and said, 'No, man; there was nothing left for us. You got him right in the chest. That was a great shot.'

"I added the kill to my count. But I must admit, it had to be my luckiest shot."

Despite these exciting, successful missions, Eaton adds, "Mostly sniping is a boring, lonely job. You wait hour after hour taking turns on the scope or Starlight with your partner. Sometimes one shot, one kill. At other times you spot so many of the bad guys that you have to call in artillery and air support while you just watch and direct the show. Then you pick up and go home, only to go out on another mission and then another. Sniping in Vietnam was not always a perfect science. Charlie would show you a different face every time—the man who was best prepared and had the best all-round weapon won, and that is what life is all about. Death may be a sniper's job, but surviving was also my goal."

* * *

*An M21 is a modified 7.62mm M14 rifle that served as the army's standard sniper weapon system during the war. For additional information see Chapter 10 "Tools of the Trade: Weapons and Equipment" and Appendix A "Sniper Rifle Systems Used in Vietnam."

White, Kugler, Eaton, and hundreds of other Marine and army snipers in Vietnam proved that long-range shooters still had a place on the battlefield—and they proceeded to take their role to a new level. Combining modern technology in weapons, ammunition, and telescopes, U.S. snipers in Vietnam used the experience and traditions of centuries of precision shooters to perfect their craft. They made such a lasting impression that even after the war in Vietnam finally ended, the one-shot killers remained an active and important component of the armed forces of the United States.

CHAPTER 2

✳✳✳✳✳✳✳✳

The First Marksmen:
From Stones to Gunpowder

BY definition a sniper is someone who uses a special weapon system to shoot at an individual from a protected area far from the target. Logically, then, the history of snipers and sniping parallels the development of weaponry. In turn, the development of weaponry follows the history of warfare, which is as old as mankind itself and varies little from the struggles of other creatures. The needs for food, propagation, and territory inevitably lead to conflict among and between all species, mankind's intelligence and culture notwithstanding.

What sets man apart is not his desire to eat, mate, or survive—or even his desire to dominate his environment. Rather, the distinguishing factor is his ability to develop weapons and master skills using them to overcome opposition. Likewise, what has set the sniper apart from other warriors is the ability to maximize accuracy and stealth to neutralize the enemy from a distance.

For hundreds of thousands of years warfare more resembled "the hunt" than modern combat. Humans were few, space and resources were vast, and little need or reason existed for men to engage in warfare with each other. Yet archaeology reveals the steady evolution in armament, from early man's throwing of stones to his constructing instruments of battle that included rocks tied to wooden clubs. Refinements led to tapered points attached to sticks, which became spears and javelins, and sharpened broad heads on wooden handles, which became axes. While brute strength and excellent reflexes remained the most important characteristics of a warrior, accuracy was a close second.

Recent discoveries suggest evidence of human, or at least humanlike, activity on Earth more than one million years ago. While clubs and rudimentary axes were the mainstay of early man's arsenal, the evolution of weaponry during most of this period focused on further shaping and refining flint spear points. At some point, man adapted eighteen-inch to two-foot wooden handles with convex ends to hold stones. These throwing sticks basically lengthened the hunter's arm, allowing him to throw projectiles with more force and for longer distances.

As early as 30,000 B.C., humans used leather slings to propel stones and short spears. About this same time the bow appeared, enabling early man to shoot arrows to kill his food and to engage his human enemies—especially from afar. The most important aspect of these early weapons is that they shared a characteristic with all arms that followed: they were only as effective as the skills of the individuals who used them.

By 10,000 B.C., man had developed agriculture, domesticated animals, mastered pottery, and established stable communities. As polished projectiles replaced crudely chipped arrow and spear points, man experimented with stronger bow materials and better strings to increase the distance and penetration power of his arrows.

The evolution of weaponry took a quantum leap when man discovered the properties of copper about 3500 B.C. and learned to mix the metal with tin to form bronze, allowing him to refine his arsenal as well as enhance his jewelry and household utensils. In about 1000 B.C., development of the technique of smelting iron into a harder, more rigid metal added to man's ability to further improve his weapons for hunting and fighting. Metallurgy technology, however, advanced slowly, and widespread use of iron did not take place until the fourteenth century B.C. in Asia Minor and the eleventh century B.C. in Europe.*

---

*All of these dates are, of course, approximate and dependent on subsequent archaeological discoveries. Also, the use of weapons and metals in one part of the world does not indicate that they were universal. For instance, the use of iron did not reach Africa until centuries after iron became common in Europe, and iron did not penetrate the New World until introduced to it by European explorers in the fifteenth and sixteenth centuries.

Any description of exactly how the ancients employed their evolving weapons must be supposition because the development of written languages did not occur until long after man had spent hundreds of centuries hunting and warring. One fairly early written record of a battle describes a confrontation between the young Egyptian pharaoh Thutmosis III and revolting tribes of Palestine and Syria. In 1469 B.C., Thutmosis defeated the rebels at Megiddo Pass, north of Mount Carmel, Palestine, using a crescent formation of soldiers armed with swords and spears and supported by bowmen.

That battle epitomizes the centuries-old tactic of using massed formations, in which overall strength is more important than individual accuracy. The only weapons capable of reaching a range farther than arm's length—arrows, thrown spears, rocks from slings, and rudimentary catapults—were usually employed in mass volleys rather than single aimed shots.

There were exceptions. An early example of a single soldier's overwhelming a larger, stronger opponent appears in the Bible's Old Testament. According to Samuel, chapter 17, when the Philistine and Israelite armies met (about the eleventh century B.C.), Goliath, a Philistine giant standing more than nine feet tall and protected by a brass helmet, chain mail, and an iron shield, challenged the Israelites to produce a champion to meet him on the plain between the two armies in individual combat.

According to verse 11, the Israelites "were dismayed, and greatly afraid." Only a shepherd boy with no battle experience volunteered. Refusing armor and sword, David selected five smooth stones from a nearby brook for his sling before he advanced against Goliath. Verse 49 notes, "And David put his hand in his bag, and took thence a stone, and slang it, and smote the Philistine in his forehead, that the stone sunk into his forehead; and he fell upon his face to the earth."

David ran to the stunned Goliath and decapitated the giant with his own sword. The inspired Israeli army proceeded to attack and destroy the enemy army. A single, well-aimed stone had turned the battle and won the day.

From the earliest records to modern accounts, however, historical documents generally focus on the accomplishments of field commanders and their armies. Cyrus the Great is one early military commander about whom substantial records of conquest have survived. From 546 B.C. until his death about seventeen years later, Cyrus established the Persian Empire by conquest.

The key to Cyrus's strength was his concentration of great numbers into tight, mutually supporting formations. His soldiers fought shoulder to shoulder against the enemy, doing their damage with the spear and sword. At that time armies often numbered as large as 50,000, with soldiers massed twenty men deep into lines only 2,500 meters long.

Slings, spears, and arrows still played a role, but protective armor and chain mail decreased their effectiveness. A single, well-aimed projectile remained important, however, and, on occasion, alone could sway the outcome of a battle. In 401 B.C., Cyrus the Younger, supported by 13,000 Greek mercenaries, attempted to take the Persian throne from his brother, Artaxerxes II. Cyrus and his army were on the verge of victory at the Battle of Cunaxa when an unidentified Persian soldier hurled a spear at Cyrus, striking him just below the eye and killing him. Cyrus's army immediately retreated homeward.

While swords and spears dominated the battlefield for thousands of years, the use of the bow and arrow inevitably influenced combat. When communities went to war against their neighbors, bowmen, who had skillfully hunted for food and successfully competed in holiday and festival shooting contests, joined the ranks of the army in archery sections. Once in battle, bowmen fired in volley at a high angle (to send their arrows over the defenders' shields) or directly at unprotected troops. Archers also aimed their missiles at cavalrymen and horse-drawn chariots that began appearing with armies as early as 1000 B.C. The very best men with the bow, however, often operated semi-independently to deliver single, well-aimed arrows at enemy leaders.

Although bowmen contributed to the outcomes of battles, most soldiers disdained them, believing the archers to be cowardly fellows who skulked on the outer edges of battlefields in relative safety waiting for the opportunity to launch arrows against better, braver men.

As populations multiplied and nations formed around political and religious leaders, warfare increased in frequency and scale. Yet, for the time bow and arrow marksmanship remained secondary to the sword and spear, which ruled the battlefield. When those standard weapons were not enough to guarantee success, adaptations appeared. Macedonian Alexander the Great conquered much of the known world between 336 and 323 B.C. with an army built around infantrymen armed with fourteen-foot-long pikes, twice the length of his enemies' spears.

Julius Caesar, expanding the Roman Empire between 59 and 44 B.C., wrote in his third-person account of the battle that defeated the Gauls titled *The Gallic War*, "The situation was critical and as no reserves were available, Caesar seized a shield from a soldier in the rear and made his way to the front line. He addressed each centurion by name and shouted encouragement to the rest of the troops, ordering them to push forward and open out their ranks so they could use their swords more easily. His coming gave them fresh heart and hope. Each man wanted to do his best under the eyes of his commander despite the peril."

But the spear and sword tactics would encounter changes that would alter the face of warfare. Legions of Rome lost a relatively insignificant battle at Carrhae in 53 B.C. that provided a preview of the future. Parthian (Iranian) cavalry armed with bows attacked Roman infantry under the command of Consul Crassus. The 10,000 Parthian cavalry, supported by 1,000 camels that carried nothing but extra arrows to resupply the mounted bowmen, annihilated the equal-size Roman force.

The horse-mounted bowman would soon rule the battlefield, but only after another innovation. Because an early cavalryman riding bareback or on a padded blanket had only his horse's mane to hold on to, shooting arrows accurately and reloading quickly proved to be extremely difficult. The invention of the saddle with stirrups, probably in India during the first century B.C., provided cavalrymen a stable platform from which to fight, making it one of the most significant military developments in five hundred years.

In the fifth century A.D. the first army composed almost entirely of horse-mounted archers conquered much of southern Europe and challenged the might of the Roman Empire. Attila the Hun, known as the Scourge of God to his enemies, assembled an army of 100,000 soldiers. Each Hun soldier rode into battle mounted on horseback and armed with a bow and multiple quivers of arrows. He led from one to seven additional horses that carried additional arrows, water, and all the supplies need for an extended campaign.

Hun bowmen could accurately shoot arrows up to 100 meters at individual targets and double that distance by firing at a high angle. Swords, axes, and maces rounded out the Huns' arsenal for close-in fighting, but the bow became their most influential weapon on the battlefield; the proficiency of individual bowmen had finally gained status. Some accounts suggest there were Huns who could shoot down a bird in flight or pierce an enemy's eye at 100 meters.

For killing at a distance, the range of the weapon and the personal proficiency of the warrior had become the most important characteristics for successful engagement. Those traits only increased in significance with the next major advance, which had the greatest impact on warfare to date.

No records document the exact development date of the crossbow, but the Chinese historical work titled *Shih chi*, composed about 100 B.C., mentions the use of the weapon in the battle of Maling, China, in 341 B.C. The Chinese document also notes that the weapon had uses beyond the battlefield. According to the *Shih chi*, Chinese emperor Ch'in Shih, who died in 210 B.C., gave instructions for preparations of his tomb and "commanded the artisans to make automatic crossbows and arrows so that if anyone dug in and entered they would suddenly shoot and slay them."

The crossbow first appeared in Europe with the Roman

army in the first century A.D. F. Vegetius Renatus notes in his writings of A.D. 386, *De Re Militari,* that crossbowmen were a regular part of the Roman army. The fact that the author does not go into detail probably indicates that the weapon had been present for some time. Art of the period in France and Rome shows soldiers armed with crossbows.

With the fall of the Romans in the fifth century A.D., the crossbow mostly disappeared from Europe for 500 years. Because Rome's enemies did not adopt the crossbow, the bow, sword, and pike remained the primary weapons.

The crossbow did not reappear on the Continent until improvements in its bow, arming mechanism, and projectiles again brought it to the forefront as Europeans prepared to embark on Crusades to "liberate" the Holy Land. Composition materials had made the bow stronger and levers allowed the operator to more easily pull the draw string to the trigger. These modifications increased the weapon's range to 150 meters. Wooden shafts with iron tips, known as bolts, replaced the traditional arrows and could penetrate armor and chain mail.

Crossbowmen carried hundreds of bolts and copied the archers' technique of firing in volley. However, marksmen who proved their accuracy with the weapon sought and engaged individual targets. These early marksmen were often successful in bringing down enemy leaders. English King Richard the Lionhearted, after gaining success and fame in the Crusades, returned home to engage enemies in Europe. In 1199, a crossbowman in the army of the Bishop of Limoges fired a bolt into Richard's shoulder during a minor skirmish. Gangrene set in, and the single, well-aimed crossbow bolt resulted in the death of the English king.

In 1453 another crossbowman turned the tide of an entire battle with a single bolt. An unidentified soldier in the Ottoman army of Mohammed II, the Conqueror, fired a bolt that seriously wounded John Giustiniani, the leader of the defenders of Constantinople. With Giustiniani no longer able to rally his men, the Ottomans quickly overran the defenses and captured the city.

The effectiveness of the crossbow greatly increased the lethality of the battlefield and the opportunities for individual marksmen. Used by infantry and cavalry alike, the crossbow soon earned the reputation as warfare's first "ultimate weapon," and some even wondered if it would make combat so deadly that it might end war altogether. Such conjecture, of course, proved invalid, but the crossbow did provoke history's first recorded example of arms control. A Vatican edict in 1139 outlawed the use of the crossbow in warfare between Christians. Its use, however, against Moslems and other "infidels" remained within reasonable limits.

Despite its advantages over standard bows and arrows of range, power, and accuracy, the crossbow was far from being the perfect weapon. Its weight of up to sixteen pounds was cumbersome, and the levered draw string made it difficult to reload. Challenging the crossbow in range and power by the late thirteenth century was the longbow, introduced by English King Edward I. Archers with these 100-to-150-pound-pull, six-foot bows could nearly match the range of crossbows but could reload and fire six times as fast. In the Battle of Crécy in 1346, English longbowmen achieved a decisive victory over the Genoese, the elite of European crossbowmen. Even though the crossbow remained an integral part of armies across Europe and Asia, it more and more became a defensive device used to protect the parapets of fortresses during siege warfare rather than to support mobile operations.

The debate over bows versus crossbows continued until another advance in military weaponry—based on old technology—made them both obsolete. As early as 500 B.C. armies had been using flaming petroleum-based weapons, known as "Greek fire," by launching the incendiaries with catapults or pouring them from defensive walls. Not until sixteen centuries later, however, did anyone attempt to record the procedures for manufacturing such armaments. A late-twelfth-century manuscript attributed to Marcus Graecus, and titled *Liber Ignium ad Comburendos Hostes (The Book of Fires for Consuming the Enemy)*, contains recipes for explosive mixtures of various strengths. Graecus even notes that the mixtures might be loaded into "small tubes" that, when fired, would "rise into the air with a great whirring noise."

These early propulsion formulas recorded by Graecus provided little more than entertainment initially. History reveals little about the origins of the chemical mixture of potassium nitrate (saltpeter), wood charcoal, and sulfur that eventually became gunpowder. There is evidence that Roger Bacon, Fellow of Merton College, England, successfully mixed the elements into gunpowder early in the thirteenth century. Spanish inventors must have discovered the correct ingredients at about the same time, for they employed primitive cannons during their defense of Seville in 1247.

Despite this evidence, some historians credit German monk Berthold Schwartz for the invention of gunpowder, citing a drawing in *Buchsenmeisterey-Schul (School of the Art of Gunnery)* by Joseph Furtenbach published in Augsburg in 1643. The picture shows a monk, surrounded by laboratory instruments, creating a small explosion in a crucible. Above the drawing is an inscription, "Portrait of the Venerable and Ingenious Reverend Father called Berthold Schwartz, of the Franciscan order; Doctor, alchemist, and Inventor of the Noble Art of Gunnery in the year 1380." More words below the image explain, "See here what time and nature have brought today through ingenious men: the art of shooting in guns has been born, created out of nature of fire and vapors of nature."

Despite Furtenbach's claims, there is ample evidence that by 1250 the Europeans and the Chinese already knew about the explosiveness of gunpowder. While its discoverer would remain unknown, the destructive power of gunpowder and its influence on the battlefield would dominate all future history.

Apparently the Chinese were satisfied for another century or so to use gunpowder merely for the manufacture of fireworks for use on ceremonial occasions. Europeans, however, recognized its military capabilities and began developing iron tubes that would fire a projectile with the explosive powder. The English began referring to these weapons as "guns," a word apparently derived from the Teutonic words of *gunhilde* and *gundeline*, both meaning "war." By 1340 references to "gonne," "gounne," and "gunne" appeared in English documents. The expenditure accounts of Edward III for February 1, 1345, list payment for the repair and transport of "13 guns with pellets."

By the end of the fourteenth century most European armies had crude cannons in their inventories, the majority of which were dedicated to defense of fortifications. Early handguns appeared at the same time and consisted of short iron or brass tubes less than one foot long with a bore of less than a quarter inch. Shooters poured powder into the tube's open end and tamped a metal or stone shot into the closed base. A "touch hole" allowed the firer to ignite the powder with a coal. These "hand cannons" were extremely difficult to aim and became even more so with repeated firing because the barrel became hot.

Innovators added wooden stocks to control the metal barrels and protect the firer from the weapon's heat. Advances in powder production, particularly the combining of the ingredients into tiny pellets or "corns," provided a quicker firing, more uniform explosive propellent. Touch holes were replaced by a pan to hold a bit of powder to ease ignition of the main charge. Tightly twisted rags soaked in saltpeter to enable them to smolder for long periods replaced coals as igniters. A serpentine device to hold the smoldering "match" could be lowered by hand, and later by a trigger, to touch the pan and fire the weapon. These "matchlocks" allowed the gunner to look at his target and aim his weapon with some degree of accuracy.

By the beginning of the sixteenth century stocks had been shortened and curved to allow better aiming. These weapons, the early ancestors of modern sniper rifles, became known as "hackbuts" in German-speaking areas but more commonly in other areas as "arquebuses," from the French word meaning "hookgun." Arquebuses weighed approximately ten to fifteen pounds and fired a one-ounce ball about three-quarters of an inch in diameter (.75 caliber). With a muzzle velocity of approximately 800 feet per second, these early weapons had a range of 100 to 200 meters. Arquebuses were not without limitations. In rainy, or even damp, weather, the powder would not ignite. Even under perfect conditions a well-trained soldier could manage only two shots every three minutes or so.

Military leaders throughout Europe and Asia Minor began integrating arquebuses into their armies, but the new weapon did not play a major role in a battle until the late fifteenth century. In 1498, Spaniard Fernandez Gonzalo de Cordoba armed some of his men with heavy, shoulder-fired, support-braced arquebuses and integrated them into his ranks of pike-carrying infantry.

In 1503, Cordoba moved his army of 6,000 into Italy to meet an invasion from France. On the afternoon of April 28 the Spanish commander established a defensive position in a hillside vineyard near Cerignola. The Spaniards barely had time to dig shallow trenches before the French force of 10,000 charged their positions. Rank after rank of French infantrymen fell to the arquebuses; the few Frenchmen who reached the trenches died on the points of Spanish pikes. A short time later the French charged for a second time, but again the Spanish held firm. No battlefield would ever be the same again.

On December 29 of the same year, Cordoba crossed the Italian Garigliano River and attacked another French force. The arquebuses and pikes proved as lethal on the offense as they had on the defense and secured victory for the Spanish.

Despite Cordoba's success, crossbows remained the primary infantry weapon in the French army until 1566. The English did not totally adopt firearms until 1596, and the Turks did not replace their archers for another decade after that. But from the time of Cordoba, armies began to increase the number of firearms they employed, and warfare, long characterized by the arrow, the sword, and the pike, became dominated by gunpowder and shot.

Firearms also began to replace bow- or crossbow-launched arrows as the primary civilian hunting weapons. They became even more dominant in hunting and target competitions with the fifteenth-century discovery, attributed to either Gaspard Kollner of Vienna or Augustus Kotter of Nuremberg, that adding grooves to a barrel's interior made the bullet spin rapidly in flight and stabilized its path. This "rifling" gave its name to the more accurate weapons it produced, and rifle marksmanship that would ultimately lead to modern sniping began.

Shooting contests, both for sport and for the maintenance of marksmanship proficiency, rose in popularity with the advances in firearms. Early in the fifteenth century the Holy Roman Empire encouraged the formation of shooting clubs in order to maintain a reserve of marksmen in the event of an invasion by the Turks.

The earliest known, documented, club dedicated to the shooting of firearms began in Lucerne in 1466. Members used their own weapons but the club provided powder and shot for the weekly Sunday competitions. Targets were set at a maximum range of about 100 meters, and the winner of each match judged the results of the next.

Shooting guilds spread rapidly in central Europe during the first decades of the sixteenth century, and soon cities and towns sponsored competitions with their neighbors. More than 200 shooters from as far away as Frankfurt am Main and Innsbruck competed at Zurich in 1504. As shooting skills and weapon manufacturing techniques improved, competition ranges increased to 200 and 300 meters.

Despite continuing technical improvements, firearms remained dependent on dry weather conditions, causing battlefield commanders to continue to rely on pikes, bows, and crossbows in combat. When weather permitted, commanders still used arquebuses to fire in volley and placed little emphasis on marksmanship.

Rifled weapons were expensive to manufacture but their primary limitation in military use was the slow process of having to tamp a leaden bullet down the barrel to ensure it would "take" to the rifling when fired. A few well-armed marksmen, however, began to display the merits of single, well-aimed shots from firearms. Leonardo da Vinci included marksmanship among his many talents. During the defense of Florence in 1520, Da Vinci fired a rifle of his own design from the city's walls to kill enemy soldiers at ranges up to 300 meters.

Another Italian artist, metalsmith, inventor, and marksman,

Benvenuto Cellini, also displayed the merits of accurate gunfire and the spirit of future snipers. During the siege of Rome in 1527, Cellini fired the shot that killed the opposing commander and ended the battle. In his autobiography, Cellini outlined mental characteristics of a good shooter and commented on the "relaxation" produced by engaging a target at long range. Cellini stated, "I will give but one particular, which will astonish good shots of every degree; that is, when I charged my gun with powder weighing one-fifth of the ball, it carried two-hundred paces point-blank. My natural temperament was melancholy, and while I was taking these amusements, my heart leaped with joy, and I found I could work better and with far greater mastery than when I spent my whole time in study and manual labor."

Cellini would not be the last man to experience the satisfaction of skilled marksmanship. As the development of weapons continued, so did individual mastery of their use.

CHAPTER 3

✳✳✳✳✳✳✳✳

Marksmanship in the New World

*A*T the same time that the advancements in the uses and delivery systems of gunpowder were expanding the capabilities of expert marksmen, European explorers were adding to the potential territories where lone shooters would impact history. Hernando Cortés, with a force of fewer than 600 men—supported by twenty horses and ten cannonlike arquebuses—conquered more than five million people by defeating the Aztecs of Central America in 1519. In 1533, another Spaniard, Francisco Pizarro, defeated the Incas in South America with an army of 200 and less than half a dozen firearms.

Both Cortés and Pizarro depended on crossbows as their primary weapons, but the surprise and firepower of their few arquebuses directly influenced their victories over far larger forces. In less than two decades, with only a few hundred men and less than two dozen firearms, they had delivered Central and South America to the Spanish Empire. The culture, language, and religion of the entire region remains today mostly Spanish—a direct result of the introduction of firearms into the New World.

North American explorers and settlers also used firearms to occupy land where native inhabitants, initially armed only with bows and arrows, vastly outnumbered them. French explorer Samuel de Champlain used matchlocks against the Iroquois in July 1609. This account appears in Champlain's diary: "We took, each of us, an arquebus and went ashore. I saw the enemy come out of their barricade to the number of 200, in appearance strong and robust men. I marched on until I was within 30 yards of the enemy. When I saw them make a move to draw their bows upon us, I took aim with my arquebus and shot straight at one of the three chiefs, and with the shot two fell to the ground and one of their companions was wounded. I had put four bullets into my arquebus. The Iroquois were much astonished that two men could have been killed so quickly. As I was reloading my arquebus one of my companions fired a shot which astonished them again, so much that, seeing their chiefs dead, they lost courage and took flight."

While the use of firearms in the New World expanded during the sixteenth and seventeenth centuries, the major improvements in weapons design continued to take place in Europe. In the early 1600s, gunmakers experimented with mechanical devices, first designing wheel locks that rubbed steel and flint together to create sparks that, in turn, ignited the priming powder in the pan. The rotating parts quickly gave way to the "snaphance," an improved mechanism in which flint and steel were propelled together by a heavy V-shaped spring. Even though these were significant developments, both devices were too complex and expensive for general military use. As a result they remained mostly in the hands of wealthy sportsmen and hunters instead of soldiers.

It was not until the middle of the seventeenth century that manufacturers perfected the flintlock mechanism, which would dominate weaponry for more than two centuries.* The flintlock consisted of a spring-loaded hammer that held a flint. When released by the trigger, the hammer-held flint struck a steel edge to produce a spark that ignited the primer powder.

The advantages of the flintlock was that, without the need for lighted matches—which required several yards' separation between soldiers to prevent pre-ignition of each other's weapons—formations could be tighter and produce a heavier volume of fire. However, even though it was a great

---

*Advances in artillery weapons paralleled those of muskets and rifles so that by the seventeenth century artillery shared equal status with the infantry and cavalry on the battlefield.

improvement, the flintlock still had limitations. Despite having a cover for the primer pan that offered some protection against rain and damp, moisture continued to cause ignition problems.

Reliability and safety had increased, but because of the cost and time-consuming reloading procedure inherent to rifles, smooth-bore muskets remained the primary military weapon. In 1645, Englishman Oliver Cromwell's two infantry companies armed with smooth-bore flintlocks directly contributed to the defeat of the Royalists. Other countries quickly adopted the weapons for their armies. By 1670 France had an entire regiment carrying flintlocks.

But soldiers, steeped in tradition and familiar with simple, basic weapons like pikes, did not necessarily trust the new inventions, especially in unfavorable battle conditions. When a rainstorm threatened or a fast advancing enemy did not allow time to reload, infantrymen found their flintlock muskets of use only as clubs. At such times, many infantrymen rammed broken pikes into the musket barrels to form crude bayonets. This did make the weapons into pikes, albeit short ones, but, of course, it also prevented their use as firearms.

About 1680 the Frenchman Marshall Sebastien Le Prestre de Vauban invented the socket bayonet, which mounted outside the barrel and did not interfere with firing the weapon. With that each infantryman could fight as a musketeer and a pikeman. By the end of the century all major armies in Europe were armed with socket-bayonet flintlocks.

The development of paper cartridges further enhanced the flintlock's capabilities. First suggested by Leonardo da Vinci, paper cartridges became common by the end of the sixteenth century and were standard by the end of the seventeenth. With paper cartridges, which contained premeasured amounts of powder, soldiers could reload quickly by biting open the end of the cartridge, pouring the powder down the barrel, tamping the charge with the remaining paper, and then adding the shot.

By the end of the seventeenth century, smooth-bore flintlock muskets dominated civilian and military weaponry in the New World. The first American contribution to firearms manufacture occurred in the Pennsylvania Colony early in the eighteenth century. Immigrants from Germany and Switzerland brought with them skills in crafting weapons and an appreciation for marksmanship and shooting competitions.

Because of the expense of shot and powder, those early American gunsmiths modified European designs to be more economical. They reduced calibers from .69–.75 to .40–.50 and lengthened the 42-inch barrels to as long as 48 inches, which increased velocity by ensuring that all the powder burned before the shot left the barrel. They also greased patches of cloth with pork or bear fat to wrap the shot, which helped seal the charges and prevented gases from escaping. These modifications also improved accuracy by flattening the firing trajectory. As a result, Pennsylvania long rifle flintlocks became the weapons of choice for hunters and frontiersmen. However, the costs of the long rifles, which could not be mass-produced, prevented their issue to local militias or to the English troops overseeing the colonies' security.

Instead the British army used the relatively inexpensive, mass-produced English Long Land Service Musket, better known as the Brown Bess. Ten pounds in weight with a forty-six-inch-long, .75-caliber barrel, the sturdily built Brown Bess could sustain the rigors of military field action. Its one-ounce lead ball measured only .71 caliber, so it loaded quickly and easily down the slightly larger barrel.

While the smaller-diameter ball positively affected speed of reloading of the Brown Bess, it had a negative impact on accuracy. The lead balls bounced from side to side in their passage out of the barrel. Consequently, the path of the shot varied widely in elevation and windage from its intended mark.

The French, the other major military force of the eighteenth century, developed their own standard military flintlock. Other than having a slightly smaller .69 caliber, the French Charleville closely resembled the British Brown Bess—down to the lack of accuracy. Even the most skilled marksmen had little control over where the shot landed.

A common military rhyme of the period about both British and French musket shots summed up the situation:

> One went high,
> and one went low,
> and where in Hell
> did the other one go.

British Brown Besses and French Charlevilles faced each other in North America during the Seven Years' War (1756–63), an extension of the two countries' conflict in Europe. American colonists, who accompanied the British as members of local militias, were also armed with the Brown Bess or other smooth-bore muskets that were "accurate" for only eighty yards or less. Toward the end of the conflict, the British formed the 60th Royal Americans as sharpshooters equipped with Pennsylvania long rifles. There is no record, however, that those marksmen had any influence on the war's final battles, perhaps because British commanders saw little use for weapons that could not mount bayonets. Cold steel rather than hot shot remained the deciding factor in most battles.

The first accurate long-range shooters to influence a battle in America came forward in the Revolutionary War. Americans armed their rebel army with Brown Besses captured from the British, with Charlevilles purchased from the French, and with locally produced .75-caliber flintlocks—called Committee of Safety muskets, authorized by the Continental Congress in November 1775. All of these weapons shared the inaccuracy common to smooth-bore muskets. Except when fired in volley at close range or employed as holders for bayonets, they were so ineffective that Benjamin Franklin recommended arming the revolutionary army with bows and arrows rather than the unpredictable muskets.

British ordnance expert Major George Hanger wrote about the accuracy of Revolutionary War muskets of both sides, stating, "A soldier's musket will strike the figure of a man at 80 yards; it may even at a hundred, but a soldier must be very unfortunate indeed who shall be wounded by a common musket at 150 yards, provided his antagonist aims at him; and as to firing at a man at 200 yards, with a common musket, you may just as well fire at the moon. No man ever was ever killed by a musket at 200 yards by the person who aimed at him."

American military commanders quickly recognized that they had neither the manpower nor the firepower to fight the British army at close quarters. They were also aware that all the Revolution had to do to succeed was to survive. As long as George Washington and other American commanders had forces in the field, whether engaged in combat or not, the fledgling United States continued to exist. As a result, Washington and his subordinates avoided open combat and often engaged in guerrilla-like warfare, knowing that eventually Britain would either tire of the conflict or would recall its forces to Europe to engage other enemies.

The Pennsylvania long rifle was the most effective weapon for the Americans' tactics. During skirmishes and harassing attacks, the sharpshooters armed with those rifles engaged the enemy from distances the British Brown Besses could not reach. In closer, more sustained combat, the rifle marksmen could pick off British commanders behind main battle lines at ranges of 200 to 250 meters.

On June 14, 1775, the Continental Congress authorized Pennsylvania to form six companies of longriflemen, and then a few days later expanded the order to nine companies. The first company mustered into service on June 29 at Northumberland with John Lowden as its captain and James Parr as first lieutenant. In its ranks stood Timothy Murphy, who would become America's first expert combat marksman and a hero of the Revolution.

The rifle companies united into the Pennsylvania Rifle Battalion, renamed the 1st Pennsylvania Continental Regiment in July 1776, under command of Colonel William Thompson, and for two years supported most of Washington's major engagements, firing from hidden positions to slow the British advance and covering the retreat of the rebel army when it broke contact.

In mid-June 1777, Washington transferred the 1st Pennsylvania, including Tim Murphy, to Morgan's Rifle Corps with instructions that the unit oppose the British army advance, under the command of General John Burgoyne, down the Hudson River Valley. Colonel Daniel Morgan, commander of the 500-man corps and an expert marksman himself, held more than mere revolutionary zeal against the British. While working for the British as a teamster in 1756, he had struck an officer during an argument and had been horsewhipped as punishment. Throughout his command of the rifle corps, Morgan often encouraged his marksmen to "shoot for the epaulets"—uniform adornments worn only by officers.

A contemporary description of Morgan's sharpshooters reported that the men of the rugged, hard-bitten group each carried a long knife and hatchet in addition to a long rifle. They dressed in buckskins and moccasins. Many wore the slogan "Liberty or Death" embroidered on their hunting shirts or on their caps.

After the First Battle of Freeman's Farm, in New York on September 19, 1777, the U.S. commander, General Horatio Gates, credited Morgan's riflemen for the success in briefly stopping Burgoyne's advance. At the Second Battle of Freeman's Farm, on October 7, Morgan's corps—and particularly Private Timothy Murphy—might very well have influenced the outcome of the American Revolution.

Burgoyne dispatched General Simon Frazer to probe the American flank at Bemis Heights, along the Hudson River, to prepare the way for the main attack. Morgan's men rushed to cut off the British advance. Frazer, mounted on a distinctive iron-gray gelding some 300 yards from the Americans, immediately became a target of the American sharpshooters. The first two Pennsylvania rifle bullets, fired by Murphy and a counterpart, hit the general's saddle and passed harmlessly through the horse's mane. Murphy, who had climbed into a small tree for better observation, then fired the third shot, which knocked Frazer from his horse with a mortal wound.*

---

*Precise credit for individual shots in the Revolutionary War was as difficult to accurately confirm as it would be in future conflicts. None of the limited accounts of the time about the battle mention Murphy as the person who fired the shot that killed Frazer. However, Murphy claimed the kill, and several of his fellow riflemen confirmed that it was his shot that brought down the general.

When Frazer fell, his troops broke off their attack and re-treated, forcing Burgoyne to cease his offensive and withdraw northward to Saratoga, where the Americans surrounded the British positions. Morgan's sharpshooters fired at all redcoats who dared expose themselves. On October 17, the British surrendered. Burgoyne acknowledged the impact of the American longriflemen on the battle, later remarking, "Morgan's men were the most famous Corps of the Continental Army. All of them crack shots."

The surrender of the British at Saratoga was a turning point in the war because the Americans realized that they could defeat the British on the battlefield. Murphy's well-aimed shot that brought down Frazer and disrupted the British advance certainly contributed to the victory. Also, as a result of the victory at Saratoga, France recognized the United States and became a valuable ally.

Morgan's riflemen continued to harass the British, adding substantial numbers to their kills for the remainder of the war. Murphy changed units several times, and there is evidence that on occasion he dressed as a civilian or an Indian to penetrate enemy lines.

Other British commanders came to the same conclusions as Burgoyne about the efficiency of the American riflemen. They formed their own sharpshooter units and hired German jaegers—at double the going rate for mercenaries—to cross the Atlantic to fight the American rebels.* Many of the jaegers were no more than glorified sports hunters, having little ability or motivation to be military sharpshooters. The few companies of jaegers that did make their way to America had no impact on the war because of their lack of military experience and the fact that their short-barreled rifles proved inferior to the American long rifles.

Major Patrick Ferguson of the 70th Foot Regiment led a more successful British effort to employ marksmen in the American Revolution. Ferguson, known throughout Britain as the finest shot in the army, developed an extremely accurate,

*The literal translation of jaeger is "hunter."

rapid breech-reloading rifle early in the war. Capable of mounting a bayonet on its thirty-four-inch barrel, the .68-caliber "Ferguson rifle" could fire four to six rounds per minute.

Ferguson brought 100 of his rifles to the United States in 1777 and succeeded in killing and harassing the enemy forces at long ranges. Ferguson had an even greater opportunity than Tim Murphy to influence the outcome of the war. Yet he did not take it.

Early on the morning of October 4, 1777, in a heavy fog at Germantown, near Philadelphia, Ferguson went forward of the British lines with a local guide in the hope of finding an unsuspecting target. General George Washington, on a reconnaissance mission with a few of his staff, approached within range of the British marksman. The guide told Ferguson that the mounted soldier was the commander of the American army, but before the British officer could shoot, Washington and his party turned back toward their lines. Ferguson did not fire. He explained in a letter to a relative, "It is not pleasant to fire at the back of an unoffending individual who was acquitting himself very coolly of his duty, so I let him alone."

A few days later Ferguson suffered serious wounds and his company was disbanded. No written records provide the British rationale for discontinuing the sharpshooter unit and withdrawing the rifles from the service other than that the Ferguson rifles' stocks tended to crack during sustained service and that their nonstandard caliber increased logistic problems.

The real reason, however, might have been attitudinal and economic. British officers in general strongly disdained the ungentlemanly practice of shooting the enemy from hidden positions at far distances. They also believed that few soldiers could ever master the skill of range estimation required for accurate shooting. British enlisted men also disliked the sharpshooter concept and few volunteered. Most of Ferguson's marksmen came not from the ranks of the regular British army but from Carolinian and Virginian loyalists.

The British were slow to adopt rifles to replace muskets for several other reasons as well. The cost of rifles limited their production, and the long Napoleonic Wars (1792–1815) were depleting the royal treasury. Also, the longer time required to reload a rifle discouraged its use in the mass formations the British favored.

The British did, however, eventually organize sharpshooter units to combat the French and their allies on the Continent. During the campaign in Spain, the British formed the 5th Battalion, 60th Regiment, composed mostly of German mercenary sharpshooters, and the 95th Rifles, manned by British marksmen. A short-barreled .65-caliber rifle, designed by British gun maker Ezekiel Baker to weigh nine and one-half pounds, served as the primary weapon of both units. It could fire a smaller shot in a smooth-bore mode or a larger one as a rifle, but the "Baker rifle" had a limited range of about 200 meters. Baker made his product more acceptable to army traditionalists by including a long bayonet in its design.

The limitations of the Baker rifle did not prevent British sharpshooters from making their mark on the Peninsula Wars. During the battle at the bridge of Cacabelos on January 16, 1809, a member of the 95th Rifles killed French General Auguste François Colbert with a single shot.

The 60th Regiment, also known as the King's Royal Rifles, made its own lasting impression. In a letter to his minister of war in September 1813, French Marshall Nicolas Soult wrote an excellent account of the British sharpshooters' tactics and influence. According to Soult, "There is in the English Army a battalion of the 60th, consisting of three companies. This battalion is never concentrated, but has a company attached to each infantry division. It is armed with a short rifle; the men are selected for their marksmanship; they perform the duties of scouts, and in action are expressly ordered to pick off officers, especially field or general officers."

Marshall Soult also noted the effectiveness of the sharpshooters units: "This mode of making war and of injuring the enemy is very detrimental to us; our casualties in officers are so great that after a couple of actions the whole number are usually disabled. I saw battalions whose officers had been disabled in the ratio of one officer to eight men. I also saw battalions which were reduced to two, or three officers, although less than one-sixth of their own men had been disabled."

Other armies also adopted the use of special marksmen. Spanish guerrillas employed sharpshooters during the Peninsula Wars. The Russians issued as many 20,000 rifles, known as "Mupa muskets," to their regular infantry forces during the conflict on the Continent. The single most influential shot of the Napoleonic Wars, however, was fired by a sharpshooter attached to the French navy.

On the morning of October 21, 1805, Private Robert Guillemard clambered into the rigging of the French man-of-war *Redoubtable* as the British fleet closed off Spain's Cape Trafalgar. When the HMS *Victory* came alongside the *Redoubtable*, Guillemard spotted a man in an admiral's uniform complete with glittering cords and decorations. The French rifleman fired a shot that struck Admiral Horatio Nelson in the spine and killed him. The British would ultimately win the battle and the war, but on that day in October, a French private brought down a British admiral with a single round.*

Back in the United States, American gun makers continued to make improvements to muskets and rifles. However, because of its lower manufacturing costs and speed of reloading, the smooth-bore musket remained the primary weapon of the small post-Revolution U.S. Army. Springfield, Massachusetts, and Harpers Ferry, Virginia, became the American arms-manufacturing centers, producing a series of musket models that incorporated improvements and standardized parts while staying with a caliber of .69 and a barrel length of forty-two to forty-four inches. During the first decade of the nineteenth century, smooth-bore muskets constituted more than 80 percent of U.S. long-weapon production.

Meanwhile American gunmakers, still mostly in Pennsylvania, continued to improve what were already the finest rifles in the world, but the handmade weapons, primarily in private

---

*Guillemard certainly deserves credit for the shot that killed Lord Nelson. However, it is interesting to note that, with the ships locked together, the French marksman's range to target was at most forty to fifty feet.

hands for use in hunting and sports shooting, remained too expensive for the military and most civilians.

While muskets dominated the fighting of both sides in the War of 1812, between the United States and Great Britain, the rifle made a significant contribution in several battles and gained further notice as a weapon to fear. At the Battle of Lake Erie on September 10, 1813, Commander Oliver Perry employed one hundred Kentucky infantrymen armed with long rifles to sweep the decks of the British fleet and ensure victory for the American navy.

The rifle proved even more influential to the American victory at the Battle of New Orleans. On January 8, 1815, more than 8,000 British soldiers attacked a force of about half that number of Americans on the Chalmette Plains outside the city. U.S. General Andrew Jackson commanded a mixed army of regulars, militiamen, blacks, sailors, and frontiersmen protected by mud banks and cotton bales. Two thousand of Jackson's force, mostly frontiersmen from Kentucky, carried Pennsylvania long rifles* and engaged the approaching British at several hundred meters. In a brief battle, the Americans brought down more than 1,500 enemy soldiers, most from rifle fire, and handed the British their worst defeat of the war. The Americans lost only 60 men.**

While armies on the Continent and in America were perfecting the use of the flintlock rifle, two European inventors were designing changes that would place dependable rifles in the hands of every infantryman. In 1807, the Reverend Alexander Forsyth of Scotland secured a patent for a percussion firing system that used the strike of a cock upon a plunger to explode a bit of detonating powder. Because the Forsyth lock proved reliable in all types of weather, gun makers around

---

*The marksmanship of the Kentucky riflemen on Lake Erie and at New Orleans virtually renamed the weapon; no longer called the "Pennsylvania rifle," it was now the "Kentucky rifle."

**Unfortunately, the casualties on both sides were for naught. The United States and Great Britain had signed the Treaty of Ghent to end the war on December 24, 1814, but slow communications did not bring the news to New Orleans until after the battle.

the globe copied and improved the system. By 1820 American gunsmiths had refined the ignition system by using fulminate of mercury in a one-eighth-inch copper cap inside the mechanism to stabilize the firing process of the main charge.

After extensive tests, the British army adopted the percussion system in 1839, and the United States followed with its Model 1842 percussion musket three years later. Other armies also adopted the percussion system because of its reliability and its design, which allowed both flintlock muskets and rifles to readily be converted. By 1850 flintlocks were relics in armies and among sports shooters.

The advances in ignition systems came simultaneously with innovations in munitions. In 1848, French Captain Claude E. Minié created a cylindrical lead bullet with a conical head and an iron cupped base to replace the round shot that had been used for the first 500 years of firearms. Grooves around the base of the bullet expanded to tightly fit into the rifling and to scrape out powder residue as the bullet exited the barrel. The "minié ball," only fractionally smaller than the barrel, loaded easily yet produced more power and accuracy. Its first wide-scale use was in the Crimean War of 1853 to 1856, where it proved its worth on the battlefield.

The percussion system, the minié ball, and improved powder were common in the "first modern war," the American Civil War. The .58-caliber U.S. Model 1855 rifled musket and its subsequent modifications in 1861 and 1863 became the standard individual weapons of both sides in the Civil War,* although both the North and the South imported British Enfields of similar design. Soldiers then carried weapons capable of a sustained rate of fire of three rounds per minute with reasonable accuracy at up to 500 meters and outside ranges in excess of 1,000 meters.

---

*The Confederacy stockpiled many U.S. weapons prior to its secession and captured more in the early months of the war. Confederates also took over the gun-making machinery at Harpers Ferry and moved it to Fayetteville, North Carolina, where James H. Burton, the former master armorer at the Federal gun works, became the superintendent of Confederate armories. The only way the Southern-made weapons differed from the North's rifled muskets was the "CSA" (rather than "USA") stamp on the rifles' lock plates.

Regardless of improved accuracy and range, small arms proved no better than the soldier pulling the trigger. Some men were better shots than others, and commanders on both sides, knowing marksmen could be better employed than just as regular infantrymen, formed special units of sharpshooters.

Shortly after the fall of Fort Sumter, Union Colonel Hiram Berdan, a New York City engineer and weapons inventor with a competition shooting background, lobbied for and received permission to form regiments of outstanding marksmen. In the summer of 1861 he recruited volunteers for the 1st and 2nd U.S. Sharpshooters Regiments, often called "Berdan's Sharpshooters," although he actually commanded only the 1st Regiment; Colonel Henry A. Post commanded the 2nd Regiment.

A recruiting poster dated August 19, 1861, appealed to "Sharpshooters" and announced, "Your Country Calls!! Will You Respond?" The poster proclaimed that the regiment was "destined to be the most important and popular in the service" but warned that all who reported to Bellow Falls, Vermont, would not be accepted: "No person will be enlisted who cannot when firing at the distance of 200 yards, at a rest, put ten consecutive shots in a target, the average distance not to exceed five inches from the center of the bull's eye to the center of the ball."

Recruited from throughout the Union, but organized into subordinate companies by state of origin to maintain cohesiveness, soldiers in both regiments initially provided their own rifles. Senior U.S. Army officers recommended that Springfields replace the private weapons, but Berdan requisitioned the Sharps Model 1859, which he received only after President Lincoln approved the request as a result of viewing a spectacular shooting exhibition by the colonel, for his sharpshooters.*

---

*The word *sharpshooter* did not evolve from the Sharps rifle. The first written reference to a sharpshooter appears in an 1802 English dictionary description of Austrian infantry. By the height of the Napoleonic Wars, a decade later, the term "sharpshooter" had become common in most armies. By the time of the American Civil War, its use was so prevalent that Berdan's Union regiments readily adopted the description.

Accurate at up to 600 yards, the percussion-fired .52-caliber Sharps rifle contained a breech block loading device that allowed the sharpshooter to reload in the prone position, thus limiting his exposure to enemy fire. By pushing forward a lever that doubled as a trigger guard, the shooter could lower the breech block to gain access to the chamber for loading a paper or linen cartridge. The closing of the breech cut the end of the cartridge to aid in ignition. A trained soldier could reload and fire up to ten rounds per minute with the Sharps, three times the firepower of men armed with Springfields or other muzzle loaders.

Although Berdan proved an excellent organizer and trainer of sharpshooters, his combat leadership abilities fell short of his shooting prowess. Fortunately, the companies of both sharpshooter regiments were usually detached to divisions and Berdan's shortcomings did not endanger his marksmen or the commands they supported.

The 1st and 2nd Sharpshooter Regiments saw action in most of the war's major battles, including the Peninsula, Antietam, Chancellorsville, and Gettysburg. Used mostly as skirmishers, similar to the British 95th Regiment in the Crimea, the sharpshooters also became proficient in hitting enemy artillery crews and senior officers. Several accounts credit the two sharpshooter units with inflicting more casualties on the enemy than any other regiment in the Union army and with killing at least six Confederate generals.

While the 1st and 2nd Regiments primarily used the Sharps rifle with a post front sight and a folding-leaf adjustable rear sight, they also employed a few special weapons designed strictly for them. Gun maker Morgan James produced several dozen rifles for the sharpshooters complete with telescopic sights that ran the length of their barrels.* The rifle's weight of more than thirty pounds and its sensitive scope limited its widespread use.

---

*Telescopic sights were first made in England about 1640 and in Germany almost immediately thereafter. Their first use in extended combat, however, did not occur until both sides employed scopes with two or three times amplification power in the American Civil War.

Southern commanders organized their sharpshooters much differently, but the rebel marksmen experienced the same success as the Union shooters. Instead of forming dedicated regiments, the Confederates allowed their sharpshooters, selected from unit competitions, to operate semi-independently in acquiring targets. Rarely joining skirmish lines, these marksmen, like their Union counterparts, focused on artillery crews and senior officers.

Confederate sharpshooters carried either personal weapons or issue Springfield and Enfield rifles. Although the typical Rebel rifleman did not have the advantage of the breech-loading Sharps, a few of them received the most accurate and deadly rifles yet used in battle.

In early 1863 Confederate agents in England purchased twelve Whitworth rifles and blockade-runners delivered them. Six were issued to the Army of Northern Virginia; the other six went to the Confederate units in the West. Two riflemen in each Confederate corps earned possession of the English rifles through shooting contests.

Using the .45-caliber Whitworths with the fourteen-and-one-half-inch-long telescopic sight that mounted on the left side of the stock, Confederate sharpshooters were soon hitting targets at ranges of up to 1,000 meters. In July 1863, the Confederates procured eighteen additional Whitworths, and the following February purchased twenty more. During the war's final months, the Confederacy secured another twenty-two Whitworths.

Only the most proficient marksmen had the opportunity to shoot the Whitworths because of their prohibitive price. Each Whitworth cost the Confederate States $500, payable not in Confederate script but in gold. In contrast, producing a Springfield or purchasing an Enfield cost less than $40.

Despite their small numbers, Whitworth-armed Rebel sharpshooters made their mark during the war. At Chickamauga, Georgia, on September 19, 1863, a Whitworth sharpshooter mortally wounded Union General William H. Lytle of Ohio. The following May 9, another Whitworth sharpshooter

engaged Union General John Sedgwick at the Battle of Spot-
sylvania, Virginia, where Sedgwick and a group of subordinates were reconning the area for their artillery positions.
Spotting Confederate riflemen more then 800 meters across an
open plain, Sedgwick's men took cover while the general criticized their caution, saying, "They couldn't hit an elephant at
this distance," At that instant a Whitworth bullet slammed into
his head. Sedgwick's death delayed the Union offensive and
contributed to the eventual Rebel victory in that battle.

Confederate agents in England also procured .44-caliber
muzzle-loading Kerr rifles in limited quantities. The exact
number is unknown, but it is likely that fewer Kerrs than
Whitworths made their way to the Civil War.

Rebel sharpshooters acted more independently than their
Union counterparts, but marksmen of both sides generally
concentrated on similar targets. Officers remained a priority,
but artillery units also drew the attention of marksmen. The
range of most of the period's artillery allowed batteries to set
up beyond the normal range of infantrymen and fire their
lethal cannons from positions of reasonable safety. Sharpshooters of both sides quickly ended this artillery advantage
and frequently interrupted or delayed their fire. In a few instances, a lone marksman rendered an entire artillery battery
useless by killing its leaders and preventing crewmen from ex-
posing themselves to serve their cannons.

Throughout the war, Union and Confederate commanders sought effective countersharpshooter methods. The most
common was simply to deploy sharpshooters against sharpshooters. Artillery units initiated a type of countersharpshooter
technique that would remain a tactic in future wars: when artillery crews came under sharpshooter fire, their observers,
who had previously only adjusted cannon fire, attempted to
identify the enemy shooter so that the entire battery could fire
at the location. While such an expenditure of ammunition
against a single rifleman might not have been economical, it
did tend to decrease the number of sharpshooters targeting the
artillery.

By the conclusion of the American Civil War, sharpshooters

were a fixture on the battlefield. Both Union and Confederate soldiers learned that being visible was being vulnerable. While Americans did not originate the concept, their sharpshooters in both blue and gray did, however, refine sharpshooting into an art form that would forever influence individual marksmanship on the battlefield.

CHAPTER 4

✳✳✳✳✳✳✳✳

Snipers Come of Age:
The World Wars and Beyond

*A*T the end of the Civil War, America possessed the largest number of military weapons in its history. Regular-issue Springfields as well as Sharps and special rifles imported and then surrendered by the South filled armories across the country.

Eliminating sharpshooter regiments and special marksmen went hand in hand with "mothballing" the arms of the war. Although marksmanship training for all infantrymen remained an important part of the postwar soldier's life, some of the conflict's innovations caused concerns over the future of firepower—individual and otherwise. Breech loaders and the newly introduced repeating rifles so enhanced the rate of infantry and calvary fire that logistics officers worried about their ability to meet ammunition requirements.

Some field commanders even concluded that volume of fire could negate the need for individual accuracy. In a letter to the president of the New Haven Arms Company dated March 15, 1865, Major Joel W. Cloudman of the 1st District of Columbia Cavalry praised the firepower and efficiency of the .44-caliber Model 1860 Henry Repeating Rifle. According to Cloudman, "I often heard the enemy discuss its merits. They all feared it more than any arm in our service and have heard them say, 'Give us anything but your damned Yankee rifle that can be loaded on Sunday and fired all week.'"

The increased rate of fire and general distaste for marksmen who fired from relative safety at specifically designated targets might have ended the U.S. Army sharpshooter program, but they did not deter the continued evolution of ammunition,

44

arms, and optics. The years just prior to and following the Civil War brought a parade of armament advances.

Self-contained metal cartridges, first patented by New York City inventor Walter Hunt in 1848, shortened loading time and added to the barrel gas seal that produced greater bullet velocity. Edward Maynard improved the cartridge design in 1856, and in the same year Horace Smith and Daniel Wesson introduced advances in primers.

The problems with metallic cartridge reliability and costs that limited their use in the Civil War were resolved during the decade following the conflict. By 1870 the U.S. Army and other armies had adopted center-fire brass cartridges, modifying old weapons or designing new ones to accommodate the improved ammunition.

Alfred Nobel of Sweden and other manufacturers introduced in the 1880s smokeless powder made from nitrated cellulose that eliminated the giveaway cloud of white smoke that had compromised the positions of Civil War sharpshooters. It also eliminated much of the smoke that had previously covered battlefields.

Gun makers next decreased caliber size and added steel, copper, and alloy jackets to lead projectiles to increase their velocity and heat resistance. By the 1890s various models of bolt-action, clip-fed rifles firing .30-caliber metal-jacketed bullets propelled by smokeless powder were available. Telescopic sight technology developed three-power scopes with a larger field of vision. Except for the introduction of automatic assault weapons, the basic infantry and sharpshooter weapons and ammunition for the twentieth century had been perfected by the end of the nineteenth.

The U.S. Army was slow to adopt many of those innovations because it spent the two decades following the Civil War mired in the Indian Wars in the West. Because of limited military funding, cavalry and infantry units fighting the Indians carried Sharps or Springfields. In several battles, the Native Americans, some of whom had repeating rifles, were better armed than the soldiers.

During the Indian Wars, the U.S. Army did not conduct specific sharpshooter training, nor did it issue special marksman weapons. Limited military budgets often failed even to provide sufficient training ammunition for the infantry and cavalry.

Superior shooting in the West came not from the ranks of the soldiers but from frontiersmen and buffalo hunters. On June 27, 1874, several hundred Comanche Indians attacked about thirty buffalo hunters and merchants at an isolated trading post known as Adobe Wells in the Texas Panhandle. After the hunters drove them away with long-range, .50-caliber Sharps fire, the Indians referred to the Sharps as "the gun that shoots today and kills tomorrow."

The Battle of Adobe Wells produced the best-known single shot of the long conflict between whites and Indians. Early on the morning after the initial fight, a dozen or more Indians appeared on a ridge distant from the trading post. Buffalo hunter and sometime-army-scout Billy Dixon took careful aim with his Sharps .50 and fired. One Indian fell from his horse and the others hastily retreated. Estimates about the range of the shot vary from 1,200 to 1,600 yards.* Years later, Dixon remarked about his shot, "I was admittedly a good marksman, yet this was what might be called a 'scratch' shot."

There were other extraordinary marksmen around the world. As armaments improved so did the skills of the shooters, and superior mastery of hitting distant and difficult targets garnered a new name. Although various definitions would define and redefine the term many times in the future, from the late 1800s to the present day, the soldier or Marine armed with special weapons and trained to deliver single well-aimed shots to kill enemy troops would be known as a "sniper."

The term probably originated with the British army in India, where officers hunted snipes, a slender-billed bird related to the woodcock. Snipes, fleet of foot and wing, were difficult targets, and shooters proficient at hitting them became known

---

*Regardless of the degree of truth about Dixon's shot, the fact that the story exists provides an indication of the accuracy attributed to the buffalo guns and the hunters who used them.

as "snipers." The British then began referring to well-aimed shots both toward and from the enemy as snipes, and those who fired the rounds as snipers.

The earliest confirmed written reference to snipers is in a 1773 letter from India by a British officer. Another letter from India, this one dated 1782, states, "The individual will be popped at or sniped as they call it from time to time." Still another correspondent in India wrote in 1824 that "several sepoys were killed and wounded by the enemy's snipers who generally stalk the sentries from behind stones." By the time of the Boer War, at the end of the nineteenth century, sniper had become the preferred term for long-range shooters throughout the British Empire.

In the post–Indian War period, the U.S. military again emphasized individual marksmanship with the standard issue .30-caliber Krag-Joegensen rifle and benefitted from that when the United States engaged in a brief and decisive war with Spain over Cuba and the Philippines. Due to the war's short duration—war between Spain and the United States was declared on April 21, 1898, and the fighting lasted only three months, even though the treaty ending the war wasn't ratified by the U.S. Senate until 1899—the regular army did most of the fighting.

The army did not conduct sniper training or issue special weapons to its troops bound for Cuba. However, at San Juan Hill and several other battles, various U.S. regiments assigned their better shots as sharpshooters to engage Spanish riflemen and to keep the enemy pinned down during ground advances.

It was World War I that provided conditions favorable to advancing the sniper's art. After only a few months of fighting, the Western Front aligned into two opposing sides dug into trenches that extended for more than 450 miles from the Swiss border to the North Sea. Periodic offensives resulted in enormous casualties but virtually no significant ground gains. During these battles, and especially during the many days between offensives, snipers accounted for a growing body count.

Germany entered the war prepared and willing to commit snipers to the battlefield. With its superior gun-manufacturing plants, the world's best optics and telescope makers, and a tradition of training young men in hunting marksmanship, Germany fielded large numbers of proficient snipers early in the war. In addition to rifles and scopes specifically designed for military use, German logisticians secured civilian hunting weapons and telescopes to supply their marksmen. In 1915 alone the German supply system provided 20,000 rifles with telescopic sights to the frontline infantrymen.

Britain countered with snipers of its own, recruiting former big-game hunters from Africa and expert marksmen from Canada and Australia as well as training additional troops in England and France. The British trained their snipers not only to engage and kill individual targets but also to be observers and to gather intelligence. In 1916, the British army formed intelligence sections composed of eight snipers, eight scouts, and eight observers in each infantry battalion. The snipers worked in two-man teams using elaborate personal camouflage and sandbagged, steel-plated "sniper hides." The armored "hides" protected the British marksmen from observation and from the enemy's snipers—the most common countersniper tactic—and from concentrated infantry and artillery fire.

Americans entered World War I late but fairly well prepared in individual sniper equipment. During the decade following the Spanish-American War, the U.S. Army and the U.S. Marine Corps conducted numerous studies of rifles, ammunition, telescopic sights, and silencer devices. As a result, the U.S. military adopted the .30-caliber bolt-action M1903 Springfield rifle in 1906, and subsequent models of that durable, highly accurate weapon remained the primary American infantry and sniper rifle for more than three decades.

Scope production also advanced during that period. The Army Ordnance Department conducted its first field test of telescopic sights in 1900. The department's test board found the sights provided by the Cataract Tool and Optical Company of Buffalo, New York, "to be of especial value in hazy or foggy weather and at long ranges" of up to 2,000 yards. The board concluded its June 8 report by recommending that the army purchase more scopes for field tests by soldiers, and stated, "If found to be satisfactory, a sufficient number should be purchased to supply such a number to the sharpshooters of each organization."

The introduction of the early models of the M1903 Springfield preempted tests on equipment for the military Krag rifles and the Cataract scope. Instead, the Army Ordnance Department turned to the Warner and Swasey Company of Cleveland, Ohio, for telescopic sights more suited to the '03 Springfield. Over the next year the army procured twenty-five of the scopes. It became obvious immediately that, although the civilian scopes needed modification for the rigors of military use, they definitely had a place in the army of the future. An obscure entry, paragraph number 269, in the army's *Small Arms Firing Regulation* for 1904 recorded the first official acceptance of those telescopic sights in the U.S. military.

Four years later the army adopted a Warner and Swasey product as the Telescopic Musket Sight, Model of 1908, along with mounting brackets for the '03 Springfield. Subsequent models over the next few years added stadia lines within the scopes to mark ranges at 500-yard increments from 1,000 to 2,000 yards. The manufacturer delivered more than 2,000 of the improved scopes to the military over the next four years.

Concurrent with the development of military scopes by the Warner and Swasey Company, other manufacturers worked to perfect silencers for the '03 Springfield. The first acceptable silencers procured by the army came from the Maxim Silent Firearms Company of Hartford, Connecticut, in 1910.

The Warner and Swasey Company continued to improve its scopes, and its 1913 model, with a 5.2 magnification capability, found use in the U.S. Army as well as with Canadian forces deploying to the European war. Within the American army, the Ordnance Department issued Pamphlet Number 1957, which outlined the care and maintenance of both the M1908 and M1913 telescopic sights.

The Winchester Repeating Arms Company of New Haven, Connecticut, also manufactured telescopes used by American, Canadian, and British snipers during World War I. Winchester

introduced its A5 telescopic rifle sight in 1910 primarily for
civilian sports shooting. Despite its lack of durability under
battlefield conditions, the A5, mounted on '03 Springfields,
became the telescopic sight of choice for U.S. Marine Corps
snipers. Canadian and British snipers also adapted the scopes
to their rifles.

Unlike the American Civil War, in which generals fre-
quented the front lines and artillery crews were easily visible,
World War I found senior officers only in rear areas and artillery placed mostly out of sniper range. As a result, the primary targets of snipers on both sides were junior frontline
officers and regular infantrymen—as well as their counterpart
marksmen on the other side of no-man's-land.

Most of the noted snipers of the period were officers who
gained their recognition through postwar writings. Many in
uniform, as well as the civilian population, still saw the sniper
as a somewhat sinister character who killed indifferently from
a great distance. Most accounts of successful World War I
snipers mention the number of their kills without providing
complete identifications of the shooters. Several World War I
sniper stories mention a "former Canadian trapper" who
claimed 125 kills but do not include his name.

In 1915, a Viennese newspaper printed an account of German snipers identified only by their last names. According
to the article, German "Private Herrenreiter" had accounted
for 121 sniper kills of French soldiers. It also claimed that a
sniper by the name of "Fark" killed sixty-three Russians in a
single day.*

The late entry in the war of the United States limited its opportunities to innovate sniper operations, but the influence of
the single, well-aimed shot, both outgoing and incoming,
made an impression on those who occupied the trenches.

---

*Neither of these stories can be confirmed. It is interesting to note that the ar-
ticle shared space in the newspaper with an advertisement for Reichert telescopic sights, to which both snipers credited their success. Confirming sniper
kills, whether during World War I or in subsequent conflicts, proved to be extremely difficult, and any claim of an exact sniper count should be looked
upon with some skepticism.

American snipers talked and wrote little about their work, and few first-person stories of their experiences exist. Interestingly, "The Sniper," one of the most descriptive accounts, originally appeared not in official reports but in the popular pulp fiction periodical *Weird Tales*. Even then it did not make its way into print until nearly a decade after the war and focuses on Allied and enemy rather than American snipers.

The Marine Corps magazine *Leatherneck* eventually reprinted the article, by Arthur J. Burks, in its August 1926 edition. According to "The Sniper," a Canadian infantry company had just taken over a portion of the frontline trenches when a single round struck one of the soldiers in the forehead. Over the next three days, eleven more of the company's infantrymen fell to the unseen sniper's fire.

Although the shots came from a cemetery at the edge of no-man's-land, the Canadians could not locate the sniper's lair. Finally, on the third night, a sergeant and a private requested that the company commander permit them to conduct a countersniper patrol. Reluctantly, the captain agreed.

The article continued by stating that the two men departed and returned. Early the next morning the captain asked, " 'Did you get him, Sergeant?' "

The sergeant replied, " 'Captain, there will be no more bullets from that particular sniper. But for the sake of your own peace of mind, don't ask us what happened in the still watches of the night! Yet, rest assured, sir, that whatever we did to him was not enough to pay him for the death of twelve of our buddies; that he had twelve lives to give that would still have been insufficient. On his part it was cold-blooded murder!' "

According to the story's narrator, the sergeant would reveal nothing further except that there had been a crypt. The captain let the matter rest. He did nothing about the incident until shortly before shipping out for home after the war ended. The captain once again visited the former front lines, easily finding the cemetery because it was "etched unforgettably" in his mind.

In the graveyard he found the concrete-and-metal crypt the sniper had used as a "hide." Next to the heavy slab covering the grave lay a short stick for propping open the cover just enough for a rifle and scope to protrude. The former infantry officer continued, " 'I lifted the slab and drew it away. Then horror seizing me in its grip, I turned hurriedly away and did not look back again. One look had been enough. Within the narrow retaining wall lay a moldering skeleton, to which clung rotting folds of gray uniform! Beside the body lay a rusty rifle and the remains of a light pack. What a ghastly revenge!' "

The captain paused, according to the author, and then continued, " 'For the sergeant and the private had crept upon the sniper and made him prisoner. Then they had thrust him back into that horrible retaining wall—ALIVE—after which they returned the slab to its place. But they had made retribution doubly sure. For wrapped around and about that moldering skeleton, fold upon fold, was a veritable maze of rusty barbed wire.' "

Whether or not they had such horrors in mind, it is not surprising that the United States and its allies once again shelved their snipers at the end of the war. Besides expressing resistance to men who cold-bloodedly killed with no warning from hiding, many world leaders thought that World War I was "the war to end all wars" and that neither snipers nor armies themselves would be needed in the future.

Unfortunately, "the war to end all wars" did not live up to its billing, and by the end of the 1930s combat once again swept across the plains of Europe and expanded around the world. Renewed interest in snipers surfaced in the earliest battles of World War II. During the Spanish Civil War, Loyalist snipers had experienced particular success in engaging the flanks and rear areas of the attacking Nationalist forces. Both Russian and German observers of the Spanish war returned to their countries with recommendations that they include snipers in the pending global conflict.

Once World War II began in earnest with the German blitzkrieg across Europe, however, the swift Nazi offensives did not require the skills of individual marksmen. The Germans had snipers with their infantry in the war's initial months, but they found little opportunity to use them.

The British were as ill prepared to field snipers against the blitzkrieg as they were to stop the attacks. British sniper expert Captain Clifford Shore wrote in 1948, "I have spoken to many men who were in France from September 1939 until the time of Dunkirk [June 1940] and to date have not met anyone who could tell me that he saw any sniper rifles in that campaign."

It was not until the German offensive on the Russian front stalled outside Stalingrad in late 1942 that the sniper emerged as a viable weapon in World War II. When the lines stagnated outside the Russian city, German and Soviet snipers began to make it extremely deadly for anyone to leave the protective foxholes, bunkers, and reinforced positions in the city's buildings. Soviet snipers armed with 7.62-mm bolt-action Model 1891/30 Mosin-Nagant rifles and German marksmen with Gewehr 98ks, slightly modified into a shorter-barreled version of the World War I rifle, engaged enemy infantry as well as each other throughout the long cold winter.

The snipers so impressed the Soviet commanders at Stalingrad that they began a training school within the city inside a section of the Lazur Chemical Plant. Firing at targets painted on the factory's wall, Soviet riflemen trained for only two days with scope-equipped Mosins before rejoining the front lines as snipers.

According to articles written by Soviet officers that appeared in U.S. military journals shortly after the Battle of Stalingrad, the Russian snipers worked in teams of two, one shooter and one observer, and focused on officers, machine gunners, mortar crews, and enemy snipers. Vassili Zaitsev, a former hunter from Elininski in the Ural Mountains, honed his skills at Stalingrad and by the end of the war is said to have achieved 242 confirmed kills of German soldiers. That number included several of the Nazi's top snipers.

Although the story of Zaitsev appears valid, the Soviets did not hesitate to greatly enhance tales of the proficiency of their snipers and other soldiers to bolster morale. The actual contribution of Soviet snipers in securing Stalingrad and counterattacking into the German heartland is impossible to calculate, but the Germans were known to respect and fear the single shot from the Soviet lines.

Joseph Stalin, the leader of the Soviet Union, also appreciated the skills of his marksmen. On May 1, 1942, Stalin issued an order that advised, "Line troops must learn the rifle thoroughly, must become masters of their weapons, must kill the enemy without fail, as do our glorious snipers, the exterminators of the German invaders."

The German army was bested at Stalingrad, but the German sniper remained an efficient killer for the balance of the war. An article written by an officer that appeared in the *Hamburger Fremdenblatt* on May 9, 1944, praised German snipers for their service to the Fatherland. Referring to the performance of snipers against the Russians as "very satisfactory," the unnamed officer provided an excellent description of the expert marksmen that would remain true for the rest of the war—as well as today: "Not everyone becomes or is able to become a sniper. Not everyone meets the necessary requirements. Natural proclivity, passion for the chase, fanatical love of firearms—these assure the results required of a sniper."

The German army continued to recruit and train snipers until the last days of the war. In 1944, to promote volunteers and encourage those already in the program, the German army authorized a special oval sniper badge composed of an eagle's head and oak leaves. Twenty confirmed kills gained a sniper the first-degree badge, forty the second-degree badge, and sixty the third-degree badge.

Despite the successes of German and Soviet snipers on the Eastern Front, the British high command remained unconvinced of the need for special riflemen on the mobile battlefield. Not until they encountered increased German sniper activity in North Africa and Italy did the British finally reactivate the sniper training they had used in World War I. In September 1943, the first British sniping school began training at Llanberis, in North Wales.

In conjunction with the training school, the British decided to present to infantry battalion commanders two-day orientations on sniper operations before they deployed for the battle zones. This training provided information on sniper capabilities as well as instruction on their proper deployment.

The acceptance of snipers in Commonwealth regiments accelerated steadily during the war. By early 1944 sniping instructors had established schools in the rear areas of battle zones to provide immediate replacements. Members of the unit that eventually became the 21st Army Sniping School landed at Normandy on August 17, 1944, and began their first instruction two days later. The unofficial definition of British sniping became "the art of drilling round holes into square heads."

Despite years of warning, the United States Army entered the conflict as ill prepared to field snipers as the British had been. German marksmen immediately took a toll of U.S. infantrymen from their earliest battles in North Africa and continued to do so until the war's final fights. Despite their losses to German snipers and the success of Allied marksmen, the U.S. Army did not establish a central sniper training program or policy during the war.

In the European Theater, the U.S. senior command left sniper training and employment to the individual units. Some division, regiment, and battalion commanders did not use snipers at all, while others actively recruited soldiers with extensive hunting or competitive shooting experience. The army's minimum standard for designation as a sniper became the ability to strike a dummy target at 400 yards and to hit a head-size target at 200 yards.

The War Department did provide some written guidance. Its Field Manual 21-75, "Infantry Scouting, Patrolling, and Sniping," which appeared in various editions and updates before, during, and after the war, provided extremely brief and basic sniping principles. For instance, the February 6, 1944, edition of FM 21-75 included a mere twelve pages of sniping information in a chapter at the end of the manual. War Department technical manuals of the period also included useful guidelines on the maintenance and care of the various sniper rifles and scopes.

Once trained—to whatever degree—by their units, U.S.

Army snipers in Europe generally employed the same procedures and tactics as other countries' snipers. They primarily
worked in two-man teams and focused on engaging officers
and heavy weapons crews. Most American snipers, especially
early in the war, used the same '03 Springfields that had
proved successful in World War I and adapted several advanced telescopic sights to these weapons.

American snipers also used the M1C and M1D models of
the .30-caliber M1 Garand that became the basic U.S. infantry
rifle of the war. Between 1937 and 1945, the Springfield and
Winchester arms companies produced more than 4.5 million
of the gas-operated, clip-fed, air-cooled, semiautomatic weapons. The M1 proved to be a highly durable, accurate rifle that
significantly contributed to the U.S. military victory. However,
although ordinary World War II infantrymen coveted their
M1s, many snipers continued to use the extremely accurate
'03 Springfields even after the C- and D-model M1s with
sight-mounting adaptations became readily available.

Americans deploying to the Pacific also faced formidable
snipers. Japan, particularly after losing the offensive momentum and beginning a defensive war, used snipers throughout the Pacific Theater. Japanese snipers initially carried the
6.5-mm Type 38 rifle that had been in use since 1905. As the
war progressed, many of those were replaced by Arisaka Type
97 rifles with a 2.5 power scope. The relatively small-caliber
rifle and low-power scope limited the accuracy and range of
Japanese snipers to about 300 yards. However, the long-
barreled, small-projectile weapon produced little smoke or
muzzle flash, making Japanese sniper fire extremely difficult
for opponents to pinpoint.

Disciplined Japanese snipers combined shooting skills with
excellent concealment and camouflage techniques. More important, the marksmen, like all Japanese soldiers, swore to
fight to the death for their emperor. As a result, to gain better
fields of fire Japanese snipers, not worrying about escape or
surrender, willingly established their "hides" in the tops of
trees.

Individual Japanese infantrymen with open-sighted, non-scoped rifles also frequently engaged the Americans with sporadic fire, causing U.S. soldiers and Marines to refer to almost any low-volume shooting as "sniper fire." Colonel James A. Donovan, USMC (Retired), served from 1940 to 1945 with the 2nd Marine Division, including time as the executive officer of a battalion of the 6th Marines during the battles for the Mariana Islands. In an interview more than fifty years after World War II, Donovan explained, "In the Pacific all Jap riflemen were dubbed 'snipers' by Marines. Of course, they were only riflemen—but were all good at cover, concealment, and patience. They were fair shots and caused many delays in our advances. They were more effective than they deserved to be."

One of the most common countersniper measures employed by the army and the Marine Corps in the Pacific was the same as that used in Europe. A training note for the 1st Battalion, 163rd Infantry Regiment, provides an excellent summary of countersniper measures. According to the report, when the 163rd replaced an Australian unit during the Battle of Sananada in New Guinea on January 2, 1943, the American infantrymen immediately came under Japanese sniper fire that killed and wounded several.

Initially, the 163rd used observers to locate the snipers and then raked the treetops and ground level with automatic rifle and machine gun fire. That neutralized some of the sniper fire but casualties continued. After several days, the 163rd brought their 37-mm antitank gun section forward and in response to sniper fire blasted nearby treetops with the cannons. Even though the sniping significantly decreased, the 163rd never completely ended it until the offensives overran and destroyed the last Japanese units.

Other army units in the Pacific employed similar antisniper techniques, but like their comrades in Europe, they never had support from an army- or theater-level sniper-training program. In the Pacific, sniper training within the army remained an individual decision of unit commanders down to battalion level.

Marines in the Pacific also practiced the mass-firepower tactic, but senior corps leaders recognized even before the war began that trained individual marksmen themselves were the most efficient countersnipers. The Marine Corps had no formal sniper program prior to U.S. entry into World War II, but it did encourage improvements in civilian manufacture of telescopic sights and assigned officers and enlisted men to study the possible uses of advanced marksmanship.

Two years before the war began, Captain George O. Van Orden and Chief Marine Gunner Calvin A. Lloyd of the Marine Barracks, Quantico, Virginia, Rifle Range Detachment studied the history of sniping and drew conclusions about the future need for such marksmen. Early in 1941 the two men published their findings in a seventy-two-page, single-spaced report titled "Equipment for the American Sniper."* The Marine Corps reproduced the report and forwarded 1,000 copies to units around the world.

The first twenty pages of the document extensively quote World War I personal memoirs on sniping. The last section discusses the merits of various rifles and scopes. Despite its brevity, the study stands alone as the best summary of sniping prior to World War II and the best predictor of future U.S. sniper developments.

The theme throughout the writing of Van Orden and Lloyd is that snipers are a necessary part of any ground combat force and that these special marksmen required and deserved weapons, scopes, and ammunition specially manufactured for their difficult missions. At the conclusion of Chapter 2, the two Marines emphasized, "The sniper has not survived merely because of the romantic, adventurous glamour which surrounds his campaign of individual extermination—the private war he wages. He is present on the battlefields because there is a real and vital need for him. It is safe to say that the American sniper could be regarded as the greatest all-around rifleman

---

*The document itself is undated and few copies have survived. According to the "Date Received" stamp on the front of the copy on file in the Marine Corps Museum in Washington, D.C., it arrived there on November 12, 1942.

the world has ever known, and his equipment should include the best aids to his dangerous calling that the inventive genius of the United States can produce."

Yet, in the first months of World War II, Marine commanders selected marksmen from their units and procured what weapons and scopes they could to arm their snipers. The weapon of choice of these Marine marksmen was the same as that recommended in the study by Van Orden and Lloyd—the .30-caliber Winchester Model 70 with an 8-power telescope manufactured by the John Unertl Optical Company.

The Winchester Repeating Arms Company shipped 373 Model 70s to the Marine Corps on May 29, 1942, and filled smaller orders over the next months. Many of the rifles found their way to the Pacific, but the Marine Corps did not officially adopt the M70 as its sniper weapon, citing the logistical difficulties in supplying and maintaining an additional rifle type.

As a result, when the Marine Corps opened its formal sniper schools (at New River, near Camp Lejeune, North Carolina, in December 1942; and at Green's Farm, north of San Diego, California, in January 1943) the M1C and M1D Garands and the '03 Springfield became the official Marine sniper weapons. Nevertheless, many Winchester Model 70s showed up at training camps and in actual field use during the Pacific campaign.

Both New River and Green's Farm conducted training under the name of Scout and Sniper School. The first half of the five-week training period focused on fieldcraft, including map reading, movement techniques, and the use of cover and concealment; the second half was dedicated to actual shooting.

Typical of the training staff was First Lieutenant Claude N. Harris, commanding officer of the Green's Farm site. Harris, fifteen years in the corps and a combat veteran of the Pacific Theater and brief campaigns in Haiti and Nicaragua, had won the national rifle championship in 1935. He passionately believed in the importance of marksmanship and reminded his classes about the influence of snipers at Stalingrad: "Snipers can save a country, sometimes. Look what they've done for Russia."

Captain Walter R. Walsh, a former FBI agent and winner of international shooting competitions, conducted similar training at New River. Although Walsh and Harris had great latitude in running their schools, their sniper-training courses were remarkably similar. Both took volunteers who had qualified as expert riflemen, coming either from pistol and rifle marksmanship teams or straight from boot camp.

Upon completion of their training, scout snipers were assigned in three-man teams to Marine infantry companies, where commanders retained discretion in their use. Most deployed scout snipers to counter enemy snipers and to neutralize crew-served weapons. Although assigned in threes, the scout snipers worked in pairs, holding the third member in reserve to replace a casualty or to rotate on missions to ensure an alert shooter. Usually the primary shooter carried the '03 Springfield while his spotter sported a C- or D-Model M1. Battle conditions and personnel shortages, of course, often altered that arrangement.

Studies and reports in army and Marine World War II files more accurately reflect the tests on various scopes, rifles, and associated equipment than they do the actual field performance of the pieces. Some investigators considered the Winchester Model 70 and the Unertl 8 and 10 power scopes too fragile for sustained combat use. Other reports found faults in the accuracy and durability of the '03 Springfield and the C- and D-Model M1s. The services and the shooters never came to any consensus, but their debate did lead to improvements and advances that influenced future sniper operations.

One innovation that would produce long-term benefits to precision marksmanship was the introduction late in the war of an electronic device known as the "Sniperscope." Capable of being mounted on either M1 model, the scope used infrared rays, a converter, and a 4-power telescope to permit the acquisition of targets during darkness. Although the scopes cost $1,200 each, required an auxiliary six-volt storage battery powerpack, and produced a fuzzy, reddish-green image, they gave snipers the capability to fire at night without the benefit of artificial light from flares or spotlights.

Marine and army snipers performed well during World War II, but their efforts made little lasting impression on their services' senior commanders. Improved individual weapons, machine guns, artillery, close air support, and naval gunfire—combined with an advanced logistic system for resupply—convinced most military leaders that massed, concentrated firepower could replace the marksmanship skills of individual riflemen.

An anonymous article in the January-February 1946 issue of *Army Ordnance* aptly summarized how volume rather than accuracy had won World War II. The article, "Sniping—a Neglected Art," stated, "The riflemen, automatic riflemen, and machine gunners which we sent forth to war from training camps in the United States were essentially machine operators who got results by shooting a greater tonnage of ammunition than the enemy."

By the time Germany surrendered in Europe and the atomic bombs had brought a quick end to the Japanese empire, few military leaders supported the continuation of snipers or sniper training. Snipers, never fully accepted by senior military commanders during the war itself, had few champions outside their own ranks to promote the skill as a peacetime specialty. A study conducted by the Headquarters, U.S. Army Ground Forces, Pacific Ocean Areas, verified this. The study, "Training and Use of Snipers" (Report Number 183 of January 5, 1945), noted that the 8th Army Headquarters found no use for sniper training and recommended that expert marksmen at company level be issued scoped rifles only under special circumstances. The report also included statements from I Corps Headquarters that said it had conducted no sniper training for more than a year and did not see the employment of special marksmen as necessary or practical.

Report Number 183, summarizing the army's use of snipers during World War II and the service's philosophy on future employment of such marksmen, concluded, "Specific training of snipers is not at present being carried on by units assigned to this theater. The individual selection for sniper missions of expert riflemen within small units has been found sufficient and is the method currently employed."

Despite having established sniper schools during the war, the Marine Corps's leadership also did not support the post-conflict retention of snipers. In a letter dated April 20, 1945, the quartermaster general of the Marine Corps referred to the commandant's lack of enthusiasm for maintaining snipers and noted that current tables of allowances "do not include any reference to a sniper rifle." The letter recommended disposal of excess sniper rifles, scopes, and associated equipment.* Three days later the Marine Corps Operations and Plans Section approved the disposal of excess '03 Springfield rifles and their scopes.

Many soldiers and Marines disagreed with their superiors' conclusions. The same 1946 *Army Ordnance* article that recounted the tonnage of ammunition fired by "machine operators" for victory in World War II concluded, "The cheapest and most effective way to kill the enemy is by the skillful use of snipers."

Yet no one in authority paid any attention. Snipers and the tools of their trade virtually disappeared from the Marine Corps and the army. The only military marksmanship training and competition shooting instruction came mostly from former snipers. Over the next five years, few efforts were made to improve existing sniper weapons or to invent new ones.

Peace, however, did not last long. On June 25, 1950, Communist North Korea invaded South Korea, pulling the United States and its United Nations allies into the escalating conflict. The initial rapid advances and retreats resembled World War II combat; the following two years of static, trenchlike standoff resembled World War I fighting. Once again the need for specially trained and equipped marksmen surfaced.

Both the army and the Marine Corps immediately updated

---

*The last two paragraphs of the letter provide an interesting insight into the early use of sniper rifles by the U.S. Navy. According to the quartermaster general's letter, the navy's Bureau of Ordnance, on April 14, 1945, requested "400 rifles fitted with telescopes for use in minesweeping operations."

manuals and training programs for sniper training and printed doctrine on how to use the marksmen. They had adequate quantities of weapons and scopes, albeit mostly the outdated World War I '03 Springfields and the C- and D-Model M1s in storage. Yet there were no formal sniper-training schools.

North Korea was not at all reluctant to use snipers, employing them from the outbreak of the war. With rifles and scopes from the Soviet Union, Communist China, and even the United States, a small number of North Korean marksmen inflicted a large number of casualties. The United States responded with massed fire against the enemy snipers. However, many commanders were aware that snipers themselves were the best countersnipers, and just as they had in World War II, field commanders in Korea developed their own sniper training and employment techniques in the midst of battle. Many company commanders simply designated one or more of their best shots as snipers and procured whatever rifles and scopes were available through the supply system.

A typical scenario of a field commander's prerogative against enemy snipers was chronicled in an article, "Team Shots Can Kill," in the December 1963 issue of the *Marine Corps Gazette*. According to the article, shortly after the new commander of the 3rd Battalion, 1st Marines assumed command on a shell-scarred Korean hillside in the summer of 1952, an enemy sniper bullet smashed into the binoculars with which he had been observing the battlefield. The battalion commander selected a gunnery sergeant who had fired on several marksmanship teams and gave him the task of recruiting and training snipers. The sergeant found men who had scored expert with their basic rifles and who had exhibited excellent field skills and patience since arrival in Korea. Just to the rear of the battalion lines, the gunnery sergeant established a firing range and soon had his future snipers training with '03 Springfields and C- and D-Model M1s. After three weeks of training, the former riflemen returned to their units in two-man sniper teams. According to the article, the battalion commander reported, "In nothing flat there was no more sniping on our positions. Nothing moved out there but what we hit it."

Army commanders likewise designated their best marksmen as snipers and provided them with scoped rifles. Some units conducted limited training at makeshift ranges just behind the lines while others merely issued the sniper equipment to riflemen and pointed them toward the enemy.

Few records about Korean War army snipers exist. Once again the best summary of their performance comes not from the official files but from periodicals of the period. An article* in the October 1951 *Infantry School Quarterly*, "A Warning," notes the equipment and training manuals available for sniper instruction but concludes, "There is no army training program that allots time for this training nor any policy that makes it compulsory. The result is that we have produced few if any, qualified snipers.

"Having no official record of the use of snipers in Korea," the article continued, "we must seek the opinion of the men who have served there." The authors then explain that in interviews with officers and enlisted veterans of Korea they found that 95 percent of those they questioned responded that the enemy used snipers against them and 74 percent felt that the North Korean marksmen were effective. Only 35 percent were aware of U.S. Army snipers in the conflict, but 88 percent thought that they would be useful if available. Those who did recall snipers in their units reported that each company usually had one sniper rifle and its operator had received no special training.

Most field commanders in the Korean War recognized the need for snipers to limit enemy movement and to provide a countersniper capability. Weapons, scopes, and mounts, while not perfect for their mission, existed, as did basic literature on sniper training and employment. However, the U.S. military concluded the Korean conflict in regard to snipers much as it

---

*A good insight into the army's official view of snipers, and perhaps a look at its control over "unofficial" publications by subordinate schools, appears in a note just below the title and the byline of the article's infantry captain and warrant officer authors. The note warns, "The views expressed in this article are those of the authors and do not necessarily represent current army doctrine."

had entered the war—no official school existed in the army or the Marine Corps to train special marksmen. When the cease-fire finally went into effect along the DMZ separating North and South Korea on July 17, 1953, the status of snipers in the army and Marine Corps remained much as it had been at the close of World War II.

CHAPTER 5

✳✳✳✳✳✳✳✳

The Battles of Peace: Snipers Between Wars

WHEN the last echoes of gunfire sounded across the Korean DMZ, the army and Marine Corps placed their sniper weapons in storage and returned their few special marksmen to the ranks of regular infantrymen. Once again, snipers, so needed in time of war, had no place in the peacetime military, in part because of a lack of general acceptance of their role.

American bombardiers released tons of bombs on enemy soldiers and innocent civilians alike from 20,000 feet. Artillerymen fired large-caliber guns with no warning at targets miles away. Anonymous killing at a distance was acceptable—unless it was by an individual marksman sighting his individual enemy through a telescopic sight and squeezing the trigger to fire a single deadly bullet.

Some American leaders, especially those in protected rear areas who never heard a shot fired in anger or smelled the smoke and decay of the battlefield, professed an aversion to "bushwhacking" and compared sniping to murder. Peace resurfaced scruples and pangs of conscience that, by necessity, had been set aside in time of war. Once combat ceased, most American civilians and elected officials, as well as many of the military leaders they controlled, reverted to a prewar unwillingness to train young men to kill in such a personal manner.

Even though authorization for snipers and sniper training quickly disappeared after the Korean cease-fire, many of the special marksmen and their instructors remained in uniform. Some did indeed revert to regular infantry positions, but many more ended up in unit and installation marksmanship schools and on competition shooting teams.

Such assignments frequently provoked resentments and jealousies within the services. While respecting the skills of marksmen, many soldiers and Marines in regular line units believed that men in marksmanship units had easy assignments. They resented the fact that the shooters were exempted from such duties as guard, kitchen police, and other after-hours jobs. Many of the line troops viewed the shooting instructors as "prima donnas" who went to work late, left early, and fired a few rounds downrange in between. Many soldiers and Marines viewed the skilled marksmen as shooters of paper targets, not as one-shot killers.

The reasonably good publicity for the services that came via victories at national and international shooting competitions only fueled bad feelings within the ranks. Most infantrymen thought the specially manufactured, precision competition rifles were a waste of money because they were not adaptable to the rigors of prolonged battlefield service.

In addition to the personal objections and jealousies against the few Marines and soldiers who maintained the special skills of marksmen essential to snipers, the overall advances in weaponry and the beginning of the Cold War also discouraged any renewal of formal sniper training. Since the United States and the Soviet Union each had an arsenal of atomic and nuclear weapons capable of mutual destruction, the armed forces trained for a new type of combat. U.S. military leaders pictured the next war as taking place between massive armored forces supported by tactical nuclear weapons on the vast European plain. Riflemen would ride to war in armored personnel carriers and unload only to mop up objectives before remounting their track vehicles and continuing the attack.

Advances in individual weapons mirrored that focus. In 1957, the 7.62-mm M14 rifle with its twenty-round magazine replaced the M1 as the basic infantry weapon of the U.S. armed forces. Most M14s came fitted with a selector switch locked in the semiautomatic mode (one shot fired for each pull of the trigger), but each rifle contained all the components to make it fully automatic by replacing the lock with a fire selector switch and spring. Telling, however, of the prevailing ideas about infantrymen on future battlefields was the fact that the M14 had barely been delivered to units before designs for a lighter, smaller, full-automatic rifle were on the boards. The USSR also began to convert from longer-barreled, more accurate rifles to shorter weapons with increased firepower. Less than fifteen years after the Korean War, the Soviets adopted the 7.62-mm AK-47 as its basic infantry weapon. Different models and copies of the AK-47 soon became the standard weapon of Communist forces and revolutionaries around the world.

In the mid-1960s the United States and many of its allies adopted the M16 as their basic rifle. Each rifle came with a simple selector switch that changed it from semi- to full-automatic and back again. Almost two pounds lighter and five inches shorter than the M14, the M16 used 5.56-mm cartridges, significantly lighter than the former standard 7.62-mm ammo.

With the advent of the M16, every soldier and Marine could easily carry twice the ammunition and deliver a tremendous amount of automatic, if not particularly accurate, firepower. The smaller M16 also adapted well to use by soldiers in the close confines of mechanized vehicles. After modifications to decrease jamming, the M16 proved as adequate as its design promised. Unfortunately, its full-automatic capability reinforced the decreasing emphasis on individual marksmanship. Mass fire, rather than accurate fire, dominated the rules of individual shooting.

While the military services focused on increasing firepower and adapting tactics for a Cold War gone hot, sniper potential received little attention. During the decade that followed the Korean War, the army and Marines did conduct a few official marksmanship studies, and various unofficial periodicals published articles touting the need for snipers and modern sniper weapons.

The most detailed document about the future of snipers in

the Marine Corps appeared before the cease-fire in Korea even went into effect. On February 9, 1951, the commandant of the Marine Corps directed that a study be conducted on available sniper weapons and equipment to determine what sniper materials should be procured for the future.

On August 31, 1951, the Experimental Branch of the Marine Corps Equipment Board at Quantico, Virginia, responded with a lengthy paper, "Project No. 757: Sniper Rifles, Telescopes, and Mounts, Study Of," which concluded—following a painful amount of history, data presentation, and interview accounts—that since the corps trained no snipers, it required no sniper equipment.* The report's summary stated, "It is believed that unless personnel are extensively training in the use or employment of sniper material, these items may be placed in the luxury item, or 'be nice to have' category."

The summary added that, if the corps did authorize snipers, the U.S. .30-caliber rifle M1C was "sufficiently accurate." The study, declaring the '03 Springfields and their Unertl 8X scopes obsolete, recommended the Stith 4X (Bear Cub) telescope with the standard Griffin and Howe fixed mount to go with the M1C. For all practical purposes, Project No. 757, in combination with the cease-fire in Korea, put an end to Marine Corps snipers.

Snipers in the army fared no better in the post-Korea years. An article in the April 1954 *Infantry School Quarterly*, "The Case of the U.S. Sniper," declared, "The U.S. Army has no trained snipers." It went on to point out that, while FM 21-75 outlined an eighty-hour sniper-training program for squad snipers, commanders "generally ignored" the requirement. The author summed up the army's policy on snipers by concluding, "It has not produced snipers in the past, and it will not produce them in the future."

In February 1957, an article in *Army* magazine showed that little or no subsequent progress had been made by the army

---

*According to the historical overview, Marine snipers in World War II "contributed little to the war effort."

in sniper development. According to the author of "Let's Get the Most From Our Shooters," snipers remained a rarity. The article stated, "In reality, most companies have none who are properly trained and qualified."

The same periodical published a piece the following June that noted that, even if the army properly trained its shooters, snipers had no adequate rifle with which to practice their craft. In the aptly titled "Modernize the Sniper Rifle," the author claimed, "Our snipers are equipped with makeshift weapons!" He then recommended that a new sniper weapon be acquired to produce "the most psychologically terrifying force of combat: the precisely placed bullet."

What is now a faded, yellow report, dated April 19, 1960, resides on the shelves of the U.S. Army War College Library at Carlisle Barracks, Pennsylvania, apparently having made its way through several army commands without comment before coming to rest in the archives. The report's condition and content are indicative of the army's pre–Vietnam War outlook on snipers. The report, "Snipers, We Need Them Again," by Colonel Henry E. Kelly, states, "Apparently the sniper is no longer considered essential in our infantry. The squad sniper, actually only a designated and specially armed infantryman, has been dropped from the rifle squad of the future. Likewise no provision is included for a sniper detachment in the battle group organization."

No decision makers paid any attention to Kelly's report or to the few other supporters of sniper training, because overall planning remained focused on the mechanized battlefield. The ramifications of this thinking were widespread. In the mid-1950s, for instance, the services began reorganizing marksmanship training and replacing the known distance (KD) ranges.

Since the Civil War, soldiers had fired their rifles at "bull's-eye" targets at set distances of 100–500 meters. On the KD ranges, shooters learned to hit what they aimed at and to fear the waving of "maggie drawers"—a red flag raised from the protective trench by the target pullers when a round completely missed. Each soldier's score depended on where he hit the target—the bull's-eye, of course, being worth the most points.*

The army now replaced the KD ranges with the Trainfire system, consisting of pop-up targets of various sizes that unpredictably appeared at different ranges and in random sequences. The targets remained exposed for only brief periods, forcing the shooter to find, aim, and fire quickly—and often to shoot low in order to kick up sufficient dirt and debris to knock down the pop-up target and thus get credit for the kill. Some aspects of the Trainfire system made sense, for the pop-ups resembled enemy soldiers much more than did the KD bull's-eyes. Unfortunately, however, the new quick-fire procedures further deteriorated the accurate shooting skills of soldiers.

Also extremely telling about the army's post–Korean War lack of interest in snipers was the mass issue that began in 1957 of M14 rifles to replace the M1 Garands. Each new M14 had a groove and screw recess on the left side of the receiver for mounting a telescopic sight or a night vision scope. However, the services failed to adopt a mount that would fit the M14.

The first attempt to adapt the M14 for more accurate shooting came in 1958, when Captain Frank Conway of the U.S. Army Marksmanship Training Unit (USAMTU) at Fort Benning, Georgia, devised his own base to mount Weaver K-6 scopes on two M14s. Conway's purpose was not to convert the M14 into a sniper weapon but to adapt it for international shooting competition.

By the late 1950s most senior military leaders perceived the uniformed shooting teams as luxuries that depleted units of much needed junior officers and sergeants and that diverted resources through worldwide travel to participate in shooting competitions. A few of the more perceptive members of the

---

*The number of targets and rounds fired varied with time and weapons. Generally, point standards for qualifications were the same as those used later in Trainfire qualification: expert at least 90 percent, sharpshooter at least 75 percent, and marksman at least 60 percent.

shooting teams realized that those seeking to disband the marksmanship units put their positions and skills in jeopardy.

According to Charles Henderson, one of the first marksmen to come up with a rationale to preserve the shooting units and their long-range skills was Chief Warrant Officer Arthur Terry, a member of the Marine Shooting Team in Hawaii. In *Marine Sniper*, Henderson quotes Terry as saying to Officer-in-Charge Lieutenant Jim Land, "If we don't provide a service as a rifle and pistol team, we're going to wind up losing our happy home. They're not going to pay for us to run around the country and shoot—we have to deliver something worth the money . . . we might give the team a new meaning by pushing the sniper angle."

Over the next few weeks Land researched sniper history and developed a proposal recommending the initiation of sniper training. Land wrote "The Neglected Art of Sniping," which began, "There is an extremely accurate, helicopter-transportable, self-supporting weapon available to the Marine Infantry Commander. This weapon, which is easily adapted to either the attack or defense, is the M1C sniper rifle with the M82 telescopic sight in the hands of a properly trained sniper."

In presenting his case, Land related the success of snipers in previous conflicts, including quotes from the World War I books of Herbert W. McBride and Neville A. D. Armstrong, and noted the sniper equipment still available. Land received permission from his immediate senior headquarters, the 1st Marine Brigade, to begin sniper training for selected infantry-men assigned to Hawaii. Late in 1960, Land and the Hawaii Marine Rifle and Pistol Team began a two-week sniper course at the Puuloa Rifle Range, near Barber's Point Naval Air Station, Hawaii. The first week focused on marksmanship, the second on fieldcraft and land navigation.

A year later Land's sniper-training program provided regular classes to Marines assigned to Hawaii. For several years it remained the only formal sniper training in the Marine Corps—as well as in the entire U.S. armed forces. The training program received little publicity and few official records of it remain. The best summary of Land's sniper classes comes from a press release issued by the 1st Marine Brigade Informational Services Office on January 26, 1962, that states, "There is very little printed information presently available on snipers and their methods."

The press release added that the school's instructors used reference materials from other countries and their own experience as well as that of their students to teach sniping and scouting techniques. It concluded with an excellent perception of snipers at the time as well as a warning about the future. "In this age of push-button warfare," the release stated, "little thought is given to the common infantryman who has nothing but a 10-pound rifle and a lot of courage. But beware of the sniper—he is deadly."

CHAPTER 6

✳✳✳✳✳✳✳✳

Snipers in Vietnam: U.S. Marine Corps

ON March 8, 1965, lead elements of the 3rd Marine Regiment, 3rd Marine Division arrived at Da Nang as the first American combat troops in support of South Vietnam against the North Vietnamese Army (NVA) and their Vietcong (VC) allies. From the time they landed in Da Nang until their withdrawal from the war zone more than five years later, Marines recognized that Vietnam was a different kind of war that required constant adaptation and innovation.

Except for the brief periods of the three unsuccessful major offensives, the VC and NVA mostly avoided combat and fought only if they absolutely had to or if all factors favored a quick firefight victory with ample time and suitable terrain in which to escape. It was the type of war that brought the sniper and his skills to the forefront of effectiveness.

For their part, the Communists adopted a simple strategy. In 1952, the Lao Dong Party, which governed North Vietnam, announced its objective: "The ultimate aim of the Vietnamese Communist leadership is to install Communist regimes in the whole of Vietnam, in Laos, and in Cambodia."

In 1957, the Viet Minh—both those who had remained in the south after the division of the country and those who had gone north and later returned—began an armed revolt against the Diem government. Those "revolutionaries"— referring to themselves as the National Liberation Front; the anti-Communists called them Vietcong—escalated their attacks throughout the late 1950s.

The year 1959 marked a turning point. In January of that year North Vietnam's Central Executive Committee issued

Resolution Number 15, which changed its strategy toward South Vietnam from "political struggle" to "armed struggle." The following May the North Vietnamese government began to develop a supply route, later known as the Ho Chi Minh Trail, to South Vietnam along a series of roads and paths in Laos and Cambodia.

To accomplish their aim, Ho Chi Minh and his North Vietnamese government continued the same strategy that the Viet Minh had used to topple the French—a three-phase methodology originally developed by Mao Tse-tung for the Communist takeover of China. General William C. Westmoreland, commander of U.S. forces in Vietnam from 1964 to 1968, described the three-phase offensive in his book *A Soldier Reports*. According to Westmoreland, "In Phase One the insurgents remain on the defensive but work to establish control of the population and conduct terrorist and guerrilla operations. In Phase Two, regular military forces are formed, guerrilla attacks increased, and isolated government forces engaged. In the climactic Phase Three, large insurgent military units go on the offensive to defeat the government's large units and to establish control of the population. A particularly Vietnamese aspect of the final stage is the 'khoi nghai,' the general uprising, wherein the people theoretically arise and overthrow the government."

Two other major factors influenced the Communists' three-phase plan. First, instead of allowing the Vietcong to conduct the war in South Vietnam by themselves, the North Vietnamese began sending advisers in 1963 and regular NVA forces in 1964. The second important influence on the VC/NVA strategy was the Communists' patience and tenacity. From the beginning of the war, Ho Chi Minh stated that the Communists would willingly fight a "twenty-year war" and that the revolution was not a short-term undertaking.

Throughout the conflict, the Communists did indeed remain patient as they consistently were successful in executing phases one and two of their strategy. Despite overwhelming U.S. and South Vietnamese superiority in firepower, mobility, and technology, the Communists conducted guerrilla warfare at will and frequently massed for small-scale attacks against units and bases. Whenever they felt threatened, they either withdrew to sanctuaries across the border in Cambodia or Laos or changed into civilian clothing and blended in with the local population.

Despite their patience before the Americans withdrew and left the war to the South Vietnamese, the Communists did attempt on three occasions to escalate their offensive into phase three. In the Ia Drang Valley in 1965, the Tet Offensive of 1968, and the Easter Offensive of 1972, the Communists found that they could not defeat the Americans in sustained open warfare and that the general population did not rise up to help them. After each defeat, the Communists dispersed, withdrew, and waited for more opportune times. Each defeat reinforced the need for patience and the belief by the North Vietnamese leaders that they would be willing to accept defeat longer than the Americans would remain dedicated to the defense of South Vietnam.

To meet the tactics of the enemy and to adapt to the demanding terrain and weather, Marine units at all levels began making adjustments to their methods of operations immediately upon their arrival in Vietnam. From squad to force level, the Marines changed their style of operation in order to provide security for themselves and their South Vietnamese allies while at the same time taking all measures to neutralize as many of the enemy as possible. In a war of attrition, where success came to be measured in enemy body count, the Marines quickly began to contribute to the combined allied total number of VC and NVA killed.

The two divisions, two additional regimental landing teams, and a reinforced air wing of Marines ultimately assigned to Vietnam served in I Corps. Logically, the Marines, trained in amphibious warfare, would have served best in the Mekong Delta region of IV Corps, far to the south. However, true to the spirit of Vietnam's being "a different kind of war," the Marines spent the entire conflict in the thick jungles and mountains of the north.

The reasons were simple—if illogical. In 1965, the Honolulu-based Pacific Command Headquarters developed contingency plans for "temporary" support operations in the Pacific that called for an initial Marine, rather than army, landing force. The shortage of deep-water ports in I Corps reinforced that plan since the Marines could be resupplied "over the beach." In the rapid buildup of U.S. forces in Vietnam during the two years after the Gulf of Tonkin Resolution, no one had time or impetus to transfer units from one end of the country to the other.

Once operations began, the two Force Reconnaissance Companies and the two Division Reconnaissance Battalions made quick adjustments in "outguerrillaing the guerrillas" by conducting small patrols and adopting many of the enemy's own tactics. Along with the regular infantry companies, the re-con units relied heavily on artillery and airpower to support their operations and to engage enemy targets beyond the range of their organic small arms.

Only when the VC and NVA attempted to escalate their offensive into phase three did Marine battalions and regiments fight as unified elements in what closely resembled conventional warfare. Otherwise, small unit counterguerrilla operations, in which squad leaders and platoon commanders operated with great independence, marked the long periods of the enemy's remaining in phases one and two of their strategy.

During those operations, the Marines discovered that they lacked the ability to quickly engage exposed targets at distances of more than 500 to 600 meters. The M14s, the basic infantry weapon of the first Marine units in-country, had a maximum effective range of 460 meters. The M16, initially issued in 1966 to completely replace the M14 by 1967, supposedly had the same maximum effective range, but true to its design, it proved much more effective in combat at 200 meters or less than it ever did at greater distances.

The massive amount of artillery and air support dedicated to the war zone came from those assets assembled to fight a possible massive land war in Europe against the Soviets. While that almost unlimited source of extremely deadly and reasonably accurate means of engaging enemy forces beyond the range of organic infantry weapons was available, it was also wasteful.* Virtually no target was too insignificant to merit artillery and/or air attack. Ground commanders, artillery forward observers, and forward air observers adhered to no budget and had few qualms about expending hundreds of artillery rounds on a single enemy soldier. Multiple sorties of helicopter gunships and fixed winged fighter aircraft likewise delivered rockets, bombs, napalm, and machine gun fire.

The problem with artillery and air support, aside from their "overkill" results, did not lie in their availability, accuracy, or willingness to respond to the needs of the ground commanders. Rather, the problem lay in the response time required to get the weaponry on target. Frequent delays occurred in getting clearances from adjacent units, air space controllers, and South Vietnamese officials. Further compounding the response time was the safety requirement that ground commanders call for marking smoke—a single round or rocket from the artillery, helicopters, or forward air controllers—to be sure targets were properly identified and targeted. While that usually took only minutes, it often provided the enemy ample time to disperse and disappear into the surrounding jungle or countryside.

The VC and NVA, with their very survival at stake, quickly learned to gauge the effective range of the Marines' basic rifles and to use the brief warnings prior to assault by artillery and air to avoid being caught in impact zones. Marines at all levels became more and more frustrated at observing the enemy at distances beyond normal rifle range but having no effective means to immediately engage and neutralize him. It did not take long for the "old hands" to recall the effectiveness of snipers in previous conflicts and to once again seek the skills of the long-range killers.

As more Marine units poured into Vietnam in the spring of

*Artillery and air support are designed for use against large, massed enemy forces. Artillery shells and bombs are not meant to be "point" weapons, like rifles, to be aimed at individuals, but rather they are "area" weapons, designed to inflict casualties or damage in a large space.

1965, it became evident that snipers could contribute in the fight against the Communists. By early summer, Marine commanders were requesting sniper equipment for forward combat units.* Colonel Frank E. Garretson, commander of the 9th Marine Regiment, became one of the first senior officer advocates of reintroducing snipers to the ranks. His commander, Major General Lewis W. Walt, concurred, and in late summer directed that a sniper program be formed in the 3rd Marine Division.**

The best account of the first Marine snipers in Vietnam comes from Major Robert A. Russell, then assigned to the Ground Combat Division of the Marine Corps Landing Force Development Center at Quantico, Virginia. In an address during visits to Marine and army schools and training centers shortly after his return home from Vietnam in 1967, Russell explained that General Walt selected him to establish sniper training and directed the division staff to assist in securing rifles, scopes, and other equipment.

According to Russell, except for expediting the supply system to provide equipment and asking the headquarters at Quantico to develop sniper doctrine, General Walt left the sniper program up to him. In his later speeches, Russell recalled that, despite being only a captain at the time, he was left mostly on his own. His guidance from the 3rd Marine Division Operations officer, Colonel Don P. Wyckoff, was

*Limited use of scoped rifles by U.S. advisers and Central Intelligence Agency operatives preceded the arrival of the regular Marine units. At least one former adviser, who prefers to remain unidentified, claims more than a dozen enemy kills using a scoped rifle during the early years of American support of South Vietnam. Those marksmen, however, had no central organization or training, and their role remained extremely minor.

**Exact dates of certain events in the early formation of Marine snipers are imprecise. Many official letters and messages, often not written until "after the fact," never made their way into the official archives or have been lost or misplaced since the war. It is also noteworthy that most official after-action reports focus on battalion and larger units. The small number of Marines who began the sniper program in Vietnam simply did not merit mention in most official records and correspondence. Personal recollections about the dates of sniper development in Vietnam are at times in conflict, and most refer to months instead of exact dates.

simple and direct: "You're Russell, huh? Fine. Start a sniper school. Let me know when you're ready to go."

Walt had selected exactly the right officer to "start a sniper school." Russell, a native of Vista, California, and a veteran of three wars, had spent much of his twenty-two years in the corps on firing ranges as a member of various shooting teams. In several later interviews, Russell exclaimed, "For years I've been emphasizing the fact that the purpose of the Marine Corps's Competition-in-Arms (annual shooting matches) is to make a Marine more proficient in combat."

In Vietnam, Russell had his chance to prove that skills learned in competition shooting could be successfully adapted to the battlefield. While the division staff expedited requisitions for equipment, Russell used his carte blanche authority to requisition personnel for his team. According to Russell, "I couldn't have been more fortunate. There happened to be five of the finest Distinguished Marksmen in the Marine Corps serving in various infantry outfits throughout the division. I knew them well, knew their capabilities, and I knew at that point, we were in business."

The senior sergeant of the five, and therefore the NCO in charge of the sniper school, was Master Sergeant George H. Hurt, forty-two, of Bristol, Virginia, a veteran of seventeen years of competitive rifle and pistol shooting. Joining Hurt were Gunnery Sergeant Marvin C. Lange, thirty-five; Staff Sergeant Donald G. Barker, thirty-four; Sergeant James R. Bowen, twenty-eight; and Sergeant Robert L. Goller, twenty-six. All four had won individual and team shooting honors at national and international shooting matches. Lange wore the Bronze Star with Combat "V" for valor from the Korean War.

As Russell gathered his instructor team and the logistic system procured equipment, documents to support Marine snipers floated between Vietnam, Pacific Headquarters, and Washington, D.C. Sometimes the messages initiated action; in other cases they acknowledged or approved measures already taken. At times, the need for snipers and Russell's enthusiasm often exceeded the progress of paperwork. Even though Russell had begun work several weeks earlier, the first official document that mentions "Scout-Sniper Training" is dated September 17, 1965.

Russell assembled his team at the 3rd Marine Division Headquarters, Da Nang, and in mid-September received sufficient Winchester Model 70 rifles with 8-power Unertl telescopic sights to begin training.* In their early meetings, Russell and his sergeants realized that they knew much about marksmanship but little about actual sniping. Because existing sniping literature was insufficient to make up for their own inexperience, Russell understood that the only way to gain sniping expertise was to actually take his team to the field in pursuit of the enemy.

The future sniper instructors began operations with infantry units at the end of September in the sand and scrub jungle area about fifty-five miles south of Da Nang near Chu Lai. They then went forty-five miles north of Da Nang to practice their skills in the mountains and plains around Hue and Phu Bai. During six weeks of operations, Russell and his team developed, practiced, and perfected the sniper tactics they would teach in their school and that Marine snipers would use for the remainder of the war. The Marine marksmen learned their craft well during the training phase, with several successfully engaging enemy personnel. Russell and others credit team member Staff Sergeant Don Barker with their first official sniper kill.

Back in Da Nang in early November, Russell reported that they were prepared to begin sniper training. Division Headquarters then solicited volunteers from the infantry battalions, requiring that applicants be combat veterans, qualified as expert in their last range firing, and recommended by their company commanders. Meanwhile, Russell made arrangements to use an Army of the Republic of Vietnam (ARVN) rifle range,

---

*These first sniper rifles to reach Vietnam were .30-caliber weapons with heavy barrels and marksman stocks specifically designed for competition shooting. Additional information on sniper rifles and equipment appears in Appendix A "Sniper Rifle Systems Used in Vietnam."

known as Hoa-Cam (near Hill 327, a few miles south of Da Nang) as his training center.

The ARVN range had several limitations. Because it had been designed for basic rifle marksmanship, the most distant targets were only 300 meters from the firing line. Beyond them stood thick elephant grass and scrub jungle. Russell requisitioned a bulldozer and a crew from a nearby shore party battalion to clear the range to a distance of 1,000 meters. He then gathered mess hall food cans, ammunition containers, and anything else that could serve as targets.

The second limitation to the ARVN range was that it was available to the Marines only three days a week. Again Russell had to adapt. Instead of the week-long course the team wanted, the entire sniper training program would last only three days. On day one the sniper instructors issued weapons and scopes and oriented the students on the equipment. Day two included shooting demonstrations by the cadre and dry fire by the students. For the entire day three the sniper students practiced firing at targets at various ranges.

Along with testing the sniper-training curriculum, Russell and his staff established the procedures that stood the rest of the war. In the forefront of these procedures was the marriage of man and gun. The rifle issued to each sniper student remained his weapon when he returned to his unit and stayed in his possession as long as it continued to be serviceable and he served in-country.

During the initial three-day sniper schools, Russell and his staff trained volunteers from all of the 3rd Marine Division's infantry regiments. Russell later admitted that the emphasis during the early classes focused on quantity rather than quality, but that the brief course still produced "fair snipers."

It is important to acknowledge that Russell and his team organized, prepared, and actually conducted training in the midst of the escalating fighting. Even their rifle range was not totally secure from enemy attack. Yet, despite the austere and dangerous conditions, Russell's sniper school provided the training and the weapons that quickly fielded reasonably qualified marksmen to meet the needs of the combat commanders.

Throughout the war, advances in Marine sniper training in Vietnam continued at a pace faster than rear echelon officials could produce the paperwork to authorize or record it. In the midst of combat that was increasing in frequency and intensity, the small sniper-training program received little notice—either at the time or in later official studies.*

In the nine chronologies by the Marine Corps History and Museums Division about the conflict in Southeast Asia prepared during the decade that followed the Vietnam War, snipers rarely gained a mention. *U.S. Marines in Vietnam: The Landing and the Buildup, 1965* devoted only three paragraphs to sniper development. An entry in the chronology for 1965 at the end of the study notes that on October 14, "a USMC sniper team was formed in the Hue-Phu Bai TAOR (Tactical Area of Responsibility). The team used Winchester Model 70 rifles with 8-Unertl telescopic sights and killed two Vietcong at a range of more than 700 yards in the first exercise of this new tactic."

Within the text of the study a single paragraph about sniper development explains, "The Marines experimented with specially trained and equipped sniper teams. Fifty of the best marksmen were selected from each of the regiments. These troops were divided into four-man teams and equipped with Winchester Model 70 rifles and telescopic sights. During November and December, 20–30 teams operated in the Marine TAORs daily." The paragraph concludes, "On 23 November a sniper team at Phu Bai killed two VC and wounded another at a distance of more than 1,000 meters."

While the news must have circulated quickly among the VC and NVA that the Marines had suddenly acquired long-range killers, little information about the newly fielded Marine snipers reached the States. On November 3, 1965, the Military Assistance Command Vietnam (MACV) Public Information

---

*"Little notice" can actually be considered a positive achievement of that early sniper training. Things that were not going well in Vietnam tended to receive more attention from military commanders and from the press than those programs that were operating successfully.

Office released a news story stating that ninety-two men of the 3rd Marine Division were being trained and armed as snipers. The release generated little interest among the media covering the war, and it was not until about six months later that articles about snipers began to appear in military and civilian magazines, including the *Marine Corps Gazette*, *Leatherneck*, *Saigon Observer*, and *American Rifleman*. Most of those stories focused on Russell and his fellow instructors rather than actual sniper operations in the field.

The early successes of the snipers brought official recognition and authorization for their continuation. On December 29, 1965, the commandant of the Marine Corps, General Wallace M. Greene, signed a letter that approved the organization of sniper platoons in each infantry regiment and reconnaissance battalion. According to the letter, the sniper platoons were to locate and destroy the enemy by precision fire, destroy or neutralize enemy personnel who opposed the approach of friendly personnel to an objective area, and deny enemy movement in the TAOR.

Along with the approval of sniper platoons came additional requirements for equipment and training. Beginning in December, Russell and his staff increased the number of sniper classes. During the first few months of 1966, as the regiments requested slots for volunteers who would form their sniper platoons, demands exceeded capabilities. According to participants, a group of thirty-three men from the 3rd Marine Regiment attended sniper training in December 1965, returning to their unit in January 1966. The 4th Marines also organized its platoon about the same time, but there is no official record as to which regiment can legitimately claim to have fielded the first Marine sniper platoon of the Vietnam War.

In a later interview Russell recalled that the sniper school effort could best be described as informal and that he and his staff cared more at the time about producing trained snipers than about recording history. Russell kept the records of the 3rd Marine Division Sniper School in a wooden box, which has since disappeared.

Upon completion of his tour in Vietnam in 1966, Russell, then a major, returned to the United States to continue his advocacy of sniper operations as a member of the Landing Force Development Center at Quantico. In addition to presenting lectures about the progress of sniper training and use in Vietnam, Russell began writing the first official sniper-training manual in Marine Corps history.*

When the lead elements of the 1st Marine Division arrived in Vietnam in August 1965, they quickly discovered the same need for snipers as had their fellows in the 3rd Division. Some companies brought sniper weapons with them and designated their better marksmen snipers. However, the division made no efforts to develop formal sniper training until Major General Herman Nickerson Jr. assumed command in 1966. Nickerson advocated that to successfully combat the VC and the NVA the Marines had to adopt guerrilla tactics and procedures. In addition to emphasizing the use of the battalion and force reconnaissance units, Nickerson firmly believed in the effectiveness of precision marksmanship.

To initiate his sniper training, Nickerson called on Captain Jim Land, founder of the sniper-training school in Hawaii. In August 1966, Land was in command of an ordnance company at Camp Butler, Okinawa, when General Nickerson stopped at the island for a briefing on his way to Vietnam to assume command of the 1st Division. At a chance meeting, Nickerson, aware of Land's experience as a shooter, offered the captain the chance to join him in Vietnam to organize and train the division's snipers.

Land, who had assisted in providing weapons and training materials for Russell, did not arrive in Vietnam until October. With him he brought a list of every competition shooter currently assigned in-country. The captain discovered that many on his list were already serving in the 3rd Division's scout-sniper school, but he was still able to assemble a group of proficient shooters.

---

*Additional information on the development and contents of this manual can be found in Chapter 11 "Training and Organization."

Master Sergeant Donald L. Reinke joined Land as the senior NCO along with Gunnery Sergeant James D. Wilson, Staff Sergeant Charles A. Roberts, and Sergeant Carlos N. Hathcock. All were experienced competition marksmen, but only Hathcock, soon to become legendary in the annals of Vietnam precision shooters, had previous sniper training. The young sergeant had, in fact, graduated from the second sniper class offered by Land in Hawaii.

Land established his scout-sniper training at division headquarters using a conex shipping container as a temporary office. As soon as he had assembled his staff and sufficient sniper equipment, he transferred his school to Hill 55, about seven miles south of Da Nang. In a manner similar to that of Russell in the 3rd Division, Land and his fellow instructors trained themselves in the art of sniping by actually participating in field operations.

Hill 55 itself lay in the midst of an area heavily populated by the Vietcong. Terminating enemy sniper fire and harassing fire against the Marines occupying the hill was the first objective of the newly formed 1st Division sniper school staff. Beginning in October 1966, Land and his fellow snipers accompanied infantry patrols and established observation posts on Hill 55 from which to engage enemy marksmen and to direct artillery fire on suspected enemy locations.

Land and his men learned quickly. In their first month of operations, they reduced the number of enemy firing incidents against Hill 55 from thirty a day to only a few a week. In addition to their success, Land and his NCOs gained the information and experience they needed to begin training new snipers.

A little more than a month after assembling his instructors, Land started the 1st Marine Division's initial sniper class at the Hoa-Cam Firing Range, which he shared with the 3rd Marine Division sniper school. For one week Land and his staff trained volunteers how to shoot and to employ the other needed skills of the scout-sniper. A second week of training took place "on the job," with the new scout-snipers actually conducting missions in surrounding countryside and on Hill 55.

By early 1967, graduates of Land's sniper training were operating throughout the 1st Division. The February 1, 1967, issue of *Sea Tiger*, the III MAF's newspaper, led with a page 1 headline: 1ST DIVISION SCOUT-SNIPERS KILLING TWO VC A DAY. Training continued at the Hoa-Cam Firing Range while Land also transported his instructors to regimental headquarters to train new snipers and to provide refresher skills for those already operating in the field.

For the remainder of the Marine Corps's participation in the Vietnam War, the 1st and 3rd Marine Division scout-sniper schools continued to operate. The need for trained snipers, however, often rose above the schools' capacity to turn out graduates. Wounds, injuries, illness, and the thirteen-month tour of duty depleted the ranks of snipers sometimes faster than the division schools could train new ones. In recognition of the inability of the in-country schools to keep up with the demand, the corps authorized the establishment of a scout-sniper school at Camp Pendleton, California, in the fall of 1966. Graduates of the Stateside school were soon joining their fellow snipers trained in Vietnam in operations against the VC and NVA.

Marine sniper operations in Vietnam developed and advanced quickly from the time of their arrival until their departure from the war zone. Marine units had arrived in Vietnam with no snipers, sniper equipment, sniper training, or authorization for sniper units. Less than a year later there was a sniper school in each of the divisions; each regiment had an operational sniper platoon and a variety of sniper weapons, scopes, and other equipment; and orders from the commandant of the Marine Corps authorized it all. An old concept had been adapted to fight a new kind of enemy.

CHAPTER 7

****

Snipers in Vietnam: U.S. Army

Two months after the first Marine infantry regiment landed in Vietnam, units of the U.S. Army began arriving in-country. When the Gulf of Tonkin Resolution passed on August 7, 1964, fewer than 24,000 Americans were serving in Vietnam. By the end of 1965 that number had increased to 184,000, and it continued to rise until it reached 536,000 in 1968.

When the 173rd Airborne Brigade arrived in Vietnam on May 7, 1965, from its Okinawa base, it represented one of only three U.S. Army units specifically trained for jungle operations.* The paratroopers of the 173rd, however, shared a deficiency experienced by their Marine counterparts and by every army unit that followed—not a single one arrived in-country equipped or trained as a sniper.

Army units arriving in Vietnam had much to learn in order to successfully combat the Vietcong and the North Vietnamese Army regulars. In a manner similar to that of the Marines, field commanders quickly recognized the need for accurate, long-range fire with which to engage distant targets and to provide a countersniper capability. A few units requisitioned C- and D-Model M1s with telescopes or acquired M14s to issue to their best marksmen. Some officers and enlisted men had families or friends back home mail them commercial 2X and 3X hunting scopes, which they fitted to the newly is-

*The others were the 25th Infantry Division, stationed in Hawaii, which soon followed the 173rd to Vietnam, and the 193rd Infantry Brigade, which remained in Panama for the entire war to provide security for the Panama Canal.

sued M16s. Many of these improvised snipers proved remarkably successful: one lieutenant in the 25th Division accounted for more than fifty individual kills in 1966 with his scoped M16.

More typical, however, were the experiences of James W. Sotherland of Glen Allen, Virginia. An infantryman assigned to the 1st Battalion, 8th Cavalry Regiment, 1st Cavalry Division, in the Bong Song area of Binh Dinh Province in 1966, Sotherland experienced considerable frustration. He recalls: "There were occasions when enemy personnel were observed several hundred meters away and not successfully engaged by our grunts with their M16s. I attributed this to poor state of the weapons that we had then, inadequate marksmanship training, and the lack of a proper weapon to engage enemy personnel at 300 to 600 meters."

After six months in the field, Sotherland, then a sergeant and a squad leader, located two M14s recaptured from an enemy weapons cache and on no U.S. unit-property register. Sotherland traded one of the rifles to a quartermaster company in exchange for spare parts, magazines, and cleaning materials for the second rifle. According to Sotherland, "My father sent me a Weaver 6X scope and a mount. I had an armorer install the mount and scope."

Sotherland quickly found that his homemade sniper rifle had problems. "After only a few weeks in the field my Weaver scope began to fall apart. The horizontal reticle became invisible and the lenses were fogged up most of the time. The mount would not hold zero. I reluctantly had an M16 sent out and abandoned the M14 of which I had been so proud."

Overall, no army sniper policy or training existed in Vietnam during its initial two years of combat in Vietnam. The first official evidence that the army even considered using snipers in Southeast Asia came in a letter from Brigadier General E. L. Mueller, the director of doctrine and systems of the Department of the Army's Office of Force Development.

On January 10, 1966, General Mueller wrote to the commandant of the Marine Corps, noting a news release dated the previous November 3 on the use of snipers in the 3rd Marine Division. Mueller stated, "A survey is being conducted to determine if a review of the army's current doctrine on sniping and sniping rifles is required in connection with current operations in the Republic of Vietnam. Request your comments on the use of snipers together with any statistical data available on their use in Vietnam."

The Marine Corps responded on January 28, 1966, with a brief overview of Captain Russell's efforts to initiate sniper training and the sniper school graduates' use of Winchester Model 70s and M1D rifles. Despite indications by the Marines that their early sniper efforts were productive, the army moved slowly. For the next twenty-four months the army studied sniper weapon systems for Vietnam service but took no direct measures to provide weapons or training for potential snipers.

The official doctrine for the use of snipers during the early years of the army's commitment in Vietnam remained that which had been spelled out in a series of field manuals (FMs) and technical manuals (TMs) that dated back to World War II. The 1962 edition of FM 21-75, "Combat Training of the Individual Soldier and Patrolling," provided eight pages of sniper doctrine.* Paragraph 90 noted, "A sniper is an expert rifleman trained in the techniques of the individual soldier and assigned the mission of sniping." In other words, sniping remained an "extra duty" of an ordinary rifleman in each squad or platoon.

Interestingly, as the need for written guidance about snipers increased and combat intensified in Vietnam, the army produced less on the subject than it had during the years of peace. From the earliest publication in 1944, field manuals on the M1 rifle had included a chapter on the use and care of the C and D sniper models. The 1958 edition of FM 23-5, "U.S. Rifle Caliber .30, M1," contained more than forty pages of information

---

*U.S. Army field and technical manuals are updated and republished every two to ten years, depending on changes and advances made in the particular field covered by a manual. A notation on the inside cover of each new issue states, "This manual supersedes [the name and date of the previous edition]." Between new editions, the army publishes updates with their effective dates and designates the changes as "C 1, " "C 2," etc.

and pictures on the employment and care of M1 sniper models. Yet, the next edition of FM 23-5, published in May 1965, the same month the 173rd Airborne Brigade arrived in Vietnam, completely eliminated reference to sniper rifles.

More than a year after army units began combat in Vietnam, official doctrine continued to exclude any requirement for sniper training. The field manuals for rifle platoon and company operations made no allowance for sniper training. The few references that did mention snipers provided conflicting information. ATP (Army Training Program) 7-18-1 stated a requirement for a minimum of three snipers per infantry platoon, but the then-current Table of Organization and Equipment (TOE)—the official document that authorized personnel and equipment for each unit—made no provision for snipers and sniper equipment.

In December 1966, the Department of the Army published FM 23-71, "Rifle Marksmanship," which repeated much of ATP 7-18-1. The manual included a chapter on "advanced marksmanship" and the employment of snipers, stating that one sniper should be assigned to each infantry squad. Yet, the army provided no actual authorization for sniper personnel, equipment, or training.

In the midst of combat operations, field commanders in Vietnam had little time for authors of manuals or the developers of doctrine back in the States. They continued to field the few sniper weapons available and worked them into their tactical operations on the basis of trial and error. As the war expanded, however, the need for trained, properly armed snipers became more evident to army commanders at all levels.

Considering the fragmentation and lack of focus on sniper personnel and equipment during the first two years of the war, the army approached the matter in a remarkably organized manner when it finally undertook official action. On February 23, 1967, Headquarters, U.S. Army, Vietnam (USARV), issued a "Letter of Instruction" to the Army Concept Team in Vietnam (ACTIV) to "determine the organizational, doctrinal, and material requirements for sniper operations by U.S. Army units in the Republic of Vietnam."

The ACTIV immediately began to question field commanders and gather data, quickly documenting that several units were conducting limited sniping operations despite a lack of proper equipment. They also determined that sufficient data on which to determine future material and organizational requirements was not available. To provide additional information on which to make their recommendations, the ACTIV contacted the U.S. Army Marksmanship Training Unit (USAMTU) at Fort Benning, Georgia, for assistance in securing additional sniper equipment, reference material, and advice.*

On April 19, 1967, USARV Headquarters issued a message prepared by the ACTIV to major combat units throughout the country announcing plans to conduct an evaluation of sniper operations and weapons in Vietnam. The units were informed that they would receive two models of scoped M14 along with Model 70 Winchesters and Realist telescopes for M16s to conduct the evaluation. The message also directed each unit to develop its own sniper training programs, organization, and concepts of employment.

In April and May, sniper equipment arrived for the 1st, 4th, 9th, and 25th Infantry Divisions; the 1st Cavalry Division; the 1st Brigade, 101st Airborne Division; and the 196th and 199th Light Infantry Brigades. Training took place in June and July.

The 173rd Airborne Brigade received sniper equipment but did not issue it or conduct any training during the data-collection period. In a message to USARV, the commander of the 173rd explained that operational commitments, personnel turnover, and the nature of their area of operations precluded training and employment of snipers.**

---

*The USAMTU, like the prewar Marine marksmanship units, contained mostly competition shooters with extensive experience on the rifle range but little or none in sniper operations. Nevertheless, they possessed their service's only real expertise in precision shooting, and it was from their skills that the army's sniper program in Vietnam evolved.

**Actually the 173rd's area of operations differed little from adjacent commands. Reluctance to participate in the program probably resulted from anti-sniper bias on the part of the commander and his staff rather than the cited conditions.

Data collection took place from July through October 1967, with monthly summaries of sniper activities forwarded to the ACTIV from each of the divisions and separate brigades. In the final month of the test, the ACTIV distributed questionnaires and received written responses from twelve brigade commanders, fourteen battalion commanders, forty-eight company commanders, forty-three platoon leaders, and eighty-seven individual snipers.

The results of this extensive test—remarkable in its scope, especially considering it was conducted in the midst of combat—were analyzed and assembled by the ACTIV staff with Lieutenant Colonel David S. Moore heading the study as its project officer. On February 23, 1968, exactly a year after the USARV letter directed the study, the ACTIV issued its findings in a classified report, "Sniper Operations and Equipment."

According to the report, the combat units participating in the test committed 7,512 man-days to actual sniper operations. This resulted in 124 engagements producing forty-six dead enemy and another nine wounded. "The highest KIA to man-days ratio," the report stated, "occurred in units that were operating primarily in the central highlands, coastal plain, and southern portion of the northern highlands of RVN. The lowest ratio of KIA to man-days occurred in units employed primarily in the lowlands area north of Saigon and south of the Central Highlands."

The report noted that the primary influences on sniper success were terrain and vegetation. Sniper engagements varied from an average of only 200 meters in units serving in jungle areas to 900 meters in those deployed in the more open coastal plains. The report concluded that most American units in Vietnam could benefit from assigned snipers and that nearly 80 percent of the interviewed officers supported the program. The report also assessed the M14 to be an adequate sniper weapon and said that the tested telescopes had proven satisfactory. In the final analysis, the ACTIV reported, "an adequate U.S. Army sniper-training program does not exist," and "there is a lack of definitive doctrine on employment of snipers."

Combining more than thirty-five pages of interview analysis, field summaries, and test results, the ACTIV recommended: "(1) Divisions and separate command brigades be authorized sniper equipment in addition to TOE weapons; (2) organization for sniper operations be tailored by divisions and brigades in accordance with their requirements; (3) the accurized M14 be designated as the standard sniper rifle in Vietnam; (4) a standard sniper telescope be designated; (5) a sniper-training program be provided for units in Vietnam; and (6) expanded doctrine for employment of snipers be developed and included in appropriate field manuals."

Headquarters, USARV, endorsed the ACTIV report and forwarded it to the commander in chief, U.S. Army, Pacific. The USARV endorsement also requested that the Department of the Army take the responsibility for developing "doctrine, to be included in appropriate field manuals, for employment of snipers" and for providing a sniper-training program that included lesson outlines.

During the weeks before USARV forwarded the report, the Tet Offensive exploded all across South Vietnam in the enemy's largest offensive to date. The official paper trail of "Sniper Operations and Equipment" stopped at the U.S. Army Pacific Command Headquarters in Hawaii despite the fact that the document's distribution list indicated that copies went to various offices in the Department of Defense; the Joint Chiefs of Staff; and every major U.S. Army command, school, and center, as well as the navy, air force, and Marine Corps. There is no evidence that any official action took place beyond the report's delivery to Hawaii.

Obviously, the Tet Offensive occupied the primary attention of all U.S. military commands for the next several months. Many of the participants in the sniper study either became casualties of the offensive or rotated to other assignments before additional action could take place. Those factors, combined with the fact that snipers had no senior ranking officer to champion their cause, resulted in the erosion of the foundation for precision shooting specialization that had been made during the ACTIV evaluation.

Just as it seemed doomed to revert to its pre-ACTIV state, the army's sniper program received the senior officer support that it needed to become a lasting part of combat operations. In February 1968, Major General Julian J. Ewell assumed command of the 9th Infantry Division, where he implemented a variety of different programs, among them the increased use of snipers. He later wrote in *Sharpening the Combat Edge*, "In the spring and summer of 1968 we were looking for ways to bring the enemy to battle on our terms and were willing to try anything within the limits of common sense and sound military judgment. To do this we adapted known tactical innovations to the unique [Mekong] delta environment, resulting in tactical innovations which proved highly successful."

Ewell increased the number of small-unit airmobile assaults and night operations. He also believed that his division's area of operations in the relatively open delta region south of Saigon would prove to be excellent sniper country.

Before his arrival in Vietnam, Ewell had already taken steps to establish a viable sniper program in the 9th Division by contacting the U.S. Army Marksmanship Training Unit (USAMTU) at Fort Benning, which had provided the ACTIV test with weapons and literature. The USAMTU was established in 1956 with the mission of improving the shooting skills of army riflemen. To do this the unit conducted marksmanship competitions and participated in worldwide matches. During the competitions the USAMTU staff was able to single out the army's top shooters for assignment to Fort Benning for additional training. They would then return to their units to pass along their shooting abilities to other soldiers.

At one time the USAMTU had attempted to establish a sniper-training course only to meet with resistance within the ranks. According to "The History of the U.S. Army Marksmanship Training Program" (published in November 1970), "The program was short-lived because of the lack of understanding and appreciation for the value of a sniper throughout the United States Army. In addition, the military attitude then envisioned any future conflict as a nuclear one with defeat or victory decided in hours."

In 1967, before departing for Vietnam, Ewell convinced the Department of the Army to direct the USAMTU to establish a sniper-training program. The USAMTU history explains, "The Vietnam War revived the need for snipers. Enemy forces demonstrated effective employment of snipers in varying tactical conditions. Attempts by U.S. Army elements to engage in countersniping activities were similar to attempts of previous wars: no special equipment or trained personnel and a lack of technique and doctrine for commanders at all levels. In 1968 the army decided to establish a school for snipers in Vietnam. The USAMTU was given the mission of writing the doctrine, furnishing the skilled marksmen and special equipment, and establishing a school in the 9th Infantry Division in Vietnam."

The USAMTU reacted quickly to provide equipment, doctrine, and instructors for sniper training in Vietnam. Some members of the unit began working with the Army Weapons Command at Rock Island, Illinois, the Combat Development Command of the Fort Benning Infantry Agency, and the Limited Warfare Agency at Aberdeen, Maryland. Their objective was to develop and field sniper rifles, scopes, mounts, and other equipment; the result was the adoption of the XM-21, a modified M14, as the army's basic sniper weapon.*

Meanwhile, other USAMTU members drafted copies of a sniper program of instruction. After all the modifications and rewrites were in, the Department of the Army published the program in October 1969 as Training Circular (TC) 23-14, "Sniper Training and Employment."

The most important aspect in meeting its mission of establishing a sniper school in Vietnam came with the reassignment of Major Willis L. Powell and eight noncommissioned officers from the USAMTU to the 9th Infantry Division in June 1968. Powell, a native of Guthrie, Oklahoma, had more than twenty

---

*Details are in Chapter 10 "Tools of the Trade: Arms and Equipment."

years in the army and had advanced in rank to master sergeant before attending officer candidate school. Along with the experience of years of competition shooting at the national and international level, Powell had served a previous tour in Vietnam in 1963 and 1964 as an adviser to the ARVN.

Powell and his sergeants immediately revamped the division's M16 rifle training for new arrivals at Fire Base Bearcat, east of Saigon, and began training a few volunteers as snipers. Before Powell could make his school fully operational, the 9th Division headquarters turned Bearcat over to the Royal Thailand Army and moved south of Saigon to Dong Tam. There the instructors began construction of a 500-meter known-distance range while also accompanying patrols to learn the terrain and tactics of the Delta area of operations. According to an article in the division magazine, *Octofoil*, of January 1969, during their first month of operations the USAMTU instructors killed ten Vietcong at ranges in excess of 500 meters.

Despite their individual successes, members of the marksmanship team found most commanders in the 9th Division too busy fighting the war to help establish a sniper school. Ewell, concerned about the slow progress of the program, recognized that its success depended on his personal intervention. In early August he assigned Brigadier General James S. Timothy the task of getting the sniper program off the ground. Ewell later wrote, "This gave it the needed boost."

Timothy, a West Point graduate and a decorated infantry veteran of World War II, had previously served in Vietnam as the commander of the 1st Brigade, 101st Airborne Division, and as commander of the II Corps Advisory Group. Before joining Ewell as his assistant division commander, Timothy served in the States as the assistant commandant of the Infantry School at Fort Benning and had an appreciation for the USAMTU and of snipers in general.

Powell, who served with Timothy at Fort Benning before their transfer to Vietnam, recalls, "General Ewell had a meeting with General Timothy and myself. He told Timothy to look over our shoulder to keep things progressing but more importantly to get whatever we needed to get the school going."

With Timothy's support, the marksmanship team made rapid progress. Powell, bearing the title Commandant, Sniper School, 9th Infantry Division, extended the Dong Tam range to 700 meters, and, with Timothy's backing, recruited volunteers from each infantry battalion for sniper training. After two and a half weeks of training, the school graduated its first snipers in November. On November 19, one of the newly trained marksman recorded the sniper school's first official kill north of Binh Phuoc in Long An Province.

In early December the second class graduated from the 9th Infantry sniper school. Over the next months Powell and his staff continued to train 9th Division snipers as well as those from other units in the southern part of South Vietnam, including riflemen from the 25th Infantry Division and the 199th Light Infantry Brigade.

During that period other American units conducted limited sniper training based on the experience and facilities developed during the ACTIV tests. As the only official army sniper program in place, the 9th Division provided advice and assistance on a limited basis to the training conducted by other units.

"Operational Report of the 9th Infantry Division for Period Ending 30 April 1969" (dated May 15, 1969) provides an excellent summary of sniper training to that time. According to the then-classified report, "A total of five classes were conducted and a sixth class began 27 April 1969. The outstanding results obtained by the 9th Infantry Division snipers have generated interest in the sniper training throughout USARV. As a result, the school has conducted training for snipers and cadre personnel from six U.S. divisions and one separate brigade. These cadre will form the nucleus for sniper-training schools in those units."

When Powell and his team completed their one-year tour of duty in Vietnam in June 1969, a second group of instructors from the USAMTU under the leadership of Major Gary R. Chittester took their places. Powell returned to Fort Benning and rejoined the USAMTU, where he assisted in the writing of TC 23-14.

In early 1969, with the encouragement of General Ewell and the USAMTU commander, Colonel Robert F. Bayard, the Department of the Army agreed to send additional marksmanship teams to Vietnam to train snipers. The teams were to be trained at Fort Benning by Major Powell at the newly formed Sniper-Training Course.

Each team consisted of a major, seven or eight NCOs, and a trained armorer. The first class of sniper instructors graduated from Powell's school on December 19, 1969. Over the next year, teams from the USAMTU's course established formal sniper training in Vietnam with the 101st Airborne Division, the 4th Infantry Division, and the 23rd (American) Infantry Division. Each of the schools, in a manner similar to that of the 9th Infantry, trained snipers from other commands as well as its own.

The army's sniper program in Vietnam was just accelerating when other events overtook it. Within weeks after Major Chittester's team replaced Powell's, the U.S. Army began withdrawing troops from Vietnam. President Richard Nixon had won the 1968 election with the promise to end the conflict "with honor." The dwindling support of the American public for the war caused the president to order the U.S. military command in Vietnam to turn the fighting over to the South Vietnamese and to transfer units back to the States. Two of the 9th Infantry Division's brigades were among the first withdrawn, leaving only its 3rd Brigade in Vietnam.

The 9th Infantry Division sniper school graduated its last class on July 19, 1969. Chittester and his team then transferred to the 25th Infantry Division and continued to train snipers, including volunteers from the 9th Division's 3rd Brigade, at a range they developed near Cu Chi.

As more U.S. units withdrew from Vietnam, the schools trained fewer snipers. When the USAMTU teams completed their tours, they were not replaced. The last USAMTU team joined the 23rd (American) Infantry Division in early 1971 and returned home when the unit withdrew the following fall. During the summer of 1972, the final army snipers in Vietnam turned in their rifles and scopes when the last ground units of the 196th Light Infantry Brigade departed the war zone.

CHAPTER 8

✳✳✳✳✳✳✳✳

Snipers in Vietnam: Other U.S. and Allies

As in all wars, the infantry in Vietnam bore the brunt of hardships and casualties, and, therefore, "grunt" units were the ones most in need of sniper expertise. There were several obvious reasons for this. First, infantrymen had the most direct exposure to the enemy. Second, on-the-ground grunts were in position to spot isolated or small groups of enemy with little or no warning, opportunities that required instant action. Third, infantry units on patrol had only the amount of ammunition they could carry on their bodies; the more efficient its use, the longer they could maintain combat effectiveness.

Americans were not alone in the fight against the North Vietnamese and their Vietcong subordinates. More than forty nations provided assistance to the Republic of Vietnam in its struggle against the Communists. That aid included educational, humanitarian, economic, and technical contributions. In addition to the United States, seven other countries provided direct military assistance. Known as the Free World Military Assistance Forces, they were: Korea, Thailand, Australia, New Zealand, the Philippines, the Republic of China, and Spain.

The United States, however, was the only player on the anti-Communist side to make significant use of snipers. And only the U.S. infantry units did that. By comparison, soldiers and Marines in armor, cavalry, and artillery units had little call for a sniper's long-range, one-shot capability. While armor and cavalry units operated in close proximity to the enemy, they traveled in tracked vehicles that offered them protection from small arms fire, provided them with .50-caliber machine guns and large-caliber main guns, and carried for them cases of ammunition.

Artillery batteries, usually operating from fixed positions in secured base camps, dealt with the enemy from afar, delivering their destructive power through coordinated trajectories. Even when the fighting shifted to close combat, the artillerymen had stores of ammunition at their disposal and their bases were mutually supporting.

Even further removed from direct combat with the enemy and any need for snipers were most members of the U.S. Navy and the U.S. Air Force—except the few sailors who experienced ground combat in Vietnam as SEALs (Sea, Air, Land), small gunboat crews, and pilots providing close air support. The SEAL teams, however, operating primarily in the Mekong Delta region south of Saigon with missions of reconnaissance, prisoner snatching, and ambushing, did not require sniper expertise. At no time during the war did they officially include snipers in their organization.*

Nor did they unofficially claim to do so. Gary Evans, who served in Vietnam with SEAL Team One in 1969, recalls that SEALs of the period were excellent marksmen but received neither sniper weapons nor special marksmanship training. Evans says that in the summer of 1969 he procured an M1D with an M82 scope and taught himself to be a sniper. He notes, however, that his team's missions did not really require a long-range marksman, and he is unaware of any other SEALs' carrying special scoped rifles.

Likewise, SEAL veteran of the same period Brian W. Curle concurs, "To the best of my knowledge, I am not aware that Seals used snipers per se in Vietnam." Darryl Young, who served with Team One in 1970 and wrote *The Element of Surprise* about his experiences, supports the fact that no official

---

*Although the SEALs performed well in Vietnam, their actual participation and impact have been exaggerated in the years since the war concluded. Their numbers never exceeded nine platoons, or 150 men, at any one time during the conflict—only a small fraction of 1 percent of the combat troop total.

SEAL snipers served in southeast Asia. According to Young, "During the time I was in SEAL Team One there were no SEAL snipers."

Besides the SEALs, a few sailors on gunboats operated on inland waterways and some navy pilots and aircrews engaged in close air support of ground units. Otherwise, navy personnel supported ground operations with large-caliber gunfire from distant offshore positions.

Air force personnel also provided air support for infantry units, but most of their operations took place from high altitudes. While a few (and exceptional) airmen and sailors— specifically, those crewing small boats or guarding in-country airstrips—might have procured sniper weapons, no evidence suggests successful sniper engagements in either of those services.

Even though the U.S. infantry found snipers to be an effective tool against the enemy, that was not the case for combat units from other countries—including South Vietnam. The South Vietnamese soldiers and marines, like their American counterparts, assumed the bulk of that country's combat missions and casualties. Twelve army divisions consisting of 105 infantry battalions and one marine division of nine battalions composed the ground forces of the Republic of Vietnam. The South Vietnamese army, first organized in 1949, and its marine corps, founded in 1965, were armed primarily with weapons from the United States. During the early 1960s the South Vietnamese infantrymen carried M1 Garands. These were replaced by M14s in the mid-1960s. When the United States implemented "Vietnamization" in 1969 and American units began to withdraw, South Vietnamese soldiers and marines began to receive M16s as their basic rifle.

Prior to the war, gun ownership, hunting, and shooting in general were limited to the small upper class of Vietnamese. Unsophisticated recruits and draftees from the countryside had no experience with firearms. Vietnamese city dwellers were also unfamiliar with weaponry, having seen rifles only in the hands of the military.

Marksmanship can, of course, be taught regardless of a person's previous experience, and many South Vietnamese soldiers and marines became adequate, if not expert, shots. Long-range, scoped marksmanship, however, was a skill that few South Vietnamese sought or acquired. Sniper training had no high-ranking advocate in the South Vietnamese military or government, and apparently it never received any great amount of consideration despite the results of the American long-range shooting programs. As a result of starting with such unskilled troops, the South Vietnamese army as a whole never reached the level of expertise to merit establishing its own sniper school. The available M1C and M1D rifles and scopes remained largely unused.

Because of the proximity of U.S. sniper training, the number of American advisers assigned to their units, and the reasonable availability of weapon systems, a few South Vietnamese soldiers and marines surely developed and used some sniping skills. But only one reference to these experiences made its way into the official records and correspondence of the war—and it provides information that is not entirely accurate.

In his 1974 monograph *Sharpening the Combat Edge*, written for the Department of the Army Vietnam Studies Program, former 9th Infantry Division commander Lieutenant General Julian J. Ewell mentions training provided the South Vietnamese by the USAMTU from Fort Benning in 1969. Ewell wrote, "One of the factors that gave the Vietnamese units quite a boost was the fact that we were able to help them with marksmanship training. After we had trained a sufficient number of our own snipers we established marksmanship classes attended not only by the 7th South Vietnamese Army Division but by the Vietnamese ranger and airborne troops from other areas of the country."

Ewell refers to the South Vietnamese graduates of this training as "snipers" but that is euphemistic. Major Willis Powell, who supervised the training, states that the South Vietnamese were taught basic marksmanship techniques with some advanced instruction in long-range shooting. None of the South Vietnamese were trained with or were issued sniper rifles and scopes. Powell states that while there were some discussions about securing M14 sniper equipment for the South Vietnamese, nothing ever came of them.

No other official U.S. source mentions formal sniper training for the South Vietnamese armed forces, even though there is documented evidence that the Americans did train their allies in the use of Starlight scopes, the light-enhancing devices employed by snipers. But that equipment was not limited to snipers, as infantrymen also used it for observation during hours of darkness.

Members of the USAMTU, who established and conducted the 9th Infantry Division Sniper School, provided instruction on the Starlight scopes to the South Vietnamese when regular sniper classes were not in session. A note in the "Operational Report of the 9th Infantry Division for Period Ending 30 April 1969" states, "Training conducted by the Sniper School has also included instruction given ARVN (Army of the Republic of Vietnam) personnel in the use of the Starlight scope. Several more classes of this type are scheduled for the month of May, 1969."

Members of the USAMTU also trained Vietnamese to return to their units as instructors in the use of Starlight scopes. "Operational Report for 9th Infantry Division for Period Ending 30 June 1969" reported, "The Sniper School also conducted training in the use of Starlight scopes for ARVN cadre from the 9th and 25th (ARVN) Infantry Divisions."

Despite lack of proof, it seems unlikely that absolutely no South Vietnamese acted as a sniper during the long conflict. Whether self-trained or as unofficial students of army or Marine snipers, at least a few South Vietnamese undoubtedly employed scoped rifles to go gunning for the NVA. Whatever their degree of participation, however, they made no impact and did not merit anything more than the vaguest recollection in the official records.

Of the seven other countries of the Free World Military Assistance Forces supporting South Vietnam, three provided noncombat units: China and Spain sent only small military medical and support sections totaling less than 100 men each;

the Republic of the Philippines sent a 1,500-man military engineering unit complete with its own security element, medical section, and civic action teams. Because of their missions, none of the three countries had any need to train or field snipers during their time in Vietnam.

The other four supporting countries varied in their use of snipers. Beginning in 1962 Australia provided individual advisers as a part of the Royal Australian Army Training Team, Vietnam (RAATTV), to the South Vietnamese army, and in 1965 the 1st Battalion, Royal Australian Regiment (RAR), arrived in-country as a part of the ground combat force. In 1969, at the peak of their commitment, more than 7,600 Australian combat and support troops were in the war zone. During the course of the war, nine RAR infantry battalions totaling more than 35,000 men served in Vietnam, 504 of whom were killed in action and 2,193 wounded.

Unlike the Americans, who replaced individuals after one-year tours, the Australians rotated entire battalions. These Australian units arrived in Vietnam ready after nine months of combat preparation. Australian infantrymen trained at home with the semiautomatic 7.62-mm L1A1 SLR (self-loading rifle) common to all Commonwealth forces in the early 1960s. Upon arrival in Vietnam a few of the rifles were exchanged for the American M16s, but most Australian infantrymen remained armed with the L1A1.

The Australian infantrymen, who performed extremely well in Vietnam, gained renown for their fighting spirit and marksmanship, shooting and hunting being commonplace in Australia. All Australian infantrymen received some long-range shooting training at the Canungra Battle Efficiency Course, in Queensland, or at the Singleton Infantry Training Center, in New South Wales. In addition, each platoon in the Australian regiment arrived in Vietnam with a trained sniper in its ranks. These marksmen served as "special infantrymen" much as U.S. Army soldiers had during World War II.

Australian snipers carried L42A1 rifles, which were 7.62-mm modifications of the United Kingdom Rifle No. 4, Mk1, first fielded in 1942. Weighing 9.7 pounds and measuring 46.5

inches long, each bolt-action L42A1 came with a ten-round box magazine and a 3X Mk 32 scope. In trained hands the L42A1 was extremely accurate at ranges up to 850 meters.

Most of the Australian infantry operations in Vietnam, however, were in extremely thick jungle areas and rubber plantations that did not permit long-range shooting. Also, the RAR never emphasized or supported sniping to the extent that the U.S. Marine Corps and army did. Australia considered its snipers as part of the platoons, and special shooters received neither the attention nor the publicity of their American counterparts.

New Zealand sent its first support troops to Vietnam in 1964 and followed with two infantry companies in 1967. Those two units, integrated into the Australian Task Force, served until withdrawn in 1971. Like the Australians, the New Zealand infantrymen operated specially trained snipers assigned to most platoons and armed with L42A1s. Also like the Australians, a few of the other New Zealand infantrymen traded their L1A1 SLRs for M16s shortly after arriving in-country.

New Zealand never had more than 350 infantrymen in Vietnam at any one time. Their sniper numbers were never more than half a dozen, and like the Australians they made little or no impact on the conflict.

The Kingdom of Thailand supported South Vietnam by allowing U.S. air bases on its territory and by dispatching support and combat troops to the war zone. Its ground troops served in the Queen's Cobras—the Royal Thai Army volunteer regiment—which arrived in 1967 and operated from Fire Base Bearcat, near Bien Hoa. They were replaced in 1968 by the Black Panther Division, composed of two infantry brigades, three artillery battalions, and an armored cavalry battalion. At its peak, Thailand had more than 11,500 combat troops in Vietnam.

Early plans called for the United States to issue 1,000 M16s per month from March through June 1967 to the Thai infantry in Vietnam. Theoretically, it would have been more effective to have issued the rifles to the Thai infantrymen for training before their deployment to Vietnam. However, U.S. logistic officers knew that any M16s delivered to Thailand tended to remain there to combat an insurgency in the country's northern provinces rather than being deployed with units to Vietnam.

Compounding the problem of delivering the authorized M16s was the need for rifles to supply the increasing number of U.S. units committed to Vietnam. Ultimately, only 900 M16s were made available to the Thais. To make up the shortfall, the United States planned to supply the Thais with M14s until U.S. officials realized that the Koreans, who were receiving M1 rifles from the United States, would be insulted if the Thais were first issued the more modern M14s. Instead the United States issued the Thais M1 (semiautomatic) and M2 (full-automatic) .30 caliber carbines that lacked the fire and stopping power of the other U.S. rifles. The Thai soldiers, however, were comfortable with the smaller, lighter carbines.

U.S. officials were correct in considering the feelings of the Koreans and making efforts to keep them happy. South Korea provided more than 300,000 men to the war effort and was second only to the United States in its commitment to assist the South Vietnamese. In addition to support units, Korea sent two infantry divisions and a marine brigade to the combat zone. More than 4,400 South Koreans died during their operations, which occurred mostly in the Central Highlands.

Although never available in any quantity, a small number of M1Cs, M1Ds, and M14s were accessible to both the Thais and the Koreans, and there is little doubt that at least a few soldiers from each country acquired scopes and mounts to assume the role of sniper. A few Korean officers visited the U.S. Marine Corps's sniper schools as observers but neither they nor the Thais established a formal sniping school, nor did their soldiers officially attend* the U.S. training. Snipers simply did not play a role in the operational planning or execution of those two allies during their service in the Vietnam War.

*Several American veteran snipers recall that occasionally Korean, Thai, and other allies participated in at least portions of their training. There is no record, however, of any official agreement for training of the individuals.

With the exception of the sniper training and employment by U.S. soldiers and Marines, the use of the special marksmen in Vietnam by South Vietnam and its allies was nearly non-existent. The Australians and New Zealanders did have official, trained snipers, and the other Free World countries had a few unofficial snipers who acquired sniper rifle systems and training on their own. At best, however, usage of snipers by our allies in Vietnam was symbolic rather than significant.

CHAPTER 9

�֍✶✶✶✶✶✶✶

The Men Behind the Crosshairs

MOST books and articles about military snipers—whether discussing Vietnam or other wars—place more emphasis on the rifles, scopes, mounts, and ammunition than they do on the men behind the crosshairs, almost as if the authors, as well as their intended audiences, better understand windage, caliber, magnification power, grains of powder, and other technical information than they do the personalities and mind-sets of the snipers themselves.

Some writers concentrate so much on mechanics and hardware that it often appears the rifles themselves killed the enemy, as if there were no soldier sighting down the barrel or through the scope before squeezing the trigger to send a bullet downrange; an accurate picture of sniper activity in Vietnam can come only through examining the men behind the crosshairs and their abilities to adapt to their unit and terrain environments. Snipers conducted their missions in triple-layered canopy jungle, on steep mountains, in scrub-covered coastal lowlands, and across open rice paddies. Some areas of operation were in remote regions far from any population; others were in locations with heavy concentrations of farmers and families; still others were near large villages. At times the snipers sought the elusive, loosely organized and poorly equipped Vietcong, who were less than enthusiastic about standing and fighting. On other occasions, army and Marine snipers opposed North Vietnamese regulars who were aggressive and well organized, armed, and trained for battle.

Army and Marine snipers made whatever adjustments necessary to find, engage, and destroy whatever enemy they faced in whatever environments they found themselves. While their training, organization, utilization, and equipment varied, they shared the most important commonality—they were men who *volunteered* to be snipers, a unique group in a unique war. Nevertheless, in many ways they were not "super Marines" or "super soldiers"; rather, they closely resembled their brother infantrymen in the combat line units from which they came and to which many returned. Their ranks contained the good, the bad, and the indifferent, yet as a whole, Marine and army snipers in Vietnam set the standard by which military marksmen still operate.

One important aspect of the snipers was age. While much has been written about the youth of the men who fought in Vietnam—the average age of Americans in Southeast Asia was nineteen and a half, compared to twenty-six years of age in World War II*—the U.S. armed forces in the war zone also had senior sergeants and officers with ten, twenty, or more years of experience providing training and leadership. Even though expanding numbers of combat units in the war's early years and the escalating casualty rates reduced their numbers as the war continued, at no point in the conflict were American units without some degree of senior leadership.

This mix of young, inexperienced soldiers and Marines with older, experienced senior NCOs and officers in Vietnam was equally evident in the sniper units of both services. Captain Robert Russell had twenty-two years' experience as an enlisted and commissioned Marine, much of which he spent on competition shooting teams, when he established the sniper school for the 3rd Marine Division. All but one of his instructor staff were in their upper thirties or early forties with ten to twenty years' experience as Marine marksmen. Sergeant Robert Goller, the youngest on the team at twenty-six, had

*Some of the American public's lack of acceptance of and disdain for Vietnam veterans might have been a result of the warriors' youth. The idea that teenagers, who had been unable to avoid the draft because they were from the "wrong side of the tracks," were returning to their streets as experienced killers frightened many Americans.

eight years of competition shooting experience and had received a perfect 250 X 250 score in a 1961 rifle match.

When he formed the 1st Marine Division sniper school, Captain Jim Land brought to Vietnam his expertise in having established the Marine sniper school in Hawaii in 1960 as well as having spent years on competition shooting teams. His NCO instructor staff mirrored Russell's team in rank, age, and experience.

The USAMTU team under the leadership of Major Willis Powell combined more than 170 years of active duty experience when it arrived in Vietnam to organize the 9th Infantry Division's sniper school. Each member had fired on army shooting teams, and most were veterans of previous tours in Vietnam or the Korean War.

While veteran competition shooters with decades of experience in uniform formed the instructor teams in Vietnam, the vast majority of those whom they trained as snipers came from the lower enlisted ranks and were serving their first tour of duty in the armed forces. Both services recruited sniper volunteers at the in-country replacement centers where new arrivals were in-processed. Recruits for sniper training also came from combat units in the field, which received periodic allocations for infantrymen.*

Both the Marine Corps and the army used the same basic selection criteria for entry into their sniper-training programs. Indeed, the wording is so similar—at times identical—that it suggests the writers exchanged information when preparing Fleet Marine Force Manual (FMFM) 1-3B, "Sniping," and the army's Training Circular (TC) 23-14, "Sniper Training and Employment," both published in 1969.

Under sections labeled "Personnel Selection," both manuals emphasize the importance of marksmanship, physical stamina, and mental condition of potential snipers. "The

---

*The exceptions to those sources were Marines who attended the sniper school at Camp Pendleton, California, before going to Vietnam and previously sniper-trained Marines and soldiers returning to the war zone for subsequent tours of duty.

sniper trainee," begins the selection requirements, "must be an expert marksman." In addition to requiring the candidate to fire expert with military weapons, the criteria stress the importance of "an extensive hunting background" and experience in competition shooting if possible.

The manuals note that snipers often engage in extended operations with limited sleep, food, and water—conditions that require excellent physical conditioning to maintain reflexes, muscular control, and stamina. According to the manuals, athletics, especially team sports, were a good background for building cooperation and self-confidence. Wearing glasses was a liability to a potential sniper not only because of the importance of excellent vision but also because the lenses might reflect light and compromise a sniper's concealment or render him useless if they were lost or damaged. Since the Marine snipers primarily used bolt-action rifles, their selection criteria added that volunteers should be right-handed because the additional movement required by left-handed shooters to operate the bolt over the top of the scope increased the danger of detection.

Long before the antitobacco campaigns swept across the United States, the armed forces declared that snipers should be nonsmokers. Smoke or a smoker's cough could give away a sniper's position. Even if a sniper did not smoke during a mission, the addiction might cause nervousness and irritation that would lower his efficiency.

In reference to mental capacity, the services sought intelligence and emotional balance. A trainee had to be able to learn quickly and retain vast amounts of information on ballistics, ammunition, and optical devices in order to shoot accurately. He also had to be able to operate and maintain communications equipment, to call and direct artillery and air support, and to gather and report intelligence on the enemy and the terrain.

Along with the ability to learn, the requirements for snipers called for innate talent for fieldcraft. He had to possess stealth and a sense of direction to reach his firing position undetected and to feel comfortable in the outdoors.

Mental condition is clearly one of the most important characteristics of a good sniper even though the manuals gave it the same priority as physical conditioning and intelligence. The potential sniper had to exhibit characteristics of reliability, initiative, loyalty, discipline, and emotional stability. In short, a sniper had to be able to pull the trigger at the right time and in the right place.

The 1969 edition of FMFM 1-3B explained the difference between ordinary Marine infantrymen and sharpshooters: "An infantry Marine, in the heat of battle, kills the enemy emotionally and reflexively, lest he be killed himself. A sniper, however, must kill calmly and deliberately, shooting carefully selected targets. He must not be susceptible to emotions of anxiety or remorse. Candidates, for instance, whose motivation towards sniper training rests mainly in the desire for prestige which may accrue to them in performing a unique function, may not be capable of cold rationality which the sniper's job requires. A proper mental condition cannot be taught or instilled by training."

Manuals, of course, detail optimums that are not always possible or practical in combat conditions. The cadres of the various sniper schools were aware of the manual's selection criteria and used them, and their own experience, to evaluate volunteers at the reception centers. Field commanders, although unlikely to have access to the manuals or time to peruse them while fighting the war, understood the basic physical and mental criteria for snipers from their personal combat experiences.

The school cadres and field commanders shared the knowledge that it took a very particular type of soldier or Marine to coldly peer through a telescopic sight and pull the trigger to deliver a fatal bullet to an unsuspecting and unwarned enemy. Not only must the potential sniper be able to accomplish that task, he also had to possess the mental toughness to do so repeatedly.

Jim Land strongly believed in the importance of the psychological stability of potential snipers and questioned each candidate at length to determine if he had the correct mind-set for the job. Land later wrote in a foreword to *Marine Sniper* by Charles Henderson, "It takes a special kind of courage to be alone: to be alone with your thoughts; to be alone with your fears; to be alone with your doubts. This courage is not the superficial brand stimulated by the flow of adrenaline. Neither is it the courage that comes from the fear that others might think one a coward. It is the courage born of honor.

"Honor on the battlefield is a sniper's ethic. He shows it by the standards and discipline with which he lives life in combat. By the decency he shows his comrades. And by the rules he adheres to when meeting the enemy.

"The sniper does not hate the enemy," Land continued, "he respects him or her as a quarry. Psychologically, the only motives that will sustain the sniper is the knowledge that he is doing a necessary job and the confidence that he is the best person to do it. On the battlefield, hate will destroy any man— and a sniper quicker than most."

The sniper instructor also wrote of other characteristics he sought in trainees. Further, according to Land in the foreword, "The sniper is the big game hunter of the battlefield, and he needs all the skills of the woodsman, marksman, hunter, and poacher. He must possess the fieldcraft to be able to position himself for a killing shot, and he must be able to effectively place a single bullet into his intended target."

More recently, in *One Shot—One Kill* by Charles Sasser and Craig Roberts, Land, reflecting on his own experience as a marksman and sniper, added, "When you look through that scope, the first thing you see is the eyes. There is a lot of difference between shooting at a shadow, shooting at an outline, and shooting at a pair of eyes. It is amazing when you put that scope on somebody, the first thing that pops out at you is the eyes. Many men can't do it at that point."

Senior commanders in Vietnam also had specific ideas about the characteristics of good snipers. General Frederick J. Kroesen Jr. (USA, Ret.), who commanded the 23rd Infantry (Americal) Division in 1971, simply states that a "good sniper" had to exhibit "selflessness" and "patience."

Lieutenant General Ormond R. Simpson (USMC, Ret.),

who assumed command of the 1st Marine Division at Da Nang in December 1968, also had ideas about what he looked for in volunteers for his sniper school. According to Simpson, "Of course superior marksmanship was an absolute requirement that was never waived. Given this talent or ability, a good sniper needed to have infinite patience, even nature and temperament, ability to get along with his team member, willingness to remain in his position for often long periods of time regardless of rain or wind, the skill to move quietly and to escape detection. The judgment to fire *only* when there was a good chance for a kill with a single round. We could never use 'trigger happy' people in this program."

An article in the January-March 1969 edition of the 9th Infantry Division publication, *Octofoil*, provided insights into what Major Powell's school looked for in potential army snipers. According to the article, "It [the sniper school] constantly seeks soldiers possessing special qualities—a good eye, ability to think quickly and remain cool in combat and, a prime requisite, the desire to learn."

The selection of potential snipers from replacement centers and from the ranks in the field was not a pure process. Ed Kugler, observed that firsthand as a scout-sniper with the 4th Marine Regiment. In March 1966, Kugler and several hundred other Marines arrived from the States at the Da Nang replacement center. Early on their first morning in Vietnam, Staff Sergeant Walt Sides, the platoon sergeant of the 4th Marine snipers, addressed the formation of replacements using a bullhorn. Sides, explaining that he worked with Captain Russell at the scout-sniper school, told the new arrivals they were looking for volunteers. Kugler recalls that the sergeant did such a great "sell job" of making the sniper role sound exciting that he and thirty or forty others stepped forward.

Some of the volunteers were eliminated when their records showed that they had not qualified as experts on the rifle range. The sniper school NCO then interviewed the remainder, looking for what he termed "mental toughness." At the completion of the interviews, only Kugler and three other replacements were selected by the NCO for transportation to Phu Bai.

At Phu Bai, Kugler and the others joined another eight Marines (from infantry units already in Vietnam) for the second sniper school class taught by Russell and his staff. Kugler recalls that, even though all were qualified as expert marksmen, several of the Marines had been "volunteered" by their units because their commanders wanted to be rid of them; that method of eliminating problem Marines (by sending them to other assignments) was a common practice in all units that, in some cases, worked well for both units and the transferred Marines.

Kugler says, "Two, I remember, specifically as friends today, were 'volunteered' by the grunts. They were 'shitbirds' the grunts wanted gone. Irony was, they turned out to be great snipers. Over my two years in Vietnam, I would say 30 to 40 percent of the volunteers were grunt misfits who became great snipers."

Generally, however, field commanders followed the same selection procedures that the sniper school NCOs used. They also had the added advantage of having actually observed the actions of the men under fire and knowing how they reacted to killing the enemy.

Most commanders wanted to fill their sniper school allocations with men who would make good representatives of their units and, more important, who would complete the school and return with training and a weapon that would assist the unit in accomplishing its mission. Unfortunately, the Marine and army sniper schools did not always have the capacity to train the number of snipers that the senior commanders and field units wanted, which meant that the number of volunteers seeking training frequently exceeded the limited school space.

Terry Roderick of Cocoa, Florida, joined P Company, 75th Infantry (Ranger) from the army's 5th Mechanized Infantry Division, near Quang Tri, in October 1969. In February 1970, his Ranger company received a single allocation for the 101st Airborne Division's sniper school at Camp Evans. Roderick recalls, "When the opening for the school came to our company, I think I had the highest score with the M14 from basic training and they wanted to make sure they sent someone who would represent the company well. I've always been a good shot with a rifle and it was well known throughout the company since we had a lot of 'shooting matches' at the range where we went for 'test firing' our weapons before going out on missions."

Although recruiting snipers in the war zone was an imprecise science, the Marine scout-sniper school at Camp Pendleton, California, had more time and certainly safer conditions under which to select trainees. Yet its process closely resembled that of the Vietnam schools. Joseph T. Ward of Lakewood, Colorado, notes in his book, *Dear Mom: A Sniper's Vietnam*, that a few days before completion of boot camp, he and his fellow Marines were offered the opportunity to volunteer for several schools. Ward, who had fired expert and "could put the bullet where it belonged," volunteered to become a scout-sniper along with thirty-six others.

Prolonged interviews by the scout-sniper school staff reduced that number to twenty-five, only twenty of whom would eventually graduate. That 80 percent completion rate was actually a bit above average. About a quarter of each class at Pendleton and in the army and Marine schools in Vietnam failed to complete the program successfully.

Nearly all of the soldier and Marine sniper volunteers came from the ranks of the infantry. Little official information about their ages, hometowns, or other demographics was recorded at the time, and such information can be gathered now only by analyzing the recollections of the war's veterans.

Traditionally the Marine Corps, because of its smaller size and emphasis on preserving history, has performed better in maintaining records than the army. Marine archives from Vietnam, however, are as lacking in information on snipers as are the army's. In 1984, Ronald H. Spector of the U.S. Army Center of Military History's analysis branch published a pamphlet about the deficiencies in official accounts of the Vietnam War.

Major Willis L. Powell (top), founder of the army's 9th Infantry Division Sniper School, briefs Assistant Division Commander Brigadier General James S. Timothy on the XM21 sniper rifle in October 1968. (U.S. Army)

Graduation photo of the 9th Infantry Division's first sniper class in November 1968. (U.S. Army)

A 9th Infantry Division sniper prepares to aim (top) and fire (bottom) his XM21 during a daylight sweep in the Mekong Delta. (U.S. Army)

The U.S. Army's most successful sniper in Vietnam: Sergeant First Class Adelbert F. Waldron of the 9th Infantry Division. (U.S. Army)

An army sniper in the 1st Infantry Division takes aim as his spotter provides security during operations south of Lai Khe in October 1969. (U.S. Army)

The M21 sniper rifle system as adopted by the U.S. Army in 1970. (U.S. Army)

The properly armed and equipped sniper as illustrated in U.S. Army Training Circular 23-14 published in October 1969. (U.S. Army)

A 9th Infantry Division sniper mounts an AN/PVS2 Starlight scope on his XM21 in preparation for a night mission. (U.S. Army)

The Hoa-Cam Training Center near Da Nang where the 1st and 3rd Marine Divisions trained their snipers. (U.S. Marine Corps)

Captain Robert A. Russell, founder of the 3rd Marine Division Sniper School, on the range on November 3, 1965. (U.S. Marine Corps)

(top) A 9th Marine Regiment sniper team in action during Operation Harvest Moon in December 1965. (U.S. Marine Corps)

(left) A 9th Marine Regiment sniper engages a target with his Winchester 70 and 8X Unertl telescope from Hill 251 in December 1965. (U.S. Marine Corps)

The basic U.S. Marine Corps sniper rifles early in the Vietnam War (from the top): M1D with 2.2X M86 scope; Model 70 Winchester with 3X-9X variable scope; Model 70 Winchester with 8X Unertl scope. (U.S. Marine Corps)

The M700 Remington sniper rifle system. (U.S. Marine Corps)

A 26th Marine Regiment sniper at Hill 557 near Khe Sanh on January 10, 1968. (U.S. Marine Corps)

A 7th Marine Regiment sniper team uses a .50-caliber machine gun as a sniper rifle. (U.S. Marine Corps)

Joseph T. Ward of the 5th Marine Regiment prepares to depart An Hoa on a mission in 1969. (J. T. Ward)

A 1st Marine Division sniper team in action on January 21, 1970. (U.S. Marine Corps)

Although the pamphlet addresses army record keeping, its findings apply to the Marine Corps as well.

In "Researching the Vietnam Experience," Spector explains, "In terms of sheer volume, the records relating to the Vietnam War appear to dwarf those of any previous American conflict. The war was the first to be fought in the age of the copying machine and the computer, and the influence of those innovations is reflected in the massive paper trail left by that conflict. There can be no debate about the quantity of documentation. Quality is another matter.

"During the early years of the war, unit commanders, overworked and understaffed, often neglected or ignored army requirements concerning the preparation and preservation of reports and records."

Later in the war, when officials recognized that proper documentation and records management were not taking place, they attempted to correct the oversights. Spector comments, "The result was the rapid accumulation of masses of trivial and ephemeral material." Spector also pointed out that studies as early as 1974 concluded that filing historical documents from Vietnam was complicated by the "tendency of units to destroy records rather than retire them."

Spector adds the important point that, unlike the paperwork from previous American conflicts, documentation of the Vietnam War is also extremely one-sided. At the conclusion of World War II, U.S. historians had access to masses of captured enemy archives as well as the opportunity to interview high-ranking military and political officials to determine their decision-making processes and the impact of American weapons and tactics. Nothing remotely similar exists from the Vietnam War.

Another difficulty in record keeping of the Vietnam conflict that Spector does not cover is the loss of records due to combat operations. Despite elaborate security measures, no area in the war zone was completely safe from enemy attack. Unit headquarters and their administrative records were on occasion, especially during the Tet Offensive of 1968, destroyed by enemy attack. Still other records remained in Vietnam when

Saigon surrendered in 1975 and fell into the hands of the North Vietnamese.

From what information is available, it is apparent that in most ways the American sniper volunteers mirrored the profile of other soldier and Marine infantrymen in Vietnam. Of the 2.7 million Americans who served in Vietnam, 79 percent were high school graduates. Fully 75 percent were volunteers while 25 percent were draftees.*

While the average age of army and Marine infantrymen in Vietnam was nineteen and a half, sniper cadre tended to select candidates who were a year older because they sought the more mature and experienced. Many volunteers from the ranks already had been in-country for several months, adding a bit to their age.

Common characteristics of potential snipers mentioned by their instructors and field commanders were familiarity with weapons and experience in the outdoors. An article on the selection of snipers in the May-June 1972 issue of *Infantry* says, "He must be an outdoorsman acting as a trapper and forest ranger with the cunning of a wild animal—all at the same time."

Some of the volunteers closely resembled that profile. Powell recalls that one of his best sniper students was a former big-game hunter and guide from Alaska. Many of the snipers grew up with weapons and as boys provided much of the meat for their family table through their marksmanship. A majority of the sniper volunteers were from the South, the Southwest, and the far West. Most came from rural areas and towns of less than 50,000 population.

Of course, there were exceptions. Sometimes prior experience with hunting rifles had instilled more bad habits (such as improper holds and sighting problems) than good in a marksman and retraining was more difficult. Soldiers and Marines

*Many men facing the draft and the possible assignment to the infantry volunteered for service in the relatively safer jobs in army rear echelon specialties or joined the air force or the navy. The Marine Corps did not accept draftees until late in the war, when the numbers of volunteers became insufficient to fill vacancies.

who had learned to shoot, and shoot well, in basic training were often the easiest to train. As a result, the ranks of snipers, although dominated by men from small towns or rural-route addresses, also contained shooters from New York City, Los Angeles, Seattle, and other metropolitan areas.

Most of the enlisted men selected for sniper training were from the lower ranks. The senior enlisted instructors in the sniper schools and the NCOs in charge of sniper units, particularly in the Marine Corps sniper platoons, came mostly from the ranks of the competition shooting teams. Later in the war some of those positions were filled by NCOs who had earned their stripes, either in Vietnam units or back in the States between tours of combat duty. Still other snipers volunteered to extend their tours in six-month increments and advanced from shooters to supervisors.

Sniper school officers, like the senior NCOs, generally had prewar experience on their service's competition shooting teams. Yet the officers involved in sniper positions faced a unique problem. To advance in rank, combat officers must command platoons, companies, and battalions. Leading sniper teams and instructing marksmanship do not enhance qualifications in front of a promotion board. Thus the officers had to make a choice between advancement potential on the one hand and their convictions about the importance of the sniper's contribution on the other.

Generally, officers attracted to sniper duty were drawn to it by their love of shooting and the personal job satisfaction it offered. Many, such as Russell and Powell, were "mustangs" who had lengthy service in the enlisted ranks before receiving their commissions. They were well aware that sniper service might prove detrimental to their careers, but they welcomed the opportunity nevertheless.

While "prior service" officers with competition shooting experience established and initially administered the sniper training and operations in Vietnam, the program also attracted junior officers. Marine sniper platoons each had a lieutenant in command who usually served several months in an infantry unit before joining the shooters. Other than a few lieutenants in the 9th Infantry Division who took charge of their battalion's teams and those officers assigned to the USAMTU, few army officers served with sniper units in Vietnam. In nearly every case, these lieutenants had already determined that they were not remaining in uniform after their initial tours of duty and sought sniper duty knowing that they had no future military careers.

Unlike most units in Vietnam, where African Americans composed about 13 percent of the ranks and other minorities reflected about the same percentage as did their ethnic groups in the civilian population, Marine and army sniper teams were mostly white. Neither the Marines nor the army maintained exact figures on the race of snipers, but available evidence indicates only a small number of black and other minority snipers. Based on a study of morning reports and unit rosters, the memory of the participants, and other sources,* it appears that only 3 or 4 percent of army and Marine Vietnam snipers were black. The numbers of Hispanic and Asia-Pacific Americans also amounted to only one fourth to one third of their overall percentage of servicemen.

The army and Marine Corps, with no official doctrine on racial composition of snipers, seemed unconcerned with the imbalances. When asked about the discrepancies, some officials shrug it off as a mathematical probability that some specialties would attract fewer minorities while others attracted more. Other officials say that there was no reason for the statistics—they just happened. A third school of thought suggests that minorities as a whole were reluctant to volunteer for any aspect of what they considered the "white man's war."

The first two explanations may indicate a lack of conscious effort to analyze the situation, but the third rationalization is blatantly invalid. In fact, blacks and other minorities volun-

---

*While the military did not record racial composition figures for subordinate units in Vietnam, it does today. Department of Defense figures for 1997 show that 4 percent of Marine and army snipers are African Americans and 5 percent are Hispanic.

teered in numbers far above their population averages for other elite units such as the army's paratroopers and the Marine Corps as a whole.

The only other units in Vietnam with similarly small percentages of minorities were the army's Long-Range Reconnaissance Patrol (LRRP) companies* and the Marine Force Reconnaissance companies. The reconnaissance units and the snipers both sought volunteers with "out-in-the-woods" experience, a prerequisite that automatically eliminated many minorities from densely populated urban areas.

The best explanation may lie in the sociological traits of blacks and Hispanics as a whole. African Americans and Latino cultures typically provide gregarious homes and neighborhoods where there is extensive interaction between individuals. Sniper operations, like those of the reconnaissance units, required extreme individualism where the "loner" type was much more comfortable than men who valued peer interaction.**

Ultimately, it was the man and his ability to shoot that made the difference, not the color of his skin or his background. From the time he joined the ranks of the most highly trained marksmen, each man found his life dominated by being a sniper. His friends and family were his fellow shooters, and with his counterparts he developed a camaraderie and empathy that only those few who peer through the scope at a living human target truly understand.

Snipers, like other warriors in Vietnam, came from all kinds of religious backgrounds. Battle has a way of driving some men to seek divine protection and others to give up on religion altogether. Still others, especially after surviving extended combat, begin to believe that they themselves are more powerful than any allegedly superior being. There is no evidence that, as a result of the unusual nature of their "business,"

---

*Redesignated Ranger companies and detachments on February 1, 1969.
**Like everything else about Vietnam, the exception often ruled. The best sniper serving with the author in the 199th Light Infantry Brigade in 1969–1970 was an African American from Washington, D.C.

snipers responded differently from their infantry contemporaries when it came to an increase or decrease of religious zeal.

Despite the fact that relatively few men passed through the narrow gates of selection and that those who did were dedicated and effective, recognition of the performance of Marine and army snipers in Vietnam remained extremely low-key during and after the war. The success of snipers depended upon their ability to be invisible to the enemy; advertising their existence in any manner threatened their survival.

The snipers themselves wanted no publicity that could endanger their lives or their missions. Simultaneously, the military deflected media attention away from sniper activity because of their controversial image. By 1969 many in the United States were actively opposed to American involvement in the war, labeling any unusual weapons or tactics, including the work of snipers, as an atrocity.

Snipers rarely talked to the press, and the unofficial policy of the army and Marine Corps was not to encourage news stories about the marksmen. Events proved the wisdom of that approach when in July 1968, the Associated Press acquired a draft copy of FMFM 1-3B, "Sniping." The resulting story, which ran in newspapers across the country, including the *San Francisco Chronicle* (on July 18) and the *Milwaukee Journal* (on July 22), began, "The ability to go for a long period without food or water, to control emotions and to kill 'calmly and deliberately' and without remorse are the main qualifications of a good sniper." In a later paragraph, the AP story repeated the lead, adding, "A sniper must kill calmly and deliberately, shooting carefully selected targets."

While the AP story accurately credited Bob Russell for writing much of the manual and reported its contents in a fairly straightforward manner, the sensational lead paragraph upset many readers, who, far from the war zone, either could not or would not understand the fact that young Americans were being taught to kill "calmly and deliberately."

Letters to the editors of the papers began arriving immediately, most specifically condemning the snipers and expressing the writers' general distaste for the war. The commandant of the Marine Corps received similar letters. It was a no-win situation for the military because even the few writers who concurred with the concept of snipers condemned the corps for allowing the content of the field manual to be made public.

Snipers in Vietnam were also criticized by a portion of the American public during and after the war for their "keeping score." In a war of attrition like the Vietnam conflict, where successes were measured by body count rather than by territory gained, it should be no surprise that snipers—who had the best position and equipment to confirm kills—also kept count of their individual records.

Unfortunately, a double standard prevailed. Fighter pilots, who painted a flag or a silhouette on the fuselage of their aircraft for each "killed" enemy plane, continued to be viewed as heroes while few Americans wanted to acknowledge, much less praise, men who looked their quarry in the eyes before pulling the trigger.

After the brief blitz of publicity in 1968, little more appeared in print about Marine or army snipers for the remainder of the war. Other than a few articles in professional journals and in the various "gun" magazines, the snipers went about their business with little or no fanfare.

Even the official records mostly ignored the accomplishments of snipers. With the exception of the official manuals, the several studies conducted by the army to determine the need for the special marksmen, and a few Marine division orders on sniper training, few written materials survived the war. Sniper numbers were small and military commanders in combat were more interested in neutralizing the enemy than in recording details on paper. Various brigade, regimental, and division quarterly operational reports include a sentence or, at most, a paragraph on sniper training, occasionally mentioning the number of kills for a certain period.

Initially, recognition of snipers in each Marine and army division closely paralleled the particular commander's interest and investment in the program. Both Marine divisions supported sniper training, and the corps developed the best organized system of sniper unit organization and deployment. Yet the corps's lengthy series of studies about the war, *U.S. Marines in Vietnam*, includes fewer than 200 words about sniper operations in the conflict.

Few outside the corps's small sniper and marksmanship community had ever heard of Gunnery Sergeant Carlos Hathcock before the civilian publication of Charles Henderson's *Marine Sniper* in 1986, which details Hathcock's 93 kills in Vietnam. When Joseph T. Ward wrote in *Dear Mom: A Sniper's Vietnam* about 5th Marine sniper Chuck Mawhinney and his 103 confirmed kills, even several "old hands" in the competitive shooting community expressed doubts about the story until eyewitnesses and the few existing official documents supported the account.

Although Hathcock, a career Marine with years of competitive shooting experience, has received far more acclaim than Mawhinney, the latter, a three-year-enlistment Marine, had the highest confirmed body count of any Marine sniper in the Vietnam War. His story is also more representative of the typical American who volunteered to become a long-range marksman during the conflict.

Charles B. Mawhinney hunted extensively as a boy for sport and to put meat on the table, but he never fired in a marksmanship competition. He entered the Marine Corps on October 10, 1967, and upon completion of infantry training, volunteered for the scout-sniper school at Camp Pendleton, California. Shortly after graduation he joined the 5th Marine Regiment in Vietnam, where he soon became a member of the regiment's scout-sniper platoon. Mawhinney served as a sniper for the rest of his thirteen-month tour and then extended for six more months to perform the same duties. He extended once again for a final six months to become a helicopter door gunner before returning to the States for discharge as a sergeant in 1970.

Most of Mawhinney's sniper missions occurred in the area of An Hoa, including Liberty Bridge, Arizona Territory, and

Go Noi Island. During his tour he teamed with more than half a dozen other marines. Joe Ward was among them. Mawhinney accomplished most of his kills with the M700 Remington and a Redfield scope, but he also used .50-caliber machine guns as sniper weapons from fixed base camp positions. For night shots, he sometimes used a Starlight scope mounted on an M14. Upon completion of his sniper tours, Mawhinney had 216 probables in addition to his 103 confirmed kills of enemy soldiers. That is, he personally accounted for the equivalent of about three NVA infantry companies.

With the exception of the brief mention in Ward's book, little appeared in print about the Marine Corps's top sniper in Vietnam until Peter R. Senich interviewed Mawhinney for the December 1996 issue of *Precision Shooting*. Senich quotes Mawhinney as attributing his success to his previous hunting experience, to the excellent training he received in sniper school, and to "learning Oriental habits and adapting to Charlie's domain."

After his discharge, Mawhinney returned home to the Pacific Northwest. In the 1996 interview with Senich, the Marine sniper reflected, "It was over. . . . I just wanted to forget about it and get on with my life. I don't spend much time thinking about Vietnam, but the memories that come to mind are mostly positive. I remember my friends and the camaraderie in our unit."

For nearly three decades since the war Mawhinney has worked for the Forest Service. According to Senich, the former sniper reports, "I trap and hunt in the winter, fish in the summer, and I try to keep up with my family."

Overall, the army recorded even less information on its snipers than did the Marines. Only General Ewell's 9th Infantry Division maintained any significant amount of information on its snipers, and even its documentation is woefully lacking in providing sufficient information to completely describe and document the program.

In *Sharpening the Combat Edge*, Ewell does mention the war's most successful sniper, Sergeant Adelbert F. Waldron III, who had 109 confirmed kills. Ewell notes, "Sergeant Waldron earned two Distinguished Service Crosses for his outstanding skill and bravery."*

Waldron proved to be the exception in receiving medals in recognition of his shooting prowess. Marine and army snipers were awarded the usual "I was there" campaign ribbons and most were awarded an end-of-tour meritorious medal. Generally, however, snipers did not receive the number of valor medals awarded to those in the regular line units. Few snipers seemed to care. Bits of metal and colored ribbon did not compare with the satisfaction of the hunt.

Snipers in Vietnam shared many of the same talents and characteristics of the army LRRP/Rangers and the Marine Force and Battalion Recon units. Within the army and Marine Corps in Vietnam there were many units and groups that considered themselves a bit above the rest. In addition to the reconnaissance units, various air mobile, airborne, demolitions, and medical evacuation units took extreme pride in their special accomplishments. Yet, all, including the snipers, recognized that the bulk of the war and the brunt of the casualties were sustained by the infantry. The vast majority of the snipers came from the infantry's ranks and performed most of their missions accompanying the line units, with which they felt a special bond and loyalty.

Army and Marine infantrymen consider themselves to be at the center of everything that occurs in the armed forces, the more so in a combat zone. Without their muddy boots to occupy territory, no battle or war can be won. They do the bulk of the work, shed the most blood, and determine the success or failure of every conflict. Snipers not only shared those distinctions of the infantry but also felt that their special training and talents made them an elite within the infantry.

One characteristic of any elite group or organization is its small numbers. The army and Marine snipers in Vietnam certainly met that criterion. They were so few that neither the army nor the Marines maintained records of who had qualified

---

*The Distinguished Service Cross is the army's second-highest decoration for valor in combat, ranking behind only the Medal of Honor.

as snipers. No complete list of sniper school graduates for any service exists in any official or unofficial archive. The only way to estimate the number of the war's snipers is to study the few surviving documents, the official personnel authorizations, the recollections of the school cadres, and the marksmen themselves.

Personnel authorizations offer at least a reasonable range of numbers. Marine FMFM 1-3B called for the assignment of one officer and thirty-five enlisted men in each infantry regiment's sniper platoon and one officer and thirty enlisted men in each reconnaissance battalion's sniper platoon. With eight infantry regiments and two recon battalions serving in the war zone at the height of the conflict, the formulas reflect that there were never more than 350 authorized Marine sniper positions in Vietnam at any one time. Considering the normal thirteen-month tour of duty for Marines, the arrival and departure dates of the regiments, and the date each division established its sniper school, calculations indicate that no more than 875 Marine snipers saw action during the war.

Obviously any estimate of numbers must include replacements for casualties or illness. Sniper school instructors must also be included in the number, as well as the handful of Marines who acted as unofficial marksmen in their units before the establishment of the schools. More important, however, few if any units in Vietnam ever operated at full strength, and it was rare that any infantry regiment or recon battalion had its complete complement of snipers. Those factors imply that it is extremely unlikely that more than 875 Marines served as snipers in Vietnam, and that number may well be high by at least 100.

Unlike the Marine Corps, the army had no official authorization for snipers in its combat units except for the antiquated and ignored guideline that one soldier in each infantry squad was to have a sniper rifle. General Ewell established a policy in the 9th Infantry Division for the assignment of two snipers to each brigade headquarters and six to each infantry battalion. If that had been carried over to the rest of the army's twenty-five infantry brigades and eighty-one infantry battalions, it would mean a total of a few more than 500 sniper positions at the height of the war.

Taking into account that the army did not train snipers until well after the Marine Corps established its schools, that soldiers served only twelve-month tours, that units withdrew at staggered times—and using a liberal method of computation—it would appear that no more than 1,000 army snipers ever served in the war. Even adding the 259 poorly trained and armed snipers who participated in 1967's test Army Concept Team in Vietnam keeps the total below 1,300.

But further investigation reveals the 1,300 figure to be extremely unrealistic. Major Willis Powell recalls that the 9th Division's sniper school trained about 120 men before the majority of the units began withdrawing from the war zone. The other USAMTU training teams arrived in Vietnam only in the last year or two of the U.S. involvement in the war. In addition, many army units worked in terrain unsuitable for sniper activities. Also, some commanders did not need or want special marksmen. In some cases, commanders as high as division level disdained even the concept of the sniper and so did not train or use them.

All in all, it is doubtful that the army trained and employed more than half the quasi-authorized numbers of snipers for a total of about 500. Adding the snipers who participated in the 1967 tests, a realistic number of army snipers who served in Vietnam is about 750.

Based on those calculations, no more than 2,200 soldiers and Marines served as snipers in Vietnam. A more realistic figure is about 1,250. And even that number may be 10 to 25 percent too high.

What it took to become a successful sniper in Vietnam differed little from the characteristics necessary in previous wars. In their 1942 study, "Equipment for the American Sniper," George O. Van Orden and Calvin A. Lloyd included a chapter titled "What Is a Sniper," but the authors admitted that they paraphrased a definition provided by Stephen Trask in his 1917 writings about World War I marksmen.

According to Van Orden and Lloyd, "While the modern theories deal with fast-moving columns of masses instead of companies of men, there survives one lone wolf of the battle-fields. . . . Wherever he chooses his hiding, he is there on the fringes of the fight, waiting, waiting, waiting, through perhaps all of a dreary day and a night. Little knots of the enemy may cross his vision. Still he holds the fire of his telescopically sighted rifle. His game is not to send a hail of rapid fire into a squad or a company; it is to pick off with one well-directed, rapidly delivered shot a single enemy, to send him beyond recall by skilled surgery in the brief flitting moment.

"He must harass the foe," the authors continue, "taking an officer here, a man there. He must hammer relentlessly upon the nerves of the rank and file of the opposing forces, until his rifle crack, joining with others of his kind, becomes a menace more to be feared than the shrieking shells from cannon, or the explosive hail from the mortars. His bullet must come from nowhere. It must find a mark sometimes as small as a two-inch loophole at two hundred yards, or a man standing against a hazy background."

In conclusion, Van Orden and Lloyd note, "The sniper is an institution that should and does naturally appeal to American fighting men, and before our army is complete, we will undoubtedly have thousands of his breed."

CHAPTER 10

✳✳✳✳✳✳✳✳

Tools of the Trade: Arms and Equipment

*T*HE success of the sniper program in Vietnam depended upon the man behind the crosshairs, but Marine Corps and army leaders also recognized that their marksmen had to be properly armed and equipped in order to accomplish their missions. In "Equipment for the American Sniper," Van Orden and Lloyd noted, "It is safe to say that the American sniper could be regarded as the greatest all-around rifleman the world has ever known, and his equipment should include the best aids to his dangerous calling that the inventive genius of the United States can produce."

Despite recognition of the importance of equipment, particularly rifles, the Marine Corps and the army entered the Vietnam War with antiquated sniper weapons, including M1Ds from World War II and Korea and a small number of '03 Springfields that dated to World War I.

Both services recognized that technology had improved durability and accuracy since World War II and looked for newer, better rifles with which to equip their special marksmen. In their search the two services took a variety of measures to determine which weapons systems to procure and ended up adopting different rifles.

With a maximum effective range of 600 meters and reasonable accuracy at 400 to 500 meters, World War II–vintage M1Ds were available in ample numbers for Captain Bob Russell and his sniper instructor team to secure them for their school and graduates. Or they could have adopted the more modern M14 as the sniper weapon of choice since at that time every Marine arrived in-country carrying one as his basic weapon.

Russell and his fellow instructors, however, concurred with the general consensus that the M1D lacked range and that the M14, having no scope to enhance its accuracy beyond the range of its "iron" or standard sights, was adequate only for the sniper team observer and not for the principal shooter.

Russell faced the same quandary the corps had encountered in 1942 and again in 1951, when the Marine Corps had conducted studies to determine the best sniper rifle. In both tests the investigators favored the Model 70 sporting rifle introduced by Winchester in 1937 for target shooting and hunting. This bolt-action rifle, having a five-round integral magazine and interchangeable twenty-four- and twenty-eight-inch barrels, delivered the long-range accuracy the Marines sought. However, officials had decided against its adoption because of the complications of injecting another rifle into the supply system—especially one that required 30.06-caliber (7.62 X 63-mm) ammunition rather than the standard military 7.62 X 51-mm cartridges. For that reason, the Marine Corps resisted adopting the Model 70 as its official sniper rifle for more than a quarter of a century.

However, when Russell and his staff sought a sniper weapon in 1965, they chose the Model 70 by default because it was the only rifle available that met the long-range accuracy requirement of the Vietnam battlefield.

The selection of the scopes for the Model 70s occurred in similar manner. Sufficient numbers of Unertl 8-power telescopes had remained in the Marine logistics system since their procurement as early as 1943 for use with the Model 70 and the M1903 sniper rifles in World War II.* While far from perfect, the distinctive twenty-four-inch-long Unertl 8-power scope would become one of the most recognizable pieces of equipment used by Marine snipers in Vietnam.

Russell and his team were satisfied with their selection, in part because for years they had practiced and competed with

---

*The "8-power" scope actually produced a magnification of only 7.8.

Winchester Model 70 sporting rifles equipped with Unertl 8 power telescopic sights rather than standard military-issue weapons. Because they were so confident in the long-range accuracy of the Winchester Model 70, they adapted it as the "unofficial-official" sniper rifle for their students.

The first dozen Model 70s to arrive in Vietnam were the very rifles that the 3rd Marine Division—including Russell and many of his staff—had used for years in national and international competition shooting matches. Now those same sharpshooters were using the same weapons to hunt the Vietcong and to train sniper volunteers. Despite their age, the rifles had been well cared for and were in excellent condition.

Russell's request for additional Model 70s produced rifles from a variety of sources. The Marksmanship Training Unit at Quantico gathered several from its stocks and procured others from the Marine Corps Supply Center at Albany, Georgia, for transfer to the 3rd Division. Several of the Winchesters dated back to the Korean War and at least one had been used in the national rifle championship matches at Camp Perry, Ohio, in 1953. Many of the rifles were older than the Marines who would carry them into combat.

With the Marine Corps's commandant's approval of sniper units in late 1965, the headquarters staff calculated the need for 550 additional weapons for Vietnam and the U.S. training base. Searches to fill that requirement reached the entire corps, bringing Model 70s from Marine bases around the world. Some arrived with markings on their stocks showing that they previously had been assigned to Special Services facilities, which loaned them to Marines and their families for use in target shooting and hunting. The condition of the rifles varied, but most could be rebuilt or refurbished to meet sniper requirements.

While Russell and his staff began training their volunteers with the best rifle and scope available, the Marine Corps activated efforts to replace the equipment with a more sophisticated weapon system. In December 1965, the Marine Corps Headquarters instructed the Quantico Marine Schools Weapons Training Battalion to issue verbal orders to the Marksmanship Training Unit (MTU) to procure a rifle, telescopic sight, and mount suitable for use by snipers in Vietnam. The orders came with no deadline for a recommendation, but all parties involved were aware of the immediate need in the combat zone.

On February 9, 1966, the officer in charge of the Marksmanship Training Unit responded to the commandant of the Marine Corps in a brief, well-thought-out response endorsed by the chief evaluator, Colonel Walter R. Walsh, a marksman of some renown who had helped establish the Marines' World War II sniper training. "The indicated urgency for an early recommendation," the letter began, "dictated that evaluation be limited to presently available commercial items."

Because the original instructions had provided no specific guidance, the letter explained that the evaluators had operated under some self-imposed assumptions. The assumptions of the MTU reflected their thorough knowledge of the characteristics of a dependable sniping system. Under a section titled "Self-imposed Assumptions," the letter listed the requirements for the selected sniper system to use the standard 7.62-mm ammunition and "be simple, sturdy, and explainable with minimum amount of instruction." The study's authors assumed that most targets would be at ranges of less than 600 yards but that snipers would require a well-sealed telescopic sight that could sustain operations in conditions of high humidity and be "capable of adjustment at ranges up to and including 1,000 yards."

To meet the requirements, the MTU tested five rifles—including the Winchester Model 70, the Harrington and Richardson Ultra-Rifle, and three models of Remington—as well as seven different telescopes. The study discounted the Winchester Model 70 for its requirement of 30.06-caliber cartridges and eliminated the Harrington and Richardson because, as the evaluation reported, "These rifles are assembled from components of 3 manufacturers including a foreign made action." They also rejected the Remington Models 600 and

700-ADL and BDL rifles as too light for military sniping operations. Only the Remington 700-40X merited positive comment: "This rifle is built on an action designed for the 7.62 mm cartridge. Trigger is internally adjustable. Relatively simple to bed."

Of the various scopes tested, the MTU found problems of insufficient power, insufficient adjustment capability, and weak seals that allowed moisture in the sight. Only the Redfield Accu-Range 3X-9X received positive comment: "Well-sealed, adequate internal adjustment, built-in range finder to 600 yards."

In analyzing the rifle and scope test data, the letter stated, "Based upon physical examination and use of the above equipment, coupled with personal experience of testing personnel with the above and similar equipment, it is believed that the Remington Rifle Model 700-40X, in combination with the Redfield Accu-Range 3X-9X variable power telescopic sight in Redfield mount, is the most suitable equipment now available for the purpose expressed."

Walsh and his fellow marksmanship instructors knew that the Winchester Model 70 had supporters at many levels within the Marine Corps, so they added a paragraph before their recommendations to head off objections to their findings: "The presence in the Marine Corps Supply System of a number of Winchester Model 70 rifles was considered. However, these are all chambered for the .30-06 cartridge. Modification to the 7.62 mm cartridge could be accomplished, but would be expensive and not especially desirable. Additionally, rifles that are nominally Winchester Model 70s are now found, due to factory modifications made over the years, in 3 different types. Many of these parts are not interchangeable."

The MTU letter also recommended "a hard carrying-shipping case with protective foam-padding containing desiccant and fungicide be provided for each rifle/scope unit."

The corps's leadership acted with remarkable speed. On April 7, 1966, the Marine Corps adopted the rifle, scope, and mount as recommended, designating the system as the M40, although for the remainder of the Vietnam War some would refer to it as the Remington 700, Model 700, or Remington M40.

Remington had marketed several types of 700s, including the two other models that the MTU found to be "too light," as hunting rifles for several years, and had found wide acceptance of the Model 40X as a competition rifle before its selection by the MTU as a sniper weapon.

On May 17, 1966, the Marine Corps issued a supply contract to Remington detailing the specifications of the Model 40s and an order for delivery. By the end of the year Remington had completed 700 rifles and then produced nearly 300 additional weapons over the next five years. Remington modified the finish and added military swivels (for a sling) at its Custom Shop in Ilion, New York, and redesignated the rifle the Model 40 to comply with Marine specifications.

The M40 shared several characteristics with the Winchester Model 70 that it replaced. Both had a five-round magazine and a bolt action. Some critics at the time noted that bolt-action rifles required additional physical motions by the shooter to eject a spent shell and to reload a round into the chamber—movements that might compromise a sniper's "hide" position—and they argued that semiautomatic rifles made better special marksman weapons.

Others countered that the additional moving parts in semiautomatic rifles made them less steady and therefore less accurate than bolt-action weapons. Marine marksmen admitted the slight weakness of "bolt-guns," but believed both the Winchester Model 70 and the Remington M40 to be superior to any other bolt-action or semiautomatic rifle available.

The supply contract for the Remingtons also spelled out the specifications for the Redfield scopes and mounts to match the new rifles. The Redfield 3X-9X variable power telescope had entered the commercial market in 1962. At slightly less than thirteen inches long, the scope weighed only three quarters of a pound and proved to be rugged as well as resistant to humidity and moisture. More important, a simple power-selection ring allowed the marksman to enlarge or reduce the image between a magnification of 3.3X and 9.1X. Movement of the power-selector ring also adjusted internal stadia wires that provided the range-to-target measurement on an internal indicator scale.

Of all its characteristics and capabilities, the Redfield scope's ability to accurately indicate range proved the most vital. Snipers, even those with extensive "trigger time," had difficulty in determining the distance to the target. Adoption of the Redfield scope ended the sniper's having to make his own range estimate.

The Marines sent 150 of the sniper systems to the Camp Pendleton scout-sniper school. A few of the rifles and scopes arrived in Vietnam during the final days of 1966, and by the end of the first quarter of 1967 adequate systems were in-country to arm the instructors and field snipers.

The final subparagraph of the MTU's letter to the commandant of the Marine Corps recommended that "action be taken to insure availability of match-grade ammunition for use in the rifle." Thus, along with the M40 sniper rifles came special ammunition manufactured for the marksmen's use on the range and the battlefield.

Target shooters and snipers alike knew that, regardless of the sophistication of their rifles and scopes, much of their accuracy depended on the quality of their ammunition. The optimum ammunition contained no variance in the amount of propellent, the size or weight of the bullet, or the shape of the cartridge. Each round should have the same characteristics and strike at the same place when fired under the same conditions.

At the time of the Vietnam War, ammunition manufacture had become extremely standardized, producing highly accurate cartridges. The tolerances of mass production, however, allowed *slight* variation, and while that had little influence on the fire of conventional riflemen, it did affect the consistency and accuracy of target shooters and combat snipers.

In the later part of the nineteenth century, ammunition manufacturers began to produce limited numbers of cartridges made with special care to ensure that each possessed identical characteristics and capabilities. Specific demand for such special-made ammunition increased with the Olympic and other international shooting competitions that became popular after the turn of the century. Since those rounds were specifically made for and used in competition shooting, they became known as "match ammunition."

Ammunition, including match, is manufactured in lots, that is, the rounds made in a single run on the cartridge plant assembly line. The manufacturer then assigns a lot number to each such batch and records the number on every ammunition container. Each round in a lot, especially those manufactured under match conditions, theoretically performs in the same manner. A sniper who zeroes his weapon with rounds of one lot can expect the remaining cartridges in the same lot to act identically.

Although the U.S. military had considered match ammunition for combat marksmen as early as World War II, it had not acted to acquire that type of round. Postwar marksmanship teams used match ammunition exclusively, but until Vietnam the most accurate rounds were limited to use on the target range. Logisticians resisted adding the more costly ammunition to already overburdened supply systems.

When Russell and Land established Marine sniper schools in Vietnam with the Winchester Model 70s, they never considered reverting to standard-issue cartridges. Instead they added match ammo to resupply requests. Because of the small number of snipers and the small number of rounds they fired, ammunition sources in the States had no problem keeping up with demand.

The Lake City Army Ammunition Plant in Independence, Missouri, manufactured the match ammunition used in Vietnam. Built during World War II, the plant operated under management by the Remington Arms Company through a contract with the U.S. government, which actually owned the facility. Lake City first made .30-caliber ball ammunition for the Winchester 70s in 1957, and in 1962 became the sole supplier of the match-grade cartridges designated M72s. In 1964, the plant began manufacturing 7.62-mm NATO match ammunition as M118s.

Quality control requirements for both the M72 and M118 match rounds were the same. The Lake City plant tested each lot of match ammunition at its 3,400-acre facility, which hosted ranges that extended to 2,400 yards.* According to the military contract for match ammunition, "The acceptance test requirement is a mean radius of 3.5 inches for nine 10-shot groups from each of three test rifles at a range of 600 yards. The mean radius represents the average distance of each shot in the group from the group center."

The U.S. Army approached its selection of a sniper rifle and scope in a manner similar to that of the Marine Corps, the primary difference being that it conducted the evaluation in combat in Vietnam rather than back in the States at a marksmanship training facility. When the Army Concept Team in Vietnam (ACTIV) began its study of sniper operations and equipment in 1967, it worked under specific instructions to test and evaluate rifles and scopes to determine which models the army should adopt as the official sniper system.

The ACTIV operated under the same restrictions as the Marine MTU. The immediate need for a sniper system meant it had to come from present inventory or via "off the shelf" civilian procurement. Time to develop a new rifle simply did not exist during the escalation of U.S. involvement in Southeast Asia.

Between April and June 1967, the ACTIV, with assistance of the USAMTU at Fort Benning, secured four different sniper systems for evaluation. These included the M14 accurized rifle with a 2.5X M84 scope, the M14 National Match rifle with a 3X-9X adjustable range telescope (ART), the M16 rifle with 3X Realist commercial telescope, and the Winchester Model 70 with a 3X Weaver scope.

Selection of the four weapon systems resulted from their availability and from the biases of the evaluators. For ease of

---

*Match ammunition arrived in Vietnam packaged in paper boxes containing twenty rounds each. The white containers with red and blue markings were much more appropriate to the rifle range than to field use, where proper camouflage often meant survival.

procurement and maintenance, the members of the ACTIV favored adaptation of a rifle already in the supply system. In fact, it is unlikely that the Winchester Model 70 would have been included at all but for the fact that eight of the rifles were already in the possession of the 1st Brigade of the 101st Airborne Division in Vietnam.*

Except for a brief mention buried deep in Annex A of the ACTIV's final report, there is no evidence that the army ever considered testing the rifle the Marines had chosen for their sniper system. The comment in the Annex about the Remington 700s stated that it and the Winchester Model 70 possessed "very close to the same potential" as the M14 National Match Service rifle and, therefore, "would not warrant their purchase."

The M16s used in the evaluation were standard issue, without modifications. No plans had ever been made to use the M16 in competition shooting so no match ammunition had ever been manufactured for it. As a result, regular-issue 5.56-mm rounds were used during the test. The Realist 3X scopes, commercially manufactured by the Colt Arms Company, also came without modifications for military use.

Little difference existed between the "accurized" and the National Match M14s except for adaptations to the former for mounting the M84 telescope and the latter for the ART system. Both rifles had been modified to prevent automatic fire, and parts had been selected and fitted to increase accuracy. Stocks of the M14s were bedded with a glass fiber and epoxy resin to make them impervious to water and the swelling or warping that would decrease accuracy. The army supply system made available 7.62-mm M118 match ammunition manufactured by the Lake City plant for use in the rifle's twenty-round magazine.

The ACTIV post-test survey of snipers and their commanders

*The presence of the rifles is an example of the unofficial efforts by army ground units to field their own snipers early in the war. The exact source of the Winchester Model 70s in the 101st is unknown, but they probably came from the division's prewar marksmanship team.

found that while the snipers engaged three quarters of their targets between the ranges of 300 to 600 meters—the average at 400 meters—and the maximum at 1,300 meters, the shooters' satisfaction in their weapon systems varied greatly. Of those using the Winchester Model 70, only 18 percent expressed satisfaction. Although reasonably happy with the rifle's accuracy, the marksmen had concerns about its durability in the field. The Model 70 users also found that the Weaver 3X scope failed to provide adequate magnification and tended to collect moisture, which made it ineffective. Those snipers with M16s also expressed doubts about the rifle's accuracy at ranges beyond 300 meters. They also found that moisture affected their Weaver scopes and that the instruments were difficult to adjust. Despite its drawbacks, a surprising 48 percent expressed approval of the M16 sniper system.

Snipers using the M14s were much more satisfied. None found problems with the rifle itself; their only complaints were about the lack of resolving power of, and moisture buildup in, the M84 telescopes. In the survey, 74 percent of the users expressed approval of the M14 with the M84 scope system, while 100 percent declared the M14 with the ART scope satisfactory for sniper operations.

The commanders of units with test snipers seconded the conclusions. According to the ACTIV final report, "The major reason for preference of the M14 was greater range and accuracy. The limited number of commanders who had experience with the M14 w/ART preferred it to the M14 w/M84 because of the power and the range finding feature of the telescope."

In conclusion, the final report recommended that "the accurized M14 be designated as the standard sniper rifle for Vietnam." While the wording "for Vietnam" resulted from the ACTIV's restricted authority to the war zone, everyone understood that the recommendation extended to army units worldwide.

The final report did not recommend a telescope for the M14 because, while the ART came closer to meeting specifications than any other, none of the scopes tested possessed all the desired characteristics. As a result, the ACTIV recommended that more telescope development and testing be conducted. Ultimately, the Redfield 3X-9X proved to be the best available telescope for use with the M14.*

Many of the army units kept the test sniper weapons after the conclusion of the evaluation and then requested additional M14s and scopes to increase their inventory. Both the Marksmanship Training Unit at Fort Benning and the Army Weapons Command produced accurized M14s and sent them to the war zone along with scopes from the Redfield plant.

Official funding approval for the procurement of additional accurized M14s came in a Department of the Army message on February 14, 1969. The Rock Island Arsenal subsequently manufactured more than 1,200 M14s as sniper rifles and shipped them to Vietnam. Together with the ART scope, this weaponry was called the XM21 system (although that did not become the formal designation until the following November). The XM21 name remained for most of the remainder of the war. In 1972, staffing and paperwork finally caught up with actual field developments; the official system name then became the "Rifle, 7.62 mm Sniper M21" or simply the M21.

Neither the Marine Remington M40 system nor the army XM21 proved to be perfect for sniper use in Vietnam, though each did have its advantages. The M40 demonstrated a slight edge in accuracy but the XM21 exhibited greater durability. The most positive aspect of the XM21 lay in its capability to mount night vision devices, allowing shooters to see in the dark. That was a particularly significant tool because the hours of darkness, in guerrilla warfare tactics important for obscuring movement, had virtually neutralized the Allied aerial observation and firepower.

Night vision devices were not unique to Vietnam. During the later months of World War II and throughout the Korean War, the United States had experimented with various infrared

---

*Modifying rifles, scopes, and mounts was an unending process in both the Marine Corps and the army. Some modifications took place at the factories, others at Stateside armories; still others were made by the marksmanship training teams, unit armorers, and the shooters themselves.

instruments that allowed night observation. But problems with the infrared systems, which used light rays just below the red end of the visible spectrum, were many. In the early models, the combined weight of the device and its power source was nearly thirty pounds. The second obstacle was that a decent picture through the view finder at ranges of 100 to 200 meters required total darkness. But most problematic in terms of popularity with field troops was the fact that, although infrared was invisible to the naked eye, an enemy with a similar device could easily pinpoint the infrared source.

In the late 1950s, U.S. manufacturers began experimenting with "passive night-observation" devices that enhanced available moon, star, and ambient light sources many thousands of times to produce a green-tinged field of view. Despite advances in technology after the Korean War, the instruments were still too heavy and cumbersome for any widespread early use in Vietnam except at fixed defensive positions such as base camps and fire support facilities. The war created an urgent need for a portable device that allowed soldiers to "see" at night.

Developers tested several models of passive device in Vietnam on a limited basis. But it was not until November 1966 that the United States fielded the Starlight scope—the "Small Hand-Held or Individual Weapons Model No. 6060." After a few final adjustments, Model 6060 became widely available to field units in 1967 as the AN/PVS-1 (Army-Navy Portable Visible-Light Detection Series Number 1). Measuring 18.5 inches long and weighing six pounds, the AN/PVS-1 enhanced available light 40,000 times. In 1969, the U.S. military in Vietnam replaced those scopes with the AN/PVS-2. An inch shorter but weighing the same, those replacements magnified available light 75,000 times.*

---

*Subsequent generations of Starlight models appeared in Vietnam near the end of the war along with much larger, higher-magnification models, but the AN/PVS-2 was the only night vision device commonly employed by snipers in the conflict. Starlight scopes were also widely used, unmounted, by the infantry to observe approaches to their nighttime defensive and ambush positions. By late 1969 the scopes were so plentiful that every American rifle platoon had at least one, and often two or more, in its inventory.

The Starlight scopes, as the AN/PVS-2s were more commonly known, came with mounting brackets for the M14 and the M16, which made them highly desirable to snipers. A report, "Sniper Training and Employment in the 9th Infantry Division," illustrates that they had become an integral part of army sniper training by 1969: "Students learn the methods of zeroing their weapons equipped with the adjustable ranging telescopic sight (ART), Starlight scope, and the fixed power M84 telescopic scope. Night firing is included in the course and each student learns to engage targets with his Starlight scope at ranges of 150, 300, and 600 meters."

Written by the division's assistant operations office, Major Robert G. Hilchey, in July of that year, the report continued, "The AN/PVS-2 Starlight scope has proven more effective for sniper use than the AN/PVS-1. Focusing is improved on the AN/PVS-2, and the windage/elevation controls are more reliable than on the latter sight. The sight reticle in the AN/PVS-2 better lends itself to engagement of long-range targets. Students bring a Starlight scope and mount to the sniper school when they report for training. The scope is mounted on the rifle and zeroed during training. The sniper retains that scope/rifle during subsequent operations. This procedure assures retention of zero even though the sight is dismounted during daylight operations and remounted for night operations."

Although the 9th Division snipers trained with the Starlight scope at ranges up to 600 meters, that proved to be a realistic distance only under optimum conditions. Most night shots were at less than 400 meters, and, in fact, the majority of snipers zeroed their Starlight scopes at 150 meters. Because of the limited range at night, sniper teams as well as infantrymen often mounted the Starlight scopes on M16s for use during darkness.

Marine infantry units used the Starlight scopes for night observation, both unmounted and on M16s, in the same manner as the army. Marine armorers also made a prototype mount to affix the AN/PVS-2 to the Winchester Model 70 and discussed doing the same for the Remington M40. No modifications of this sort proved successful,* however, so the corps's marksmen in Vietnam did not employ the night observation devices with their primary weapons.

Even though not generally mounted on their sniper rifles, the Starlight scopes did prove beneficial to the marksmen. On October 14, 1967, a 4th Marine sniper team joined the regiment's 2nd Battalion in defense of a bridge on the supply route to Con Thien, near the DMZ. In the middle of the night the sniper team, using an unmounted Starlight scope, spotted a large group of NVA massing for attack. The snipers warned the 2nd Battalion Marines, whose fire broke up the enemy assault and killed most of its attackers.

The Starlight scopes also allowed snipers to be innovative. Frustrated at visual and ground-radar sightings of enemy personnel at ranges beyond the capabilities of their M40s or XM21s, the shooters sought other methods to "reach out and touch" enemy soldiers. Both army and Marine snipers experimented with mounting telescopes and night vision devices on .50-caliber machine guns to hit targets at long range. Because of its slow rate of fire, its traversing and elevating (T&E) mechanism, and its stable M3 tripod, the Browning .50 caliber fired accurate single shots. Using them primarily at fixed installations such as firebases, snipers could prefire the .50 calibers at identifiable targets downrange and work the data into a range card to provide increased first-round accuracy.

An article, ".50 Caliber Sniper," by army Captain Albert R. Amos Jr. in the September-October 1970 issue of *Infantry* magazine discussed the heavy machine gun sniper program in the 1st Battalion, 5th Infantry, 25th Infantry Division. Amos described how the unit constructed twenty- to thirty-foot-high shooting platforms at firebases, added steel base plates and posts to further stabilize the .50 caliber's M3 mount, and

_____

*Despite adaptations, neither the Winchester nor the Remington offered a stable enough platform or a satisfactory "sight line" to mount the relatively large, heavy Starlight scopes. Also, some snipers and Marine officials did not support pursuing an adequate mount because they believed that replacing the normal day-scope with a night-vision device under field conditions would decrease the accuracy of the weapon system.

trained gun crews to use them. In conclusion he wrote, "The end result more than made up for the intensive work that was required. Base defenses were strengthened through more efficient use of long-range night observation devices and the enemy no longer could operate securely within 1,000 meters of a sniper team without putting his life on the line."

Marine marksmen also experimented with .50 calibers. In February 1967, Sergeant Carlos Hathcock used the large-bore machine gun to accomplish what is generally accepted as the longest-range confirmed sniper kill of the Vietnam War. Firing from a hillside position using an Unertl 8X scope on a .50-caliber machine gun stabilized by a sandbag-supported M3 tripod, Hathcock engaged a Vietcong pushing a weapon-laden bicycle at 2,500 yards. Hathcock's first round disabled the bicycle; the second stuck the enemy soldier in the chest.

These shots at a little more than 1.4 miles were, of course, extraordinary. Many former snipers reflect that, even with scopes, targets beyond 1,200 yards are extremely difficult to see, much less hit with any consistency. The .50 caliber snipers undoubtedly harassed the enemy and caused them to move with even more circumspection than usual in the vicinity of U.S. bases. However, the extremely heavy, nonmobile machine guns are a mere footnote to Vietnam War sniper history, and their use and impact were extremely limited.

Yet to the sniper, every little innovation helped, and so the marksmen tested and experimented with any tool that could provide an advantage. Snipers of both services also tried, in addition to the .50-caliber machine guns, a wide variety of noise and flash suppressors, because remaining undetected was essential to the sniper's success in killing the enemy and his own survival. Muzzle flashes and rifle discharge noise were the greatest threats to the sniper. The commercial-manufacture Winchester and Remington sniper models did not have flash suppressors which resulted in a sound signature that was distinct from those of the M14 and M16 military rifles, which did have devices to disperse the fire and gases that follow a bullet from the muzzle.

Soldier and Marine snipers experimented with various suppressors to reduce muzzle flash but none worked to any degree.
The most widely used method of reducing the visual firing
signature was quite simple. Many snipers carried a one- to
two-foot-square of olive drab canvas that they placed beneath
the rifle muzzle when firing from a prone position. This cloth
prevented the muzzle blast from kicking up dust or vegetation.

Along with a visual signature, each sniper's shot also provided an audio compromise to the firer's position.* Not only
did the Winchester and Remington sniper rifles lack flash suppressors, they also lacked the threaded barrel end for attaching a silencer—usually a tube containing sound baffles that
was screwed onto the rifle's muzzle. Although Marine snipers
and armorers and commercial developers worked to design
effective noise suppressors for the bolt rifles, none proved
successful.

The army made a slightly greater, if misguided, effort to develop silencers for snipers and other special operatives, but the
noise-suppression program focused on M16s instead of M14s
and XM21s. In May 1966, the army sanctioned development
and procurement of M16 silencers and tested various models,
including a 12-inch H4 and a 9.5 inch H4A, in Vietnam during
1967 and 1968.

Because those noise suppressors did decrease the audio signature of a gunshot and decreased its flash, development continued, and in the fall of 1968 the army selected the 12.5-inch
Noise and Flash Suppressor Assembly MAW-A1 manufactured by the Sionics Company of Atlanta, Georgia, for use
with the M16 rifle. Then, and only then, did the fabricators of
the XM21 adapt the same basic design of the MAW-A1 to
what they called the "M14SS-1 Noise and Flash Suppressor
Assembly" for the sniper system.

While the Sionics and other silencers certainly *looked* im-

---

*A combat veteran quickly learns the distinctive sound of each weapon,
friendly and enemy, used on the battlefield. Even the newest arrivals in the
combat zone, U.S. or North Vietnamese, could distinguish between an AK-47,
SKS, M16, M14, and the bolt-action sniper rifles.

pressive when mounted on weapons, they looked much better than they actually performed. Each shot still produced a flash, albeit somewhat reduced, and the sound became more a "spew" than a "crack," so the wise sniper still moved to a different position after each shot. Most veteran snipers viewed the devices as extra weight rather than as real security.

Subsonic ammunition provided still another method of reducing the audio signature of sniper weapons because they produced no sound-breaking "crack." Subsonic cartridges also made less noise simply because they contained less powder, which, of course, resulted in reduced power, range, and accuracy. The special ammunition was available in ample supply for the M40, XM21, and M16, but its actual use in the field was extremely limited. The quieter ammunition simply did not outweigh the disadvantages of reducing range and accuracy. And the smaller charge of the subsonic cartridge did not provide enough power to automatically eject spent cartridges in the semiautomatic XM21 and M16 systems, requiring manual ejection of each used shell case. Ultimately, the snipers relied more on their hunter's instincts than on high-tech solutions.

While the rifle and scope were the dominant tools of the sniper trade, the special marksmen required other equipment and supplies to sustain themselves in the field. Sniper operations rarely lasted more than a few days so the marksmen did not need to carry the heavy burdens of the typical infantrymen. There were many items necessary, however, for their survival and for the success of their missions.

The two-man sniper team, composed of a shooter and an observer, nearly always operated as an attachment to an infantry or a reconnaissance unit.* They nevertheless equipped themselves individually and as a team to act independently. However, as with all other aspects of sniper operations in Vietnam, the weapons, ammunition, and equipment carried by the two-man teams varied greatly from unit to unit and from individual to individual. Snipers in Vietnam procured or adapted

---

*Additional information on the two-man team concept can be found in Chapter 11 "Training and Organization."

any item they thought would aid their ability to success-fully hit enemy targets while increasing their own chances of survival.

Scoped rifles were ill suited for defense in a sustained fire-fight, so snipers and their observers armed themselves with a variety of supplemental weapons. Many snipers carried pis-tols, the .45-caliber M1911A1 being the most common choice because it required little care and maintenance, ammo was plentiful, and its use by the U.S. armed forces since 1911 spoke well for its reliability. Other sidearms included .38-caliber revolvers procured from aviation units and various civilian models sent by family or friends back home.

Some snipers also carried M16s. Others, especially the bolt-gun-armed Marines, brought full-automatic M14s. The weap-ons of the observer, or the second man in the two-man sniper team, also varied with situation and personal preference. Ob-servers most often carried either M14s or M16s, and they, too, frequently added .45s or other sidearms to their web gear.

On occasion sniper teams carried M79 40-mm grenade launchers with high-explosive rounds for use at up to 400 me-ters and buckshot canisters for in-close combat. Experimental models of an over-and-under combination of the M16 and M79, known as the XM148 and later adopted as the M203, also became a popular weapon of the sniper team observers.

Two important factors influenced weapons selection by the sniper teams. In relatively static areas of operations with lim-ited movement, the sniper teams could and did carry larger loads and maximum firepower. If accompanying units on pa-trol or long-term operations, they had to leave some items behind. The second factor that influenced backup weapon selection was compatibility of ammunition. The marksmen typically carried forty to eighty rounds of match ammunition for their sniper rifles, and the M40s, XM21s, and M14s were all capable of firing standard 7.62-mm rounds as well. The 5.56-mm ammunition for the M16 was lighter and easier to carry, but it could not be used in the sniper rifles.

Again, mission requirements and distances to be covered greatly influenced the amount of other munitions carried by sniper teams. Each man added two to four or more hand grenades and two or more claymore mines for defense. Each also carried several smoke grenades and star-cluster canisters along with a strobe light to mark their positions for supporting fires and for extraction. Some snipers even included CS and other types of tear gas canisters and white phosphorus (WP) grenades to their arsenal. In the event of compromise, the sniper team could move upwind, then pop the gas and WP behind them to mask their withdrawal and slow pursuit.

Intended primarily for cutting camouflage vegetation or opening rations, a variety of knives rounded out the list of sniper weapons. Because snipers worked at great distances from their targets—the greater the distance the better—the idea of their using knives in combat was neither popular nor practical.

Snipers attached to infantry platoons and companies usually relied on the radio communications organic to those units. At times security elements assigned to sniper teams carried radios to maintain contact with higher headquarters and air and artillery support units. In the extremely rare instances when sniper teams worked independently, they carried their own PRC-25 and its later replacement, the PRC-77. With their standard antennas, the twenty-two-pound radios provided communications over a range of eight to twelve kilometers. This distance could be doubled using various field-expedient antennas made with WD1 commo wire extended into overhanging tree limbs.

No Americans in Vietnam, including snipers, went anywhere without communications. The radio lifelines not only provided artillery and air support but could also call in extraction helicopters and maintain contact with nearby units to avoid friendly fire incidents.

Sniper team observers also frequently carried 20-power M49 spotting scopes along with a tripod. The scopes provided a wider field of vision and greater magnification than the rifle telescopes. Binoculars of various manufacture and magnification also added to the observation power of the sniper teams.

Maps, sometimes supplemented by aerial photos, and a lensatic compass rounded out the sniper team's working gear.

Other adjustments to the snipers' operations involved clothing, supplies, and creature comforts. The first Marines in Vietnam arrived wearing olive drab cotton "utilities" while the early soldiers came wearing similar clothing known as "fatigues." More suited to garrison and parade field activities than to jungle and rice paddy action, those uniforms quickly gave way to lightweight jungle uniforms that dried rapidly and withstood the rigors of long-term wear in the field.

The jungle uniforms had trousers with a cargo pocket on each thigh large enough to hold a map, a ration packet, or other cumbersome items; two hip pockets on the front; and a couple of traditional pockets over the buttocks. The leg openings had drawstrings that allowed blousing at the boot tops to prevent leeches and insects from crawling up the leg. The jungle uniform shirt, cut long to be worn outside the trousers, had four large pockets on its front. Each pocket on both shirt and trousers had a small, thread-reinforced hole at the bottom to allow water to drain after stream crossings or during monsoon rains. Tops of the shirt pockets slanted inward to further assist in shedding water.

After their introduction, the jungle uniforms went through several modifications, such as changes in pocket placement and the addition of draw tabs to shirts and trousers for tailoring their fit. The most practical modification was replacing the ordinary cotton material with a ripstop poplin that made the uniform much more durable. Because of the heat, humidity, and frequent downpours, most snipers, like their fellow infantrymen, wore no underwear beneath their jungle uniforms in order to reduce rashes, ringworm, and jungle rot.

For the snipers, the most significant problem with the uniform was that it came in only solid olive drab, a color that did not always blend in with the terrain. Some snipers procured various types of camouflage uniforms that ranged from Korean War–vintage green-and-black-spotted "leopard" fatigues to a variety of green-and-black irregularly striped "tiger" uniforms available from in-country manufacturers. Since those uniforms were generally made for the smaller-in-stature Vietnamese, snipers had to special-order larger uniforms.

Snipers sanitized their field uniforms by removing all emblems of rank, unit, name, or other identification. Beyond the "USMC" stenciled on Marine pockets or the "U.S. Army" sewed above them, sniper uniforms were bare of adornment, in part to support counterintelligence but mostly to prevent anything that might give away the sniper's position.

The issue black leather boot common to the army and Marine Corps early in the war quickly gave way to a black-leather-bottom, olive-drab canvas-top jungle boot that came with drain holes along the sole to evacuate water. Some snipers and infantrymen wore their jungle boots without the heavy green issue socks.

Snipers of both services frequently camouflaged their skin with green and black grease sticks, and they sometimes added cloth and vegetation to their weapons and equipment. They did not, however, wear the "gillie suits" made of net, burlap, and artificial shredded garnish that have come to symbolize post-Vietnam snipers because those were not available in Vietnam.* Even if they had been, the weight and resultant discomfort from heat would have limited their use. Many snipers did carry a lightweight camouflage-pattern poncho liner to assist in their remaining unobserved in their "hides." The poncho liner also came in handy as a blanket in the cooler night hours.

Headgear for the snipers also varied greatly. The most preferred hat was the circular-brimmed "floppie" or "boonie" hat that came in various shades of olive drab and camouflage patterns. In addition to providing reasonable protection from the sun and rain, the flexible brim assisted snipers in blending in with the environment and proved useful as a pad to hold hot weapon barrels. Snipers also wore various issue and nonissue

---

*The suits gained their names from Scottish hunting guides and gamekeepers known as "gillies" who used the camouflage covers to conduct game counts in their preserves and to watch for poachers. The first American use of the gillie suit is credited to Captain Jim Land, who used one made by his wife, Ellie, at the 1st Marine Brigade sniper school in Hawaii in 1961, but they were in common use on Soviet reconnaissance and sniper missions during World War II.

soft caps as well as headbands made from the olive-drab triangle bandages found in standard-issue first aid packets. Tied bandanna-fashion around the forehead, the cloths kept perspiration out of the eyes and obscured light-colored skin.

Few snipers used the standard-issue steel helmets because of their weight and easily recognizable profile. The only times they were likely to wear them were on operations with regular infantry units or when they supported base camps or fire bases, especially those vulnerable to enemy mortar and rocket fire. In those cases the snipers also added flak vests to their uniforms.

To carry ammunition and supplies, snipers wore issue web gear, wide-woven canvas belts supported by canvas suspenders officially labeled "load-bearing equipment" (LBE). On the LBE, like other infantrymen, snipers attached canteens, ammo pouches, first aid packets, and a variety of other equipment according to unit policy and individual preference.

Although the web gear generally held everything necessary to sustain the sniper for brief periods, he often needed heavier equipment, creature comfort items, more rations, and additional water. Those he stowed in a rucksack suspended from shoulder straps on his back. The standard-issue canvas, multiple-pocket, aluminum-frame rucksack came with a quick release on one of the straps so it could be quickly jettisoned during contact. Some snipers preferred the more compact tan rucksacks captured from the NVA while others constructed their own rucksacks using whatever was available, including issued and captured gear.

Water, the item most essential for sustained field operations, added the greatest weight to the sniper's load. Snipers carried multiple plastic one- and two-quart canteens along with canvas-covered plastic bags that held up to five quarts. Although they also carried iodine and halazone tablets to purify water from streams in the field, they generally tried to carry sufficient water because the enemy often maintained observers at water sources.

Food for the snipers consisted of canned C rations and

freeze-dried meals—known as "LURPs" in honor of the reconnaissance units for which they were originally fielded. However, because of the need to remain hidden to successfully engage targets and for their own security, most snipers ate little in the field. To light a heat tab or other combustible in order to warm their rations or to make a cup of coffee might compromise their position.

Along with the standard first aid kit, many snipers carried additional "pill packets" containing anything from basic anti-malaria tablets and vitamins to stimulants that helped them maintain alertness. As with many of their other supplies, the amount they carried depended on how closely they were working with other ground units. In their usual duty as attachments to infantry platoons or companies, the sniper teams looked to the unit medic or corpsman of their hosts to provide medical supplies.

Water, food, medical supplies, and other creature comfort items were carried to enable the sniper to transport his weapon and ammunition and to use his telescopic sight. Along with a few personal items, such as a toothbrush and toothpaste and an extra pair of socks, snipers sometimes carried an olive drab jungle sweater or undershirt in a plastic bag for the cooler evening hours at higher elevations.

Most snipers also maintained a "log" or a "kill sheet" detailing their observations and actions on each mission. The written accounts provided intelligence analysis of each mission as well as proof of each successful engagement. Some units, particularly in the Marine Corps, required the signature of an officer on each entry to verify a kill. This usually meant a direct contact with the dead enemy's body. In instances where the approach to a distant kill might be too dangerous, long-range ground or air visual observation would suffice. In a few special cases, officers signed kill sheets on the basis of the sniper teams' report when direct contact or observation was not possible.

The tools of the sniper's trade varied greatly from unit to unit and from individual to individual. All were important, but the sniper's arms and equipment merely delivered, protected, or sustained the individual marksman so that he could properly align the scoped rifle.

CHAPTER 11

✻✻✻✻✻✻✻✻✻

Training and Organization

*T*HE selection of personnel and the acquisition of weapons and equipment were key elements in the success of army and Marine snipers in Vietnam. However, quality men and material alone could not accomplish the mission of long-range shooting. Sniper candidates required specific training to master their rifles and the many other components of effective sniper operations.

Training, varying in time and content, began with the formal sniper schools, taught either at in-country training facilities or in the States. The objectives of the training were simple and specific. To successfully complete the course, each student had to develop the confidence, will, knowledge, and skills required to become an effective sniper. Along with those skills, he had to display the ability to apply, instinctively, correct procedures and techniques when functioning in combat as an individual and as a team member.

The learning process, however, did not end with completion of the formal schools. Snipers continued to add to their knowledge by gathering information and techniques from their teammates on the job and through their own personal experiences. Although refresher training courses—especially in marksmanship—became common in Vietnam, it was each mission that provided snipers, regardless of their time in the field and their number of personal kills, the opportunity to perfect their craft.

Marine sniper training during World War II had lasted five weeks, and in the 1960s most experienced shooters still believed that marksmen required at least three to five weeks of

157

intensive day and night training to become proficient snipers. In fact, when the Marine Corps published FMFM 1-3B, "Sniping," in 1969, it included a syllabus for sniper training consisting of more than 200 hours of formal classes and practical exercises.*

Unfortunately, because the Marines and the army arrived in Vietnam with no sniper capability, they had to train their marksmen in the midst of combat operations. Time to structure the in-country sniping schools according to peacetime training guidelines or requirements simply did not exist. Other factors, such as limited access to ranges—experienced by Captain Russell when establishing the 3rd Marine Division sniper school—also curtailed the length and content of training.

Because of range limitations, the 3rd Marine Division offered only three days of training in its initial classes. That became a week when facilities became available. Captain Land likewise used a five-to-seven-day training schedule for the initial sniper classes in the 1st Marine Division. The length of both in-country Marine sniper programs eventually extended to eighteen to twenty-one days.

The army's sniper training in Vietnam also was brief when first established. When it began sniper evaluation in 1967, the Army Concept Team in Vietnam (ACTIV) provided to the infantry divisions and separate brigades guidance for training programs averaging forty-six hours in length. Two years later, when he founded the 9th Infantry Division's sniper school, Major Willis Powell used the eighteen-day curriculum that he had developed at the USAMTU at Fort Benning.

Because of the limited time available, the initial, week-long sniper schools focused almost exclusively on marksmanship and the care of rifles and scopes. Subjects included telescope orientation, range estimation, target detection, zeroing, wind effects, and weapon maintenance. Once the students mastered those skills, they began live firing.

Despite the abbreviated schedule, most soldiers and Ma-

---

*See Appendix B for the entire training syllabus.

rines believed that the training provided sufficient practice for them to master the basics of long-range marksmanship. According to ACTIV surveys, about 85 percent of those trained for the army test expressed satisfaction with their instruction. Marines who went through the early sniper-training schools in both divisions expressed an even greater degree of approval of their training, frequently commenting positively on the skills and experience of their instructors. Ed Kugler, who joined the 4th Marine Regiment Sniper Platoon in March 1966, states, "My training was excellent. It was real, it was hard, but it was effective. No hype, just do it."

Powell's 9th Infantry Division students, as well as those in the Marine schools, recognized the experience of their instructors and respected their expertise. An article in the January-March 1969 issue of the 9th Division's *Octofoil* quoted one of Powell's early students: " 'I couldn't believe how great the NCOs were. They really know their business and treated us like professionals.' "

Ultimately, all sniper training, in-country and Stateside, followed basically the same program. Training began with an orientation on the sniper weapon system, its ammunition, and its care and maintenance. Following lectures and demonstrations the cadre moved the students to the firing range, an area that dominated the entire course. Other instruction included classes on techniques in camouflage and concealment, individual movement, escape and evasion, land navigation, communications, intelligence gathering and reporting, and air and artillery fire request and control.

Depending on time and available facilities, instructors modified or combined subjects, frequently teaching fieldcraft and other nonshooting skills to students awaiting their turn on the range. The concurrent instruction allowed everyone to maximize the limited number of training hours.

Regardless of hours available or content modification, marksmanship remained the focus of all the sniper-training courses. Other portions of the schools might be shortened or combined, but range firing remained a priority because many students, even though they had scored expert with their individual weapons, had little or no experience with scoped military weapons or firing at long-range targets.

The all-important marksmanship training began with the basics of sighting and aiming, trigger control, and sight adjustment in dry-fire mode. Only then did the students begin to place rounds downrange to learn how to zero—to adjust the weapon sights so the bullet struck where aimed—their weapon systems. Once satisfied with their zero, the student fired from both supported and unsupported prone, kneeling, and standing positions. Even though the prone position with the weapon supported by a bipod, sandbag, or other steadying device provided the most accuracy, snipers had to be able to fire quickly from unprepared positions as well. Students fired at targets at ranges of 150, 300, 600, and 900 meters.

Due to the lack of standard silhouette targets in Vietnam, both the Marines and the army used the expended canisters of 155-mm artillery rounds as targets. Mounted on short poles, the readily available canisters served as reasonable facsimiles of the body area of enemy targets, held up well in all types of weather and after repeated strikes, and they rewarded snipers with a satisfying *ping* when bullets struck the target.

Marine and army sniper schools included night training as part of their curriculum. Marine snipers received limited instruction on how to shoot under the artificial light provided by aerial flares and searchlights. Because of their greater use of the AN/PVS-2 Starlight scope with the XM21 weapon system, army sniper students spent more time shooting during hours of darkness.

During training the sniper cadre attempted to instill a hunter's mind-set into the students and to prepare them for the extremely personal aspects of killing. Because of the sniper-selection process, most candidates arrived at their training prepared to pull the trigger. Many were veterans of extensive combat before volunteering for sniper school and had already developed mechanisms for dealing with killing. Instructors and students alike maintained the attitude that sniping, albeit more personal, was just one more method of killing the enemy. "A sniper feels nothing but the recoil," became a common saying among the Vietnam marksmen.

While nonsnipers in Vietnam sometimes referred to the marksmen as "Murder, Inc.," snipers, who understood their role in the conflict, on occasion promoted such attitudes. A sign at the 1st Marine Division sniper school, near Da Nang, proclaimed, "War Our Business, Death Our Only Product."

Sniper training did not end with graduation from the schools; completion of the formal training merely signified the beginning of the sniper's learning and perfecting of the skills of a superior marksman. New graduates returned to their units to continue their education by gleaning information from other veterans and by learning from their own firsthand experience. Each mission provided additional opportunities for improvement. All one had to do to add to his sniper skills was to survive.

The Marine Corps and the army in Vietnam did offer refresher courses that varied in depth. Some programs provided only unit armorers to maintain and adjust sniper weapon systems and shooting ranges for confirming zeroes; others provided full refresher training lasting as long as a week.

The 3rd Marine Division established the most lengthy and sophisticated of the programs on September 3, 1968. Division Order 1510.5, "Scout-Sniper Refresher Training Course," provided information and instructions for a five-day program at Quang Tri. According to the order, the refresher training focused primarily on newly arriving snipers trained at Camp Pendleton before their deployment to Vietnam and on infantrymen serving in sniper platoons who had not undergone formal sniper training.

The refresher course included the same subjects contained in the basic schools: land navigation; communications procedures; and air, artillery, and medical evacuation support.* As with other sniper instruction, the curriculum emphasized

---

*The 3rd Marine Division's five-day "Scout-Sniper Training Course" is reproduced in Appendix C.

range training with the rifle and scope system, and actual firing.

While their training shared similar objectives and used the same basic training schedules, the Marines and the army employed the sniper graduates in very different manners. Early draft copies of FMFM 1-3B, which contained what would become the official Marine sniper organization, were widely distributed shortly after the divisions organized their schools. The manual called for infantry regiment sniper platoons composed of a platoon commander, a platoon sergeant, a rifle team equipment repairman, and three sniper squads. Each squad consisted of a squad leader and five two-man sniper teams for a platoon total of one officer and thirty-five enlisted Marines.

The regimental sniper platoons were under the command and administrative control of the regiment's headquarters company. Operational control remained directly under the regimental commander.

FMFM 1-3B also called for reconnaissance battalion sniper platoons, which were to operate with a similar but slightly smaller organization. Personnel included a platoon commander, a platoon sergeant, a rifle team equipment repairman, and four squads, each with a leader and three two-man teams. The thirty enlisted Marines and one officer served under the command and control of the reconnaissance battalion's headquarters and supply company and the operational control of the battalion commander.

Responsibilities for personnel in the regimental and reconnaissance battalion sniper platoons were the same. The regiment or battalion commander, with the assistance of his operations officer, detached sniper teams to subordinate units. The sniper platoon commander provided input on these decisions and advised subordinate unit commanders on their employment. He remained responsible for the operational efficiency of his platoon, provided liaison for attached elements, and scheduled rotation of personnel to permit rifle rezeroing, training, and rest.

The sniper platoon sergeant assisted the platoon commander in coordinating the detachment of squads and teams to other units. He also was responsible for the discipline, training, and welfare of the platoon and for the care and condition of weapons and equipment. The rifle team equipment repairman assisted in the latter task while also ensuring the security of weapons and special equipment in rear areas.

Each squad leader carried out orders issued by the platoon commander and assumed the responsibility for the care and condition of his men and their weapons and equipment. When detached to other units in the regiment or recon battalion, the squad leader assisted the commander of the supported unit in the control of the sniper teams and made recommendations about their employment. He also provided liaison between the supported unit and his sniper platoon commander and frequently performed as a sniper on missions as a part of a team.

Team leaders reported to their squad leader and carried out his orders. Their responsibilities included the supervision of the second member of the team and the care of their weapons and equipment. The team leader performed the actual sniping while his spotter provided observation, adjustment, and security.

FMFM 1-3B provides a simple statement of sniper duty. According to the manual, "The primary mission of a sniper in combat is to support combat operations by delivering precision fire on selected targets from concealed positions."

The two-man team represented the heart and soul of the sniper platoons. Capable of attachment to any size unit or of limited independent operations, the two-man team represented the basic operational sniper element. The platoon chain of command did its best to keep teams together for as long as possible because the longer the two men worked together, the more efficient they became.

The spotter or observer learned from the team leader in the never-ending training process. Often when a team leader completed his tour, the observer moved up to assume his duties and to take over the sniper rifle.

While the various manuals and manning documents spell out appropriate ranks for each of these positions, as with everything else that occurred in the Vietnam War, there were often variations and adaptations. A first or second lieutenant usually filled the authorized platoon commander position with a staff or gunnery sergeant as the senior NCO. Staff or "buck" sergeants led the squads with corporals as team leaders and lance corporals as their observers. Because of the importance of maintaining the sniper rifle systems, units made great efforts to keep the team equipment repairman position filled with a lance corporal or above to ensure a skill level that could master the care of the weapons.

In the absence of officers, senior sergeants often occupied the officer's billet with Marines one or even two ranks below the authorized grade assuming the duties of squad and team leaders. Experience and expertise of individual snipers received more attention than rank in the teams, and it was not unusual for the senior ranking member to act as the observer while the junior person did the actual shooting. Again, on occasion some senior NCOs filled positions authorized for lower ranks in order to maximize the field time of the more proficient and experienced snipers.

The regimental and reconnaissance battalion organization allowed the sniper platoons' employment as a unit, as squads, or as separate teams. For example, the entire regimental platoon might be attached to a subordinate battalion with squads or teams further detached to companies. In the recon battalion, the platoon might be attached to a recon company for a short time, but the general organization called for the attachment of one sniper squad per company. The organizational structure of the regimental and recon battalion sniper platoons also provided for attaching a squad or team to any size subordinate unit.

These attachments were usually for the duration of a mission or patrol that might last from a few days to a week. Most of the sniper platoons attempted to send the same squad and teams to the same subordinate units to increase an awareness of capabilities and to promote teamwork.

The organization of the Marine sniper platoons centered on the ability to assign a squad per battalion in the regiments and a squad per company in the reconnaissance battalion. This concept worked fine on paper but had its shortcomings in the reality of the combat zone. Rarely were the sniper platoons at full strength. Even when adequate personnel were assigned, some snipers would be unavailable for duty because of wounds, illness, rest and recreation leaves, and administrative matters. Also, because of the nature of sniping itself and the mental and physical diligence it required, snipers could not remain effective for extended periods of time and required time to rest and refit.

While their actual operational functions rarely matched the theoretical model, the Marines did have the advantage of having all their combat units assigned in the far northern quarter of South Vietnam, where they encountered fairly similar terrain.

Unlike the Marine Corps, which had a formal, approved organization for its sniper platoons, the army never authorized or adopted official units for its long-range marksmen in Vietnam. Army separate brigades and divisions served throughout South Vietnam from the Mekong Delta in the south to the DMZ in the north, and the terrain varied from flat, wet, rice paddies to thick jungle and mountains, which required differing tactics and methods of field operations. The differences in areas of responsibility did not readily lend themselves to consistent organization or employment of army snipers. As a result, each army division, separate brigade, and long-range reconnaissance company established its own sniper organization appropriate to location, situation, and overall command support of the concept.

Senior army commanders recognized the lack of consistency in sniper organization and in the spring of 1969 directed Lieutenant Colonel Richard S. Fleming of the U.S. Army Combat Developments Command to visit field units "to discuss sniper programs, policies, and utilization." From April 6 to 10, Fleming talked with commanders, operations officers, and snipers in the XXIV Corps Headquarters, the 1st Brigade of the 5th Mechanized Infantry Division, and the 101st Airborne Division. Fleming also visited the 3rd Marine Division. Its Division Order 1510.5 on refresher training as well as other information on the Marine sniper organization and reporting procedures so impressed Fleming that he included copies as enclosures to his final report.

In his written findings, dated April 28, 1969, "Trip Report (33–69), Sniper Programs" (referred to below as Trip Report), Fleming detailed the current status of the army's sniper efforts but noted that they "are still too new in the units visited to provide any definitive figures on results." Fleming did find a "surprising consensus of opinion of all those personnel contacted" on sniper organization.

Fleming shared the consensus view that it was a mistake to allow "fragmentation into too many small specialized units within the division." He recommended that sniper teams be assigned directly to the Ranger companies* and to each battalion reconnaissance platoon, and he advised assigning an additional team to each infantry platoon. According to Fleming, the direct assignment of snipers to units would provide the teamwork and support necessary to ensure their success. To provide flexibility, Fleming further recommended a sniper unit be formed at each brigade headquarters to be detached to subordinate battalions when needed.

Fleming's ideas on sniper organization had merit, and had they been adopted they would certainly have contributed to the combat capabilities of field commands. Unfortunately, the combat units had neither the manpower nor the training capabilities—nor, in some cases, the desire—to train and maintain the number of snipers that Fleming proposed.

Much of their reluctance resulted from the fact that infantry units in Vietnam were never manned at full strength. Replacements arriving in-country often did not match rotations of tour completions. Casualties, illnesses, and R&Rs further reduced the numbers available for day-to-day duty. Men wounded or killed in firefights that took only a few minutes might not be replaced for days or weeks, and the replacements would likely be new in-country and inexperienced in combat. Many pla-

---

*The army's Long-Range Reconnaissance Patrol (LRRP) units were redesignated Ranger companies on February 1, 1969.

toon leaders and company commanders resisted the loss of a single man from the field for a week or more of sniper training. They were even more concerned that the individual might not return to the unit upon completion of his schooling. Other commanders did not believe that snipers could be properly utilized in their area of operations because of the terrain and vegetation. Some leaders simply did not have any faith in the overall concept.

Only a few weeks after Fleming wrote his report, President Richard Nixon announced the first withdrawals of U.S. forces from Vietnam. With the focus more and more on reducing the number of soldiers in Vietnam, the army paid little additional attention to sniper organization and left it to individual commands to determine how and where to assign their long-range marksmen.

As a result, a great disparity occurred in the organization of snipers in army units serving in Vietnam. Some division and separate brigade commanders simply ignored the potential capability and made no effort to acquire snipers for their units. Within those same commands, however, some battalion and company commanders who did believe in the advantage of long-range shooting procured a few sniper weapons and fielded teams or individuals within rifle squads.

Most army divisions and separate brigades did not establish their own sniper schools and received allocations to those conducted by the Army Marksmanship Training Units teams, such as the one operated by the 9th Infantry Division and, later, the 25th Infantry Division. Upon completion of the training, individuals returned to their units and became the snipers for their squads or platoons in a manner similar to what was done during World War II with the special marksmen.

Changes in command of battalions and brigades usually occurred every six months and at times even more frequently. Emphasis on snipers changed as each new commander brought his own ideas and experience to the command. In many army units, the sniper became no more than an ordinary infantryman armed with a more sophisticated weapon than his fellow grunts.

As with all aspects of army sniper operations in Vietnam, the 9th Infantry Division led the way in establishing an organization for the special marksmen. A formerly classified report, "Sniper Training and Employment in the 9th Infantry Division," written by Major Robert G. Hilchey, division assistant operations officer, provided the most official, specific, and detailed sniper organization for any army unit in Vietnam. According to Paragraph V of the July 15, 1969, report, "Six snipers are assigned to each battalion headquarters and headquarters company and four to each brigade headquarters. It is essential that sniper employment be planned at battalion level to insure command interest and optimum utilization. Sniper teams are normally composed of two snipers."

Within weeks of the publication of Hilchey's report, two of the three 9th Division brigades began to withdraw from the war zone. The remaining brigade, the 3rd, did use the sniper organization outlined in the report and continued to send volunteers to the sniper school after it moved to the 25th Infantry Division.

The organization of Marine snipers in Vietnam was more rigid and consistent than that of the army. Sniper platoons at regimental and reconnaissance battalion level worked well and provided excellent support to field operations. With their late start in sniper operations and the greater variety of terrain in their areas of operations, the army never reached anything near the level of the Marine Corps's organizational expertise. Nevertheless, the army's experience in sniper organization learned in Vietnam would leave a lasting impression and influence the service's future marksmen.

CHAPTER 12

✳✳✳✳✳✳✳✳

One Shot, One Kill: Operations

 S NIPER operations in the Vietnam War varied greatly from unit to unit, season to season, and year to year. The diversity of enemy activity, ranging from guerrilla operations to conventional offensives, required differing tactics, and the seasonal weather, changing from extremely hot and dry to monsoons, also affected sniper activities. The war zone's great variety of terrain contributed to the mix.

Another significant influence on sniper operations resulted from the frequent changes in command at all levels: battalion, regiment, brigade, division, and higher. Despite organizational charts or previous operational techniques, snipers worked not for themselves or by their own rules but rather at the desire of their senior commanders. Some commanders believed in the sniper concept and supported all aspects of the program. Others ignored the marksmen to focus on other combat factors that they thought would better accomplish the mission of closing with and destroying the enemy. Between these two opposite poles of interest and support fell a large number of commanders who were neither particularly positive nor negative about snipers or their operations.

The officers and sergeants who trained, organized, and developed operational procedures for snipers in Vietnam had little personal experience and almost no documentation from previous wars on which to base their decisions. Although the techniques of marksmanship remained the same on the rifle range and in the combat zone and the merits of the two-man team organization quickly became apparent, just how to use the trained teams remained a difficult question.

The sniper experience and documentation that did exist referred to the conventional, fixed-frontline warfare of the two world wars and Korea. But Vietnam was a very different kind of war, one in which guerrilla warfare dominated and the difficulty became not hitting targets but finding and identifying them.

Marine and army sniper leaders developed combat operational procedures to meet the unusual needs of the unconventional battlefield. These methods, however, were evolutionary rather than revolutionary. Developers of sniper tactics and operational procedures began with current doctrine, then kept what worked and discarded what did not. Some things were changed, some deleted, some added. Operations did not remain static but rather adapted to the ebb and flow of the level of enemy activity.

All sniper operations in Vietnam had, first, to deliver accurate long-range fire to kill individual enemy soldiers and, second, to plan operations to optimize the first objective while ensuring the security of the sniper team. In recent years articles, books, and even motion pictures have portrayed the sniper as a "lone wolf" hunting far "behind enemy lines" to strike high-ranking enemy officers or other targets. Evidence of such missions in Vietnam is rare to nonexistent. All U.S. forces in Southeast Asia went to great lengths to prevent the live capture of their troops and to retrieve the bodies of their dead. Commanders simply did not place lone soldiers or Marines in positions where supporting units and fires were not readily available. No one went anywhere in Vietnam without radio communication links to those resources.

In his Trip Report, Lieutenant Colonel Fleming noted, "As yet, snipers seldom, if ever, constitute the primary weapon of a behind the lines force. This is true even in the marine division where the organization and doctrine is already spelled out." Fleming explained that snipers usually accompanied a larger force that contained "reliable means of killing the enemy" on its own.

Besides the potential of capture, the "lone wolf" concept in the nonconventional combat zone did not make sense for another important reason. Lieutenant General Ormond R. Simpson, USMC (Ret.), who assumed command of the 1st Marine Division in December 1968, commented on November 8, 1996, about the stories of single snipers who wandered far into enemy territory to "take out" a North Vietnamese Army division commander. According to Simpson, "First we *never* had a fix on a NVA Division Command Post. Second, if we had, we damn sure never would have sent *one* sniper when we had 176 tubes of artillery and all the possible air we needed. It makes good reading, I suppose, for those never in Vietnam, but it is pure fiction—and not very good fiction."

The written procedures concerning sniper operations of the two Marine divisions that served in Vietnam provide detailed instructions on the employment of the special marksmen. Division Order 3590.3B, from the commanding general of the 3rd Marine Division to subordinate commanders with information copies to the 1st Marine Division, established the primary policy for Marine sniper employment for the remainder of the war.*

Paragraph 4c of the division order states, "A squad (10–14 marines) built around a sniper team is generally considered as the smallest unit which should be employed on missions beyond sight or direct communications from parent units. However, where the situation, terrain, and reaction capability permits the commander to reduce this force to exploit stealth and surprise, the calculated employment of smaller groups (4–8 marines) is authorized out to 2,000 meters from friendly positions. These forces may be made up primarily or even exclusively of scout-sniper personnel provided appropriate arms and equipment augmentation is provided."

The same paragraph concludes with authorization for commanders to employ unsupported scout-sniper teams out to 500 meters from friendly positions. However, the guidance states

_____

*The 3rd Marine Division Order 3590.3B provides the most detailed, concise outline of policy, procedures, and administration for the employment of American snipers of any Vietnam War documentation. It appears in its entirety in Appendix D.

that commanders should take such measures only if the "situation, terrain, and reaction capability" were appropriate. Paragraph 4d follows with instructions that sniper units or teams were not to be employed without appropriate communications and dedicated indirect fire support.

In contrast, army units in Vietnam did not issue such clear and detailed guidance for army sniper operations. However, in practice the army adopted many of the same general policies. The most detailed document outlining the policies and procedures for army sniper operations is "Sniper Training and Employment in the 9th Infantry Division," dated July 15, 1969.*

The 9th Division sniper policy stated that the best use of snipers was as part of an infantry platoon (thirty to thirty-five soldiers) ambush, or in a sniper hide position supported by a security element of five to eight soldiers. Again, as with the Marine Corps policy, snipers were always to be within range of radio communications and supporting fires.

Techniques for employment by the Marines and army were similar. One of the initial efforts to provide a written record of the employment of snipers in Southeast Asia appeared in a pamphlet published in late 1967 by the navy for the Marine Corps as NAVMC 2614, "Professional Knowledge Gained From Operational Experience in Vietnam" (below referred to as "Professional Knowledge"). According to the document, "Appropriate methods of employment for scout-sniper teams are as part of a blocking force, outpost security (daylight hours), as part of daylight patrols, as part of daylight ambushes, and as long-range covering fire for advancing units. Employment of sniper teams for patrols, outpost security, and as members of blocking forces constitute the most prevalent types of employment in RVN."

By the time Division Order 3590.3B appeared, in June 1968, this basic guidance for sniper employment had been expanded and further defined. Under "Considerations of Employment," the order listed appropriate employment as conventional offensive, conventional defensive, attachment to

---

*See Appendix E for the complete document.

patrols, extended daylight ambush, close daylight ambush, countersniper, and blocking positions.

In the conventional offensive section, the order noted the value of precision fire and the added benefit of better observation provided by the sniper's 9-power telescope. The conventional defense subparagraph focused again on the added observation powers of the sniper and the sniper's ability to break up, or channel, attacks by engaging the enemy at long range. Although the explanation of these employment techniques was fairly rigid, a sentence followed that stated, "Employment of snipers in both an offensive and defensive role is generally limited only by the imagination."

The explanations of extended and close ambushes, countersniper operations, and blocking positions emphasized the sniper's superior observation abilities and the influence of his accurate long-range fire. These explanations also included the importance of the sniper's maintaining communications in order to direct artillery and air strikes against targets too numerous for an individual marksman to engage with rifle fire.

The 9th Infantry Division's "Sniper Training and Employment" classified sniper operations in a manner similar to that of the Marine Corps. Under "Methods of Employment" it listed support of platoon ambush patrols, sniper ambushes accompanied by a five- to eight-man security element, and countersniper operations. It also noted that "stay behinds," sniper teams with small security elements, could observe the back trail of patrols and engage enemy soldiers who might attempt to follow units.

The army covered two additional situations that the Marine documents did not mention: offset and night hunter operations. An offset operation was night firing with Starlight scopes augmented by high-powered xenon searchlights.

Night hunter operations in the 9th Infantry Division were the U.S. Army's first integration of snipers with airpower. Colonel David H. Hackworth, USA (Ret.), described the night hunter operations in his autobiography, *About Face*. According to Hackworth, "Two snipers and three helicopters—a slick and two gunships—made up each Night Hunter team. The choppers flew in blackout, the slick just a couple of hundred meters off the deck, its sniper passengers lying prone in the back, checking out the crisscrossing Delta canals and trails with Starlight scopes. The gunships, meanwhile, hovered maybe five hundred meters overhead. If through their scopes the snipers saw enemy below, they and the slick's door gunners would take them under fire, with weapons loaded with tracer rounds. This showed the gunships exactly where in the pitch-black night the target was, and in turn, the gunships would hose the area down. The slick could also drop air force flares to light up the contact area, and a reaction force was always ready and waiting at the firebase if a target justified 'piling on.' "

In a conversation with the author, Lawrence E. Tahler of Whitefish, Montana, provided additional information on the night hunters. According to Tahler, "I had just finished a six-month tour running a platoon for C Company and was working in the battalion Tactical Operations Center. Hack [Colonel Hackworth] had just taken over the battalion and called me over to talk about the new job he had in mind. His words were something like 'Hey, Stud, I hear you won the Silver Star recently. I don't want my studs to be in operations, I want them where they can do some good for the battalion. What about setting up a sniper program?' "

Tahler recalls, "It took me about three, maybe four seconds to respond, 'Yes, Sir!' The 4th Battalion 39th Infantry's sniper program was born."

Once the battalion's new platoon was fully operational, Tahler experienced several problems common to other army and Marine sniper units in Vietnam. He found that many of the infantry company commanders did not understand how best to employ their snipers and that the other infantrymen in the battalion did not always appreciate the special marksmen. Tahler summarizes, "The snipers were the only ones in the battalion authorized to wear camouflaged fatigues and black berets with a red recondo patch on the front. The special outfit, the specialized weapons, the fact that snipers only reported to me (they were not under command of any of the line companies), they did not stay out in the field like the grunts did; all combined to make the snipers very unpopular with the troops. However, I don't remember ever being at a loss for troops who wanted to become snipers!"

Other army and Marine sniper units shared the operational problems experienced by Tahler. According to Ed Kugler, the biggest problem while he was a sniper in the 4th Marine Regiment was the small unit commander's lack of knowledge about how to use the teams properly.

In his 1969 Trip Report about the sniper program in Vietnam, Lieutenant Colonel Fleming noted that both the army and the Marine Corps were guilty of the misuse of their snipers. As an example, Fleming included the story of a Marine who built a body count of fifty-two enemy soldiers using sniper tactics and his scoped rifle only to be killed by a shot through the heart when misused by an infantry commander in a ground assault against a fortified position.

Captain John W. Pinkston, former officer in charge of the 3rd Brigade, 9th Infantry Division, snipers during 1969 and 1970, also encountered typical operational problems. In a 1971 study for the Fort Benning Infantry School, Pinkston wrote, "The sniper program in the 3rd Brigade was hindered by small unit commanders' not being well versed on the utilization of snipers. During early employment, the sniper was forced to hump the rice paddies all day and perform sniper missions by night. Obviously, this constituted poor morale for the sniper and lowered his standards and performance."

In addition, Pinkston noted that at times snipers took advantage of field commanders' lack of information about their operations, writing, "There were some cases where snipers used their knowledge to deceive commanders, i.e., the sniper would move his weapon off zero to obtain a 'sham' trip to the rear for purposes of rezeroing his weapon. Had this specific commander understood the art of sniping and sniper equipment, he would have known that a corrective measure against this malpractice would have been to write his zero setting on paper and keep it in his records."

Kugler agrees that some snipers took advantage and "weren't motivated to do what they were trained to do."

Fleming's Trip Report points out another significant impact on sniper operations: "The most important finding from this trip is an answer to the question, 'Why do so many teams rarely engage targets?' " Conversations with the snipers themselves clearly indicate that it is primarily the well known 'don't shoot, you'll give our position away'* syndrome of World War II and Korea."

The Trip Report also noted, "A second and possible contributing cause for some trained snipers' rarely engaging targets may well be an 'executioner complex.' Most officers and sergeants interviewed say that their men would not hesitate to kill an enemy 'in cold blood.' However, in the next breath they tell you that the first criterion for selecting a sniper should be: 'a good soldier—a solid citizen.' "

With these factors in mind, Fleming theorized, "It would certainly seem likely that the same moral and religious upbringing that produced such a good soldier also produced a man with serious reservations about the morality of shooting an unwarned, unsuspecting fellow human being. An historical precedent morally may be the bounty hunter of the old west; many felt this type of person was reprehensible, although the cause could be just."

Fleming included in his report that the solution to these problems was additional training and as much live-fire practice as possible. He concluded, "The more a man uses his weapon the more likely he is to use it in a combat situation."

Operational techniques used by army and Marine snipers in Vietnam evolved and improved in the same manner as did their weapons systems and training. Some maneuvers and tactics carried over from previous wars; some originated in the rice paddies and jungles of Southeast Asia. Like other military

---

*The senior member of each sniper team made the decision about whether or not to engage a potential target. Firing even a single round increased the risk of compromising their position and receiving accurate counterfire. In every war, including Vietnam, some snipers, as well as regular infantrymen, at times passed up the opportunity to shoot as a means of self-preservation.

units in Vietnam, the snipers repeated what worked and discarded what did not work. Their experiences and accomplishments varied, but they established and reestablished sniper operational procedures that would outlast the long war itself.

CHAPTER 13

✳✳✳✳✳✳✳✳

The Other Side: VC/NVA Snipers

AMERICANS and their allies were not the only participants in the Vietnam War to appreciate the merits of the sniper. The Vietcong and the North Vietnamese Army regulars also recognized the value of sniper fire to kill their opponents, to disrupt their advances, and to cover the withdrawal of detected units.

"Shoot and move" tactics fit well with the VC/NVA procedures of avoiding sustained combat while at the same time slowing U.S. field operations and destroying morale. In response, U.S. soldiers and Marines interpreted nearly all sporadic rifle fire by single enemy soldiers as sniper actions.

Most "shoot and move" operations by the VC/NVA were not actual sniper activities but merely "harassing fire" from standard-issue AK-47 assault rifles or SKS semiautomatic carbines. Both iron-sight, 7.62-mm weapons, manufactured in the Soviet Union, were reasonably accurate up to 400 meters. Many similar models made in the People's Republic of China and other Communist countries also found their way into the VC/NVA arsenal.

Harassing fire originated more often from local-force VC units than from the NVA regulars. Commanders of the VC local forces were responsible for maintaining a presence in assigned areas, inflicting their will upon people and controlling the land to whatever degree possible. For much of the long war in Southeast Asia the local-force guerrillas were not able to stand up to the U.S. and ARVN forces in their zones of responsibility and so conducted only sporadic guerrilla warfare as a show of force rather than as an attempt to demonstrate a significant threat.

Harassing fire became an integral part of the limited fighting abilities of the local forces. Many of the VC worked as farmers or posed as ordinary villagers in the day only to retrieve their weapons and assume the role of guerrilla at night. A frequent mission of the part-time soldiers was to squeeze off a few rounds or a burst of automatic fire against a government compound, firebase, or patrol. The harassing fire was rarely accurate and did little more than remind the Americans, the ARVN, and, more important, the local villagers of the guerrillas' continued presence.

Nearly every personal narrative by American Vietnam veterans contains at least one account of "four-o'clock Charlie," "Luke the Gook," or some other such nicknamed VC who popped off a few rounds of AK-47 and SKS harassment fire almost on a schedule. Carlton Sherwood of Annapolis, Maryland, related a typical account that appears in the book *Inside the VC and NVA* by Dan Cragg and this author. Sherwood, an infantryman in G Company, 2nd Battalion, 4th Marine Regiment, in 1967 and 1968 and later a Pulitzer Prize–winning journalist, recalled, "Then there was 'Teatime Charlie,' a VC sniper who'd fire four or five rounds into our positions every day exactly at 1600. He was so regular that we knew to get ready for chow at 1700 whenever he'd open up. He never hit anybody. I'm convinced that was his only mission in the war—pop off four or five rounds our way every day and then he was off duty until the next time."

Although the vast majority of enemy activity identified by Americans as sniper was actually harassing fire by ordinary VC/NVA infantrymen, the Communists did train and arm snipers during the war. In fact, NVA snipers began action against the U.S. Marines in the northern part of South Vietnam about the same time that the Americans began to experiment with their own precision shooters.

As a result of the North Vietnamese defeat of South Vietnam, much information about the organization, training, and employment of VC/NVA units, especially their elites, remains unknown because of the limited amount of data on the subject. Available information comes from documents captured in the field during the conflict and from interviews with prisoners of war and those who voluntarily surrendered. The first detailed report on NVA sniper operations came in the early summer of 1966 when a thirty-five-year-old North Vietnamese lieutenant surrendered to a South Vietnamese village chief fifty miles north of Da Nang. Armed with a Russian-made sniper rifle and telescope, the lieutenant had infiltrated down the Ho Chi Minh Trail with a sniper company in which he commanded a platoon.

The South Vietnamese interviewed the officer before turning him over to Major Robert Russell, head of the 3rd Marine Division Scout-Sniper School, for further questioning. An article by Gunnery Sergeant Jack Childs in the July 19, 1966, issue of the III Marine Amphibious Force publication *Sea Tiger* revealed much of what Russell learned from the NVA lieutenant.

According to the article, the lieutenant, speaking through an interpreter, reported that he and his unit trained in North Vietnam for three months before infiltrating south into the area around Phu Bai. All of his platoon's enlisted snipers were between nineteen and twenty-two years of age, and their families in North Vietnam received extra allotments of rice and land in exchange for their volunteering. In addition to dry- and live-fire shooting, each sniper received extensive training in camouflage and movement techniques before deploying south.

Using information from the NVA lieutenant, interviews with other prisoners, and translations of captured documents, the U.S. Military Assistance Command Vietnam (MACV) published a classified study on January 6, 1967, "VC/NVA Employment of Snipers."* The cover letter, signed by the MACV's assistant chief of staff for intelligence, Brigadier General J. A. McChristian, stated that the study was one in a series designed to describe VC/NVA tactics and tactical doctrine. It also discussed training, unit organization, and tactical employment of snipers.

*The complete document is in Appendix F.

"VC/NVA Employment of Snipers" confirmed the three-month training for snipers in North Vietnam. It noted, however, that, although formal sniper training took place only in North Vietnam, there was evidence "that local guerrillas in SVN [were] being instructed by NVA snipers." Training included live-fire practice at ranges up to 1,000 meters; instruction on camouflage, movement, and position selection; and extensive lessons in weapon and scope maintenance. Each VC/NVA sniper was expected to be able to act as his own armorer in repairing and adjusting his weapon system.

Intelligence reports from field units revealed that VC/NVA snipers often used booby traps to channel American and South Vietnamese patrols into their kill zones. The MACV study explained that there was no evidence that the training in North Vietnam contained any instruction on mines and explosives, but U.S. intelligence sources believed enemy snipers received such training after arrival in South Vietnam.

VC/NVA snipers used K44 rifles supplied by the Soviet Union. The weapon was actually a Mosin Nayant Model 1891/30, the model number derived from the original 1891 design and the 1930 modifications. The bolt-action 7.62-mm rifle had a five-round magazine and 3.5 power PU telescopic sight and was capable of reasonable accuracy up to 800 meters. It had served the Soviet army well in World War II, and, redesignated the K44, proved durable in the jungles and rice paddies of Vietnam.

The K44 served as the primary sniper weapon of the VC/NVA for the entire war. Although the Soviet Union replaced the system in its own army in the 1950s with the Dragunov SVD 7.62-mm, gas-operated, semiautomatic sniper rifle equipped with a 4X scope, it provided precious few of those to the North Vietnamese, at least before the American withdrawal from Southeast Asia.

The VC/NVA snipers wore the same uniforms as other infantrymen and carried similar equipment. Vietcong guerrilla marksmen wore a mixture of civilian and military clothing, while Main Force and NVA snipers dressed more uniformly.

The best description of the NVA snipers' apparel appears in John J. Culbertson's *Operation Tuscaloosa*, which describes a battle fought at An Hoa in January 1967.*

Culbertson records an encounter by his H Company, 2nd Battalion, 5th Marines, that killed a Communist sniper cell in a bunker: "The enemy soldiers were lying in a contorted pile at the bottom. Arms and legs intertwined in such unnatural postures that it was difficult to determine where one man ended and another began. They all wore green fatigue uniforms, rubber sandals, and green canvas cartridge belts loaded with ammunition and grenades. Green pith helmets with red star emblems on the front lay where they had tumbled off the dead soldiers' heads. Three weapons lay on the dirt floor of the bunker still within reach of the dead soldiers' grasps. Lafley pointed at one of the weapons—a long-barreled, wood-stocked, bolt action with a telescopic sight mounted on top of a polished receiver."

Organization of VC/NVA sniper units differed greatly from those in the U.S. military. Sniper units trained as companies— about 100 men—each composed of a headquarters element and three platoons. Each platoon had three squads, which, in turn, had three three-man cells and a squad leader. The three-man sniper cell mirrored the organization of all VC/NVA units and evolved from the Communist Chinese army concept that the three-man cell provided the optimum tactical and political organization.

From the limited evidence available, the NVA 32nd Regiment, which remained in the North, appears to have conducted all sniper training. In 1967, the North Vietnamese sent the 700th Sniper Battalion and C.100 Sniper Company into South Vietnam, where those units remained for the duration of the war.

There is no documentation of other sniper battalions or companies training in the north and infiltrating to the south, but it is likely that the 700th Battalion and C.100 Company received individual sniper replacements from North Vietnam's

*Ivy Books, 1997.

training center. The replacements would have received additional training alongside VC volunteers once they arrived in South Vietnam.

For security purposes, the VC/NVA frequently changed unit designations, and some used more than one letter and/or numerical designation at the same time. That probably explains why some U.S. intelligence reports refer to different-numbered sniper battalions and companies. Another security measure taken by the NVA was to conduct on-the-job training of newly arrived snipers in Laos and Cambodia, where the Americans and ARVNs could not pursue.

Despite their overall organization into companies subordinate to a battalion headquarters, after reaching South Vietnam, the NVA snipers rarely came together in groups larger than a platoon. Each sniper platoon generally had the responsibility of supporting five infantry battalions. This meant that often a squad or only a three-man cell accompanied a battalion on operations. Some prisoner interviews and captured documents refer to sniper squads being so dispersed that they rarely operated any closer than a three-day march to each other.

Although assigned to support a battalion, NVA sniper squads and cells did not usually accompany the larger unit on maneuvers or during offensives. Mostly the Communist snipers limited their operations to certain areas and employed local VC as guides and security. Their areas of operations were usually on the outer edges of VC/NVA-controlled areas or around their fortified base camps.

The three-man sniper cells established positions that provided good observations and fields of fire on possible routes of advance. They used natural terrain features such as hills, ravines, and gullies, which would channel approaching enemy into their kill zones, and supplemented their lines of fire with mines and booby traps to further control the targets' advance and to seal off avenues of retreat. Carefully selecting positions that provided concealment from ground troops and aerial detection, the VC/NVA snipers placed more mines and booby traps in front of their "hide" positions to slow enemy pursuit after engagement. Not unlike U.S. snipers, these marksmen prepared a route of withdrawal, as well as an alternate route, before the cell and its security element took their positions.

VC/NVA snipers also prepared "hides" in the outer trench-work of base camps. In the event of attack, the snipers' mission was to slow the enemy assault to provide time for the remainder of the unit to withdraw. The snipers carefully selected and rehearsed their escape plans.

Target selection for VC/NVA snipers did not differ from that of special marksmen of previous wars. Officers and their communications personnel, easily recognizable by their distinctive radio antennas, were the top priority. In order to avoid singling themselves out, most U.S. officers did not wear rank in the field; even so, the VC/NVA snipers were well aware that leaders stayed close to their radios and radio operators. Machine gunners and other crew-served weapons personnel constituted the secondary targets. The point man (the lead man of a patrol), and the rear security (the last soldier) provided other ideal opportunities for the sniper's bullet.

American helicopters were also important targets for Communist snipers. Trained to establish hide positions near clearings and other possible landing zones, VC/NVA snipers frequently fired on command and control helicopters and personnel transports.

The "shoot and move" tactic against helicopters might have looked tempting in the theoretical school environment but proved to be extremely dangerous in reality. VC/NVA snipers found themselves at risk from American observation and attack gunships as well as from lightly armed transports. Because helicopter unit commanders spared no firepower to "prep" landing zones with general suppressing fires before conducting landings, the snipers were even vulnerable to routine "unaimed" firing sweeps. If seen—or even suspected—the snipers could expect the helicopter crews to level the area with automatic grenade launcher, rocket, and machine gun fire.

Even though the training they received in North Vietnam emphasized engaging Americans as much as possible, once in the combat zone, the VC/NVA more often engaged the ARVN than the U.S. forces. The reason for this is simple: the Americans reacted faster and more powerfully, throwing artillery, helicopter gunships, and air strikes at any individual target successfully inflicting casualties.

Despite the 800-meter range of their K44 rifles, VC/NVA snipers initiated fire as close as 50 meters and rarely at ranges in excess of 500 meters. Unlike the American two-man teams, in which only one man carried a sniper weapon, each soldier in the VC/NVA three-man cell was armed with one.

That three-rifle capability also provided their basic tactic. The senior sniper usually initiated the fire, aiming at and killing his target with his first round. When other members of the targeted group maneuvered—whether to retrieve the body or against the sniper position—the senior shooter and his two cell members took aim at the new targets. Usually the snipers fired just one or two shots each, and rarely more than five rounds, before withdrawing. If the approaching unit detected the snipers' position, VC/NVA security element covered the withdrawal with automatic weapons fire.

Frequently the VC/NVA sniper teams did not conclude their missions with a single engagement. Instead they withdrew to predetermined positions from which to fire again on the pursuing enemy force. It is important to note, however, that the VC/NVA sniper teams did not often go looking for targets. Their primary role remained that of defense—and then only to defend areas the VC/NVA considered extremely important. Even in their defensive positions, the VC/NVA could expect American army and Marine ground commanders to fight back with the same enthusiasm and firepower as did their aviation counterparts.

The VC/NVA found American snipers to be their most lethal foes. The only advantage the VC/NVA snipers had against the American marksmen was that U.S. forces never had adequate numbers of snipers to supply to each army or Marine company, or even each battalion. Otherwise, the VC/NVA shooters were at a disadvantage because of the superior training the Americans received, the enhanced observation they gained with telescopes and spotter scopes, and the tactics under which they operated.

In its 1967 edition of *Professional Knowledge*, the Marine Corps outlined countersniper operations for units without attached snipers of their own. Description of immediate action included the following: "When taken under fire by a sniper, personnel often fall to the ground and seek cover. It cannot be overemphasized that the requirement to bring fire to bear on the suspected sniper location is as important as individual protection. Immediate action drills and directing immediate rapid and accurate fire into the general direction of the sniper should be emphasized in training."

While it is doubtful that the average VC/NVA sniper was aware of official American doctrine, he most surely experienced the results of it. The minute he pulled the trigger, he could anticipate return fire from rifles, grenade launchers, and machine guns in accordance with American directives. If he held his position and continued his attack, he could expect to be bombarded by American mortars, artillery, and air support.

At times, too, the VC/NVA had to worry about American firing missions directed at general locations based on the mere chance that the sniper might be hiding there. Because American field commanders had no budget restraints on ammunition expenditures, the VC/NVA sniper could never be sure what type or how much power the Americans would use to try to neutralize him.

Professional Knowledge also suggested other measures in the event that massive firepower failed. "Large search and destroy operations," the document admitted, "have little chance of killing or destroying this type of VC guerrilla, but well-planned and executed small unit patrols . . . have proven effective in coping with snipers."

Therefore, provisions of *Professional Knowledge* recommended saturation of an operational area with squad-size, daylight combat patrols whose mission was twofold: to make contact with the enemy and to become familiar with the terrain. The VC/NVA could be sure that patrol leaders of each mission would report any sign of his activity, data that would ultimately further concentrate patrolling, blocking positions, and observation posts. Night operations were also part of the effort to locate and destroy the snipers.

According to Professional Knowledge, the American tactics proved successful and "produced several significant contacts resulting in confirmed VC kills and capture of VC weapons, including one with a high-power scope." The report concluded, "To achieve maximum effectiveness, patrol members must be thoroughly familiar with the terrain and all details of the patrol plan must be known and understood by the observation posts/blocking positions and the combat patrol. Patience, alertness, and fire discipline on the part of each marine are requisites."

To defend themselves from the Americans' sophisticated weaponry, nearly unlimited firepower, and aggressive patrols, the VC/NVA snipers further adapted their guerrilla tactics. However, not all of their defensive measures were successful, as is illustrated by the following story.

In early 1967, Vietcong snipers were slowing a 3rd Marine Division offensive and inflicting casualties by popping out of spider holes, firing, and then disappearing back into the ground before the Marines could spot them. The commander of the 4th Marine Regiment dispatched a group from his scout-sniper platoon to neutralize the Communist shooters.

Staff Sergeant Jerry Sides, a former sniper instructor, led the eight-man team composed of three shooters, three observers, a corpsman, and a radio operator. An article in the February 1 edition of *Sea Tiger* describes the results: "The Marine countersnipers moved into position before daylight. After lying in wait for three and a half hours in the bone-chilling rain, Sides spotted two VC snipers through his field glasses. A silent signal was given and two of his men slipped to his side. Their weapons were snuggled into their shoulders, the crosshairs lined up, two sharp reports, and two VC snipers move no more.

"Then came three more hours of lying in the deep mud, not moving a muscle or making a sound—just waiting patiently to do the job. Patience finally paid off when another VC was spotted and downed at 1,100 yards."

The VC/NVA used the same tactics against the U.S. Army. In the May-June 1967 issue of *Infantry* magazine, Captain Patrick H. Graves, a former platoon leader in the 1st Battalion, 327th Infantry, 101st Airborne Division, recorded his observations of the VC/NVA marksmen. Graves's experiences were typical of the war's small unit leaders and provide an excellent insight into the army's stance on enemy snipers.

In "Observations of a Platoon Leader," Graves noted that the typical mission of the enemy snipers was to harass U.S. and South Vietnamese forces. "The sniper," he wrote, "is used in areas where enemy strength is nominal, and where he can demonstrate to the inhabitants that the Viet Cong can resist a larger government or U.S. force. Primarily, such light resistance is for propaganda purposes."

Graves continued by writing that the VC/NVA snipers were effective in holding up a superior force while their comrades withdrew. He warned that the enemy snipers frequently kept open areas, waterways, and roads under observation for possible targets. "To destroy the sniper," Graves wrote, "closure must be executed with speed and aggressiveness for the sniper is usually prepared to escape on preplanned routes. Thus fire and maneuver come into play—fire to pin the sniper in place while the maneuver element closes to destroy him. Grenade launchers should be used to the utmost, their fires concentrated on trees and other suspected sniper locations."

The former platoon leader added that artillery and mortar fire support could also be used to directly engage the enemy marksmen or to cut off their route of escape. In conclusion, Graves provides another warning: "Aggressiveness is often the key to success or failure in destroying a sniper; but, be cautious not to over-react to the sniper and be drawn into a baited ambush."

It is difficult, if not impossible, to evaluate the overall effectiveness of the VC/NVA snipers. The VC/NVA snipers did not have the luxury of firing as many rounds during initial or refresher training as their American opponents. In the *Sea Tiger* article about the NVA sniper lieutenant, discussed on page 180, Major Russell concluded, "Their training, although longer, can't begin to compare to ours." Russell added that although the NVA sniper trainees were new recruits straight off the farm or out of the village, Marine snipers were mostly selected from the ranks. The Marine snipers, according to Russell, were "hand-picked, already combat-hardened veterans."

Of course, many of the NVA snipers and the VC they trained also became experienced veterans. Since they were in South Vietnam for the duration, as opposed to the one-year tour of the Americans, at least some of the VC/NVA snipers who survived became skilled marksmen. In the same interview in which he discussed harassment fire by "Teatime Charlie," Carlton Sherwood noted the results and impact of a more effective NVA sharpshooter.

Sherwood recalls, "Let me tell you another sniper story. This was in Quang Tri Province. The whole battalion was walking in the bush just off Route 1. It was rolling hill country. We got a sniper who knew how to shoot. This guy was about a half mile away. Each shot got a guy right between the eyes. He got about five men. We had no idea where he was shooting from. The whole battalion went to ground. This one sniper held us up the whole day. Next day, same thing. Nobody wanted to stand up anymore. The battalion commander called in air strikes—bombs, napalm, 20-mm cannon for one sniper! They laid in on the ridge line where we thought he was. After the air strike, we walked for about an hour when 'bang!'" another guy went down. At that point we'd made about a mile and a half in two days. Then we tried to flank him with two platoons, which is what the battalion CO should have done in the first place. Night came on and do you know he actually took pot shots at us in the dark! The CO called in another air strike and do you know what? When the jets came in I could hear *ping*, *ping*, *ping*, that motherfucker was shooting at the goddamned jets.

"We never found him," Sherwood concluded. "Eleven hundred guys, the meanest fighting force in the world, held up by one man."

Despite such individual success, there is no evidence that the North Vietnamese made any attempts to expand the use of snipers beyond their initial efforts, nor did they ever assume anything other than primarily a defensive role. Stories such as Carlton Sherwood's about one sniper slowing an entire battalion are not unique even though the VC/NVA sniper role was relatively minor in terms of the overall war.

CHAPTER 14

✳✳✳✳✳✳✳✳

The Assessment

*A*LTHOUGH U.S. forces won every major battle in South Vietnam before their withdrawal, history records the war as the country's first defeat. As the years have passed, most Americans have begun to realize that the loss came not from the failure of their military but rather from the lack of national support and concessions made at the conference table.

Deciphering exactly what occurred in regard to Vietnam is complicated by a myriad of factors, not the least of which is the "fog" of combat that obscures much of what happens when weapons are in use. Men separated by only a few feet or even fighting side-by-side often see and experience entirely different aspects of the same battle. Combat infantrymen throughout history have focused on accomplishing their missions and surviving rather than recording their experiences. Senior military and political leaders who do write about their observations of war are often more interested in their own reputations than in accurately presenting events. Further clouding the real events are the war historians, who rarely fail to bring their own agendas to their descriptions.

Capturing the essence of the Vietnam War in writing has proved to be an even greater challenge than writing about other conflicts because of the complexities of the nonconventional battles and campaigns and the characteristics of the men who did the actual fighting. Most of the war's encounters occurred in remote jungles or watery rice paddy battlegrounds between small elements with no news reporters or military history unit personnel present.

Added to this void was the fact that records and files not extracted with U.S. units during their withdrawal ended up in the hands of the North Vietnamese when Saigon fell in 1975. Access to these files and those maintained by the North Vietnamese during the war remains extremely limited.

A final consideration in studying the Vietnam War is the polarization it created. Emotional views of the war still influence those who attempt to write about the period. In a 1986 letter, Lieutenant General Stanley R. Larsen, USA (Ret.), commander of the II Field Force in Vietnam from August 1965 to August 1967, provided an observation on the difficulties of recording the accurate history of the conflict: "More needs to be written about the Vietnam War, but unfortunately, these studies must consider that they are covering a 'lost' war run by politicians determined to beat out a no-win war, who were afraid to make difficult decisions, and certainly never aimed at MacArthur's famous truism, 'There is no substitution for victory.'"

Larsen was correct about the need for more written information about the Vietnam conflict. However, the publication of such material does not, in itself, necessarily remedy the situation—indeed, it often obscures the truth further. Any analysis of writings on or about Vietnam—official or unofficial—must factor in the self-interest and/or the agenda of the authors and the intended audience. While that statement applies to the assessment of all writing, it is particularly important in the evaluation of material on the already complex, emotionally laden subject of Vietnam. For example, several political leaders of the period, some now deceased, penned self-serving memoirs that avoided responsibility for their decisions during the war and placed the blame for the fall of Saigon and the South Vietnamese government everywhere and anywhere but on themselves.

A few senior military officials have recorded their stories, and thus enhanced their reputations, while other high-ranking military commanders of the time have died or can no longer physically or mentally offer recollections. For years no one seemed interested in their comments; now many are no longer able to contribute.*

Making the task of investigating the war even more difficult is the fact that to date neither the U.S. Army nor the U.S. Marine Corps has produced any definitive history of its involvement in the war. In the early 1970s, the Department of the Army published a series of pamphlet-size works called Vietnam Studies that were written by a few veteran senior commanders and staff officers. The Marine Corps has offered a somewhat better effort with its series, "U.S. Marines in Vietnam," that has been published over the last twenty years. Neither service's publications, however, devote more than a few lines to the development of snipers or to their operations, and those limited entries contribute little to the understanding of sniper employment or effectiveness.

The most detailed official explanation of sniper operations in Vietnam by either service appears in *Sharpening the Combat Edge: The Use of Analysis to Reinforce Military Judgment* by Lieutenant General Julian J. Ewell and Major General Ira A. Hunt Jr., published in 1974 as part of the Vietnam Studies series. In the four-page summary subtitled "Sniper Program," the authors include a brief history of the development of army marksmen in the 9th Infantry Division and conclude that it "was one of the most successful programs we undertook."

The three primary pioneers of sniper training and organization in Vietnam—Marine majors Robert Russell and Jim Land and army major Willis Powell—wrote official and unofficial reports for their superiors. While the content of these writings was, of course, limited by the priorities of combat, the authors still had an agenda.

---

*In 1986 and 1987, while researching what became *Inside the LRRPs: Rangers in Vietnam*, the author queried more than fifty retired officers who had served as generals in Vietnam. Less than a decade later, because of death or poor health, more than a third of that group was unable to contribute to this book. Many had had significant information to share and great stories to tell, but the long-term disdain of the American publishers for anything related to the Vietnam War and its participants discouraged the recording of that aspect of history. Much is now lost forever.

Most of the original Marine and army snipers and sniper instructors came from the peacetime shooting teams and were
very aware that they needed to demonstrate how precision
marksmanship could complement infantry units in combat,
thus guaranteeing the continuation, and perhaps expansion,
of competition shooting teams and matches after the war
concluded.

Unofficial accounts of snipers in Vietnam have done better
than the official sources in telling the story, but they, too, have
their deficiencies. The most detailed books to date on snipers in Vietnam are *The Long Range War: Sniping in Vietnam*,
published in 1994, and *The One Round War: USMC Scout-
Snipers in Vietnam*, released two years later. Both of these
books, written by Peter R. Senich and published by Paladin
Press, contain extensive illustrations and photographs in an
oversize 9-by-11-inch format.

Written for gun enthusiasts and those already familiar with
long-range shooting, those books do provide a great deal of information, and their illustrations are the best to be found in
print. Unfortunately, the $39.95 cost of *The Long Range War*
and $59.95 for *The One Round War*, combined with the lack
of wide distribution by the publisher, has prevented those
pioneer volumes from gaining any substantial readership or
acceptance.

Two books about individual Marine snipers in Vietnam and
a collection of sniper stories, which includes several marksmen in Vietnam, have also added to the general information
about snipers in the war. The first, *Marine Sniper: 93 Confirmed Kills* by Charles Henderson, presents the story of Carlos Hathcock. This work, which first appeared in 1986, is one
of the best-selling books on the Vietnam War. Although some
senior Marine commanders and other snipers and infantry veterans question portions of the stories as Henderson presents
them,* there is no doubt that Hathcock attained a deserved

---

*Editors significantly shortened and altered Henderson's original seven
hundred-page manuscript, apparently combining some events and embellish-
ing others to create more dramatic impact for market appeal in an era (1986)

reputation in the competition shooting community as one of the all-time best marksmen in the Corps. His ninety-three kills in Vietnam also place him near the top of the list of that conflict's successful snipers.

Henderson's book does provide many insights on sniper training and operations. However, Hathcock's experiences were not at all typical of the experiences of the ordinary Marine or army sniper in Vietnam. According to Henderson, Hathcock was one of the few Marine snipers—and possibly the only one—allowed to operate independently or semi-dependently rather than as a member of a two-man team secured by at least a squad of infantry. Henderson's book provides a story about a brave, sure-shot Marine but does not offer a general history of snipers in Vietnam or an account representative of the ordinary snipers who filled the regimental and recon battalion scout-sniper platoons.

The second book about a Marine sniper in Southeast Asia, *Dear Mom: A Sniper's Vietnam* by Joseph T. Ward, provides a better account of day-to-day activities of the precision marksmen as well as information on weapons and equipment. Ward's personal narrative does include a bit of sniper history, but the source is his own recollections rather than official documents. The book's greatest merit may very well be that it is the honest story of a low-ranking Marine sniper who did only one tour in Vietnam and in the corps and then quietly returned home to rejoin the ranks of civilians.

Interestingly, when Ward's book was first released, several of the "old guard" of Marine competition marksmen expressed doubts about certain aspects of his kill ranges and his number of successful missions. Apparently these doubters had difficulty accepting that a one-tour Marine with no prior experience in competition shooting could be so successful. Support

when Vietnam War books were usually shunned. Henderson admits in his preface that he took "the liberty of inventing" the dialogue of the VC/NVA; combat veterans and others knowledgeable of the "real" Vietnam War recognize that several operations detailed in the book do not remotely reflect Marine Corps sniper standard operating procedures. Even so, editorial and dramatic considerations in no way diminish the accomplishments of Hathcock.

from fellow snipers and officers in Ward's 5th Marine Regiment quickly quieted the doubters.

A third book, *One Shot—One Kill* by Charles Sasser and Craig Roberts provides stories in an oral history format about individual snipers in World War II, Korea, Vietnam, and Beirut. Linking the narrative are various bits and pieces of American sniper history, including a brief overview of the development of the marksmen during the Vietnam War.

While all of the official and some of the unofficial publications note problems and shortcomings of sniper operations, all have declared the use of the special marksmen to have been a successful aspect of U.S. forces in Vietnam. Yet no single source analyzes the "big picture" impact of specific actions. Some references provide statistics on the numbers of sniper missions and their outcomes for brief periods for specific units, but no source combines these numbers into any kind of definitive study.

Along with influences of a "lost cause" and limited access to the enemy's archives, other factors reduce our ability to provide a complete, statistical analysis of sniper activities and accomplishments in Vietnam. Some army separate brigades and divisions made few or no reports at all on the number of their snipers, sniper operations, or the number of their snipers' enemy contacts and kills. Only the Army Concept Team in Vietnam, as a part of its test, and the 9th Infantry Division, as a result of the interest of General Ewell in what he considered a personal project, kept any detailed records on soldier snipers.

Although the Marine regiments and reconnaissance battalions did a better job than the army in requiring and maintaining sniper records, they rarely collated them into external official reports. Some information that did make its way into the official record was lost or destroyed during the major offensives, such as Tet of 1968, or simply disappeared in transit.

The official records that are available are brief and contain few details. Typical of the limited accounts is the single paragraph in the twenty-page Combat After-Action Report of the 2nd Battalion, 5th Marines, describing its participation in Operation Tuscaloosa, January 24–28, 1967. On page 8 of the report, under a paragraph labeled "Execution," a short entry states that the battalion's F Company, at 1740 hours on January 27, "observed 12 enemy" whom they engaged with organic weapons and an air strike. The paragraph concludes, "Scout-sniper team accounted for one enemy KIA confirmed."

Entries in official army reports about snipers were also brief. One of the more detailed accounts appears in the "Operational Report—Lessons Learned for the 25th Infantry Division" for the three-month period ending on April 30, 1970. Page 40 of the report relates, "On April 21 at 2101 hours, snipers from B/2-27 Inf engaged five to six enemy at XS525993 with organic weapons and artillery resulting in two enemy killed. At 2050 hours on 23 April, snipers from C/2-27 Inf engaged three enemy soldiers at 260 meters southeast of the 21 April contact (XS542978) with organic weapons resulting in two enemy killed and the capture of 30 pounds of rice. Snipers from Recon Platoon/2-27 Inf engaged two enemy soldiers on 24 April at 0346 hours 80 meters southeast of the 21 April contact site (XS532996) with organic weapons resulting in two enemy killed."

The "Operational Report" of the 3rd Brigade, 9th Infantry Division, for the three-month period ending October 31, 1969, provides a better cumulative total of sniper success but lacks details. According to page 20 of the brigade's report, "From 26 July 1969 to 31 October 1969, snipers accounted for 47 enemy eliminated in Long An Province. A total of 39 kills were attained at night utilizing a Starlight scope."

Personal narratives and unofficial writing about snipers in Vietnam often rely on memory alone and contain gaps in information as well as unintended inaccuracies. In some cases, the analysis does not take into account the fact that snipers in the same unit were at times so dispersed that they never knew each other, let alone each other's accomplishments or failures. The very nature of snipers and sniping reinforced this lack of interaction and the "clouding" of whatever information was available. In addition to their discretion among themselves, snipers talked to few outside their immediate ranks about their operations and engagements.

As the antiwar movement at home gained momentum and support from the American press, the snipers became even less communicative with those outside their own units. Marine and army public information officers, even though desperately seeking a positive slant on the war to show the media, avoided mention of successful snipers. As a result, for the Vietnam era, few newspaper or other media stories exist about snipers or their effectiveness.

Despite the controversy about the U.S. military's assessing its accomplishments in Vietnam by the daily enemy body count, the numbers policy did readily lend itself to measuring the success of units and operations. Snipers, who engaged individual targets with superior weapons and scopes and had each kill verified by an officer, fit perfectly into the body count policy of attrition warfare.

Of course, because of battle conditions, distances, and the valiant efforts of the VC/NVA not to leave bodies behind, the snipers could not always determine the results of each shot. Every sniper maintained an account of both confirmed and possible kills. Snipers also kept records of each nonlethal wound they inflicted. However, because a slightly wounded VC/NVA nearly always escaped, those numbers were estimates at best.

No figures, or even reasonable guesses, are available on the number of kills made by the unofficial American snipers who acquired rifles and scopes on their own prior to the formation of the in-country marksmanship schools. Most of those soldiers and Marines acted as regular infantrymen in addition to their sniping duties. Their body counts included enemy killed by firing with conventional iron sights as well as those eliminated by long-range, scoped-rifle fire.

Once the Marine Corps established its sniper schools and organized the scout-sniper platoons in the regiments and reconnaissance battalions, the two divisions began to require regular reports on the number of engagements and kills by their sharpshooters. Individual Marine snipers kept logs and/or submitted kill sheets detailing the results of each engagement. Those reports were forwarded to the division headquarters by the regiments and reconnaissance battalions to be consolidated into a single report—at least, that was the official policy. In the midst of combat and the frequent changes in leaders and personnel due to the thirteen-month tour policy, the sniper platoons and their senior headquarters were not always able to follow the prescribed procedure. At times they were late in submitting the records or sent no report at all. In other cases reports were misplaced or never forwarded to permanent archives.

The most accessible, and in many cases the only available, information on the kill totals of Marine snipers comes from the shooters themselves.* Each Marine scout-sniper platoon maintained its own unofficial kill total and some posted daily updates to the figures. Joe Ward recalls that shortly before his departure from the 5th Marine Regiment on March 3, 1970, the tally for his scout-sniper platoon totaled 1,174 kills since its formation about four years earlier.

The 5th Regiment withdrew from Vietnam along with the rest of the 1st Marine Division a year later. At the time of its departure, the 5th Marine Scout-Sniper Platoon had increased its kills to about 1,300. The 1st and 7th regimental sniper platoons in the 1st Division had similar successes with about the same body counts. Two other regiments, the 26th and the 27th, joined the 1st Marine Division in 1967 and 1968 and together added about 1,200 successful sniper engagements. The slightly smaller reconnaissance battalion platoon added another 1,100 dead VC/NVA bringing the 1st Marine Division sniper kill count to about 6,200—or the equivalent of twenty-one VC/NVA battalions!—during its time in Vietnam.

The 3rd Marine Division organized and trained its snipers several months before the 1st Division but began rotating out of country more than a year earlier. Only three regimental sniper platoons, the 3rd, 4th, and 9th, and one from the 3rd

---

*Sniper veterans are welcome and encouraged to provide additional information about their own personal experiences as well as those of their units in Vietnam for possible inclusion in future editions of this book. For details, see Appendix G "Information Request."

Reconnaissance Battalion, were assigned to the division. Because of its smaller numbers and shorter time in the war zone, the 3rd Marine Division produced only an estimated 4,500 sniper kills.*

Unofficial army snipers who acquired Korean War–vintage rifles and scopes or who adapted civilian weapons to field use also undoubtedly built a body count prior to the official introduction of the program. The first official statistics, however, were not recorded until the Army Concept Team in Vietnam (ACTIV) sniper operations and equipment test of June through October 1967. According to the test report, 259 snipers produced a body count of only 46 enemy soldiers during a little more than three months of field operations. Of course, many of those shooters were poorly trained, and they were armed with a variety of rifles and scopes, many of which were inferior to later weapon systems. There was also great diversity in the support they received from field commanders.

After the completion of the ACTIV tests, only the 9th Infantry Division maintained records on the accomplishments of its snipers to any degree. According to its report, "Sniper Training and Employment," the division's snipers were "first assigned to maneuver battalions on 7 November 1968 and obtained their first kill on 10 November 1968. During the period from November 1968 to April 1969 seventy snipers were employed in the division. They had 286 contacts and accumulated a total of 475 confirmed kills, or 1.67 kills per contact."

A few months later the 9th Division—less the 3rd Brigade, which remained in-country for one more year—left the war zone as one of the first American units to withdraw from Vietnam. The final confirmed number of kills by the division, including the 3rd Brigade, totaled a little more than 1,200.

No other army division or separate brigade snipers came anywhere near the total kills amassed by the 9th. Most of the

---

*The number of sniper kills per week, month, or even year varied from unit to unit, depending on the level of enemy activity and the degree of support by individual division, regiment, and battalion commanders. Availability of weapons, particularly the introduction of the M40s, also impacted the pace of sniper kills.

army commands integrated their trained snipers back into their infantry platoons and their kills were merely added to the unit body counts. It would be extremely optimistic to estimate that the sniper kill total of all the other army units in Vietnam together equaled that of the 9th Infantry Division.

Based on those considerations, the combined army and Marine sniper kill total for the Vietnam War is about 13,000. Considering that only about 1,250 soldiers and Marines served as precision marksmen during the conflict, and that they expended fewer than two rounds of ammunition per contact to produce a body count of 13,000, it is difficult to evaluate the sniper program as anything but a successful contributor to the war effort.

Yet those figures are small compared to the overall number of VC/NVA casualties during the long conflict that incorporated the most sophisticated small arms, artillery, and air support of any war to that point. A conservative estimate of VC/NVA deaths as a result of combat is 666,000, though some place the figure as high as 924,000. Using the rough average of 800,000 VC/NVA deaths, 13,000 sniper kills accounts for less than 2 percent of the total enemy killed.

That minimal impact on the progress and outcome of the war is one reason for the lack of any mention of army and Marine snipers in the various almanacs and encyclopedias about the Vietnam War. The exclusion of snipers began with the publication of the groundbreaking *Vietnam War Almanac* by Colonel Harry G. Summers Jr., USA (Ret.), in 1985 and with *The Vietnam War: An Almanac* edited by John S. Bowman the same year. Despite the increased interest in snipers in more recent years, the 1997 edition of *Encyclopedia of the Vietnam War* edited by Stanley I. Kutler makes no mention of them.

Shelby Stanton's *Vietnam Order of Battle*, published in 1981, is the most comprehensive reference book on U.S. Army forces deployed to Vietnam during the war. Yet even that detailed work offers only two photos of XM21 sniper rifles and the explanation that the weapon was "the standard army sniping rifle during the Vietnam War."

Another source that usually provides insight into the effectiveness of a unit, tactic, or weapon system is the enemy himself. In Vietnam, however, that resource revealed little about the American snipers. A few VC/NVA prisoners during wartime interviews mentioned snipers but none made any reference to any great impact by the long-range marksmen. Of course, with the amount of artillery and air ordnance delivered on suspected enemy locations, it is little wonder that single shots from rifles, regardless of their accuracy, did not make an impression.

One of the most often referenced indications of the impact of American snipers on enemy operations is also one of the most controversial. Practically every book and article on American snipers mentions Communist commanders' offering huge bounties—up to a year's pay—on snipers "dead or alive." While the stories were often repeated and believed by both the snipers and their commanders, there is no conclusive evidence that a single reward for the demise of a sniper was ever offered by the VC or NVA.

Not a single reward poster, printed announcement, or prisoner interrogation manuscript exists in any archive to support the bounty claims. More telling is the fact that every elite unit—army LRRPs, Marine force reconnaissance, and the various Special Forces units in Vietnam—also claim to have had bounties placed on them. The stories even extended to helicopter crews, armored cavalry squadrons, and artillery batteries as well as to the ranks of the ordinary infantrymen.

But there is *no* hard evidence that formal rewards for snipers were ever issued by the VC/NVA. Perhaps, someday, one or more of the rumors will be verified, but that has not yet happened.*

---

*Interestingly, although there is no substantiation of the rumored bounties announced by the VC/NVA, the Americans and South Vietnamese did issue "wanted posters" for Vietcong leaders in the Mekong Delta as a part of Project Phoenix. The reward announcements, which were counter to provisions of the Geneva Convention, were implemented on an extremely limited basis. Only a few examples are known to have survived, and most remain in the hands of private collectors and Project Phoenix veterans.

Another often misunderstood or misrepresented aspect of American snipers in Vietnam is their casualty rate. The VC/NVA rarely had sufficient mortar and artillery support to "pile on" firepower against a single sniper or team. The tactic most commonly used by the Communists against the American snipers was the same tactic they used in their other operations—when engaged the VC/NVA withdrew as soon as possible.

The enemy's lack of significant countersniper measures, combined with the excellent training of the U.S. marksmen, meant that few American snipers were killed or wounded. Although there are no official statistics on U.S. sniper casualties in the war, the available information indicates that the percentage of marksmen killed or wounded is far below that of infantry and reconnaissance units. An article in the April 21, 1986, edition of *U.S. News & World Report* states that of 600 snipers trained by Carlos Hathcock in Vietnam, only one was killed in combat.

Many of the snipers who did die did so heroically. On June 6, 1967, Corporal John R. Burke of the 26th Marine Sniper Platoon joined the regiment's 1st Battalion defense of an outpost on Hill 950, near Khe Sanh, that came under attack by a numerically superior enemy force. Burke, a twenty-three-year-old from Clearwater, Florida, suffered grenade fragment wounds early in the battle. Ignoring his wounds, Burke administered first aid to several other wounded Marines and moved them to safer positions under heavy enemy fire. When it appeared the attack was about to overrun the outpost, Burke armed himself with grenades, shouted encouragement to his fellow Marines, and charged the enemy in a valiant one-man assault. The Marine sniper fell mortally wounded but his actions stopped the enemy attack.

Burke posthumously received the Navy Cross, the second highest award for combat valor. His actions, like those of other snipers, would receive little notice at the time but added to the postwar reputation of the precision marksmen.

With their minute contributions to the total body count, their general tendency to keep operations secret, the lack of enemy concern about them, and few references in official and unofficial publications, it would seem that post-Vietnam sniper service would follow the precedent of previous wars and quickly disappear, that snipers would disband into the "civilities" of peacetime. That was not to be.

As the first conflict brought into the living rooms of America via television, Vietnam took away the mystique and glamour of war for most viewers. For the first time Americans saw the blood, carnage, and death of battle on their TV screens. Some were sickened by the display and turned to or increased their pacifism and antimilitary bias. Others embraced the openness and sought more information on the lethal methods of warfare and its warriors.

Among the people interested in the Vietnam War were legitimate history buffs, fans of all things military, and "wannabes"—those who lived vicariously through combat stories and even invented their own. Weapons and marksmanship appealed to those groups, and among them the sniper gained a positive profile, becoming an object of interest—and in some cases, envy.

The image of the sniper in the post-Vietnam period received a further boost when police departments incorporated special marksmen into their forces as members of Special Weapons and Tactics (SWAT) teams to counter the growing number of criminals armed with high-power rifles and automatic weapons. In the minds of many, policemen combating serious crime with scope-mounted rifles legitimized the sniper and added to his reputation as a "special" individual.

Henderson's 1986 book on Carlos Hathcock greatly increased the visibility of Vietnam snipers. Much of the legendary reputation of snipers in Vietnam comes from this description of how Hathcock earned his 93 confirmed kills. Accounts of army sergeant Adelbert F. Waldron's 109 kills and more recent revelations of Marine Chuck Mawhinney's 103 kills have greatly added to the legend of the Vietnam-era sniper.

Although the accomplishments of those magnificent marksmen are worthy of books and admiration, they are not typical of the ordinary Marine and soldier sniper in Vietnam. Few snipers in the war built a body count into the double figures, and many of the trained marksmen never acquired a single confirmed kill.

A study of the first fifty-four snipers trained by the 9th Infantry Division reveals that during their initial five months of operations eighteen, or one third, had no confirmed kills; half, or twenty-seven, had 1 to 4 kills; seven, or 13 percent, accounted for 5 to 9 kills each. One of the snipers had 12 confirmed kills, and Waldron had accumulated 92 on the way to his final total of 109.

Many action-adventure novels of the late 1980s and the 1990s featured Vietnam-trained snipers performing various daring, and at times dastardly, acts. By the time the movie *Sniper*, starring Tom Berenger, was released in 1993, in some circles the sniper had reached a superhero status more akin to comic book heroics than actual combat.* The proliferation of the Internet in the 1990s has increased interest, and there are thousands of sniper home pages containing everything from marksmen conspiracy theories to catalogs from which to order T-shirts with logos about death from a distance.

The accomplishments of individual snipers in Vietnam are certainly commendable, but they had little obvious effect on the war or its outcome. However, their performance in combat, with a few men producing large numbers of enemy casualties, reconfirmed the importance of long-range marksmanship and, more important, provided a legitimacy and acceptance of their craft that would survive into the postwar peacetime.

Like many aspects of the Vietnam War, as well as the overall conflict itself, snipers have sparked a controversy. In *Sharpening the Combat Edge*, General Ewell, who had the greatest influence on the development of army marksmen in

---

*Except for the opening scenes of Marine sniper training, the movie adds nothing to the history or understanding of precision marksmen in combat. Later in the film, snipers in the field shout at each other, use nonmatch ammunition, and employ telescopes that resemble nothing in the United States' or any other country's inventory.

Vietnam, said, "The sniper program of the 9th Infantry Division was one of the most successful programs that we undertook. It took over a year from its inception in the States to its peak of performance in Vietnam. It also took plenty of hard work and belief in the concept and in our snipers. But more than anything it restored the faith of the infantryman in his rifle and in his capabilities."

In a letter dated November 26, 1996, Ewell repeated his praise for the snipers of two decades earlier, and added, "The program was most worthwhile. Our snipers (70–80) produced as many kills as a typical battalion plus encouraging the ordinary rifleman." In later correspondence, Ewell added, "Setting up and carrying out the program was a major effort as we had to start from scratch. The payoff was substantial."*

Lieutenant General Elvy B. Roberts, who commanded the 1st Cavalry Division from May 1969 to May 1970, also had praise for his snipers. Roberts recalls, "Snipers in the 1st Cav were very, very effective. We used them to target VC and NVA using trails in our area of operations and the snipers' accurate fire greatly limited the enemy's movement."

Lieutenant General Ormond R. Simpson, USMC (Ret.), provides a more balanced response—and perhaps the best overall evaluation of sniper operations in Vietnam. In a letter dated November 8, 1996, Simpson wrote, "When I assumed command of the 1st Marine Division (Reinforced) at Da Nang, Vietnam in December, 1968, the sniper program had been operating for some time. I was satisfied with what I found and continued the program during my tenure.

"It is difficult to accurately measure the effectiveness of a program such as that of snipers," Simpson continued, "there is little if any feedback. The number of confirmed KIA/WIA was impressive and this is certainly a plus. But the war cannot be won by such numbers. The few POWs that we got we asked about this. Most professed to know nothing, a few

---

*This reference and the letters and summaries of telephone conversations that follow result from the author's direct correspondence and conversation with the sources. Original copies are in the author's files.

showed some knowledge and indicated that it was demoralizing to the units concerned but only for a short time."

When asked about the major accomplishment of his division's snipers, Simpson responded, "Who knows? Judging from the number of kills, we assumed the program was effective but always, of course, within a very narrow scope as far as the overall division mission was concerned."

Simpson had nothing but praise for the individuals behind the crosshairs. When asked about the quality of his shooters, Simpson noted, "I recall no major shortcomings. These men were all superb marksmen with the sniper rifle."

Other Marine commanders share Simpson's praise for their snipers. Lieutenant General William K. Jones, USMC (Ret.), who commanded the 3rd Marine Division in 1969, recalls that his "outstanding rifle marksmen" were "very effective."

Not all senior army and Marine commanders shared the praise of generals Ewell, Roberts, Simpson, and Jones for snipers in Vietnam. Major General Ellis W. Williamson, USA (Ret.), included in a letter dated November 7, 1996, his observations of snipers in three wars. Williamson, who commanded the 173rd Airborne Brigade during 1965 and 1966 and the 25th Infantry Division during 1968 and 1969, said, "I am not a good witness for the sniper program. I observed this activity under many circumstances to include World War II, Korea, and two tours in Vietnam. I have not been convinced that it is a worthwhile activity. There is no doubt that many riflemen have done well; however, it did seem to me to be a waste of some well-qualified men to set this type program up as a full-time activity."

General Frederick J. Kroesen Jr., USA (Ret.), who assumed command of the 23rd Infantry (Americal) Division in July 1971, wrote, "My experience with snipers was not good." Before Kroesen assumed command of the 23rd, the division's sniper-training program had been abandoned, and the general recalls, "I did not renew it."

Kroesen admits a need for snipers in certain combat situations, such as static warfare, but states that they did not meet his division's needs during the latter stages of American involvement in Vietnam. According to Kroesen, the few remaining snipers in his command were "of little consequence" to overall operations and he found them to have "prima donna" attitudes.

Major General Kenneth J. Houghton, USMC (Ret.), who commanded the 5th Marine Regiment in 1967, states that his snipers did "a hell of a job" but were not "extra special." Houghton continues by relating that his regiment's snipers "were not a player" during his command time because of the nature of warfare and the terrain in which they worked and so they operated mostly as ordinary infantrymen.

Many other officers, at all levels of command, have little or nothing at all to say about the sniper program. At the highest level, General William C. Westmoreland, USA (Ret.), who headed the Military Assistance Command, Vietnam, as well as all U.S. forces in the combat zone from 1964 to 1968, made no mention of snipers in his postwar autobiography, *A Soldier Reports*. More recently, Westmoreland simply stated, "Snipers did play a role in the war in Vietnam, but there is nothing significant I have to add."

General Creighton W. Abrams, who replaced Westmoreland, came from an armor background and had no affinity for special operations units. He left no formal record of his opinion of American snipers in Vietnam before his death in 1974.

Snipers also made little impression on the last MACV commander, General Fred C. Weyand, who replaced Abrams in June 1972 and supervised the final withdrawal of U.S. combat forces from the war zone. When asked in 1997 about sniper operations in Vietnam, Weyand responded, "There is nothing in my personal experience that would be helpful."

Some of the recollections of army and Marine commanders in Vietnam about snipers reflect the time periods they served in-country. Brigadier General Frederick J. Karch, USMC (Ret.), who commanded the 9th Marine Expeditionary Brigade early in the war, wrote that "no meaningful tasks or duties were available for our sniper platoons." Another retired Marine, General Raymond G. Davis, wrote about his service with the 3rd Marine Division in 1968 and 1969, saying, "I cannot contribute anything substantial on snipers." Davis added that he saturated his area of operations with small recon teams with orders not to directly engage the enemy but rather to observe and report so a helicopter reaction force could attack.

Like the Marine leaders, army commanders had recollections about snipers or their effect on overall operations. Major General Paul F. Smith, USA (Ret.), stated, "During my tour in Vietnam, July 1965–July 1967, and more particularly my time with the 173rd Airborne Brigade, 1966, I had absolutely no experience with snipers. When I took command of the brigade there were no designated snipers nor do I recall my being aware of any brigade personnel who had received such training. Our operations were such that snipers could not have been employed profitably."

Smith's comments provide a good summary of the first several years of involvement by U.S. Army ground units in Vietnam. He concluded, "My other year in Vietnam was spent in two different jobs—establishing as Chief of Staff what later became I Field Force (July 1965–January 1966) and working for the Ambassador in the redevelopment business (January 1967–July 1967). While in those two jobs I do not recall ever hearing anyone mention snipers."

Even more telling are the recollections of General W. B. Rosson, who served six years in Vietnam in positions that included command of a division and a field force and deputy commander of MACV. Rosson, one of the better field commanders of the war and a man who has a deep understanding of the conflict, had nothing to say about army snipers, and only stated, "I recall, however, that the 1st and 3rd Marine divisions placed strong emphasis on snipers."

Other army generals also have little to say about their snipers. General Michael S. Davison, USA (Ret.), who assumed command of the II Field Force in April 1970, stated, "Sniping was not an issue at my level."

Major General A. R. Bolling Jr., USA (Ret.), who commanded the 3rd Brigade, 82nd Airborne Division, in 1968, added, "Ninety-nine percent of the time, the 82nd Airborne Division refrained from using snipers. We also found our fights either when we ambushed the NVA or vice versa. Early on, some of our LRRPs tried setting out snipers. They never saw the enemy."

These comments must, of course, be taken in context of the great many duties and responsibilities of commanders in Vietnam and the passage of more than twenty-five years since their service. Opinions about snipers in Vietnam, like those about the precision marksmen in previous conflicts, vary greatly. Although their collective impact on the war itself is debatable, the young men who shouldered the special rifles and viewed the enemy through the crosshairs of their scopes were certainly as dedicated, brave, and effective as the shooters who preceded them in earlier wars. Even more important, after Vietnam peace would not bring an end to authorized snipers and sniper units in the U.S. Army and the U.S. Marine Corps.

CHAPTER 15

****

Vietnam Sniper Legacy

DESPITE an uneven performance and an incomplete picture of their effectiveness, army and Marine snipers in Vietnam made an impression. For the first time in U.S. history, the military services began to investigate the retention of snipers in the peacetime force, but the decision to do so was not a straight-line action.

As American combat forces withdrew from Vietnam between August 1969 and June 1972, soldiers and Marines were reassigned Stateside and around the world to prepare for new challenges and emergencies. In an atmosphere in which the American public held the military responsible for the long war in Vietnam and in which their respect for those in uniform had reached an all-time low, the services faced budget and personnel cuts that were not conducive to innovation.*

In the austerity of the post–Vietnam War period and the general disapproval of all things military by the American taxpayer, neither the Marine Corps nor the army was able to take any immediate or direct action to include snipers in the

*Many accounts of the time, and even some today, emphasize the defeat of the Americans in Vietnam at the hands of the Vietcong. In reality, the VC ceased to exist as a viable military organization as a result of their catastrophic defeat in the Tet Offensive of 1968. It was North Vietnamese operating Soviet-built tanks who led the capture of Saigon—from the South Vietnamese, not the Americans. Only a few hundred U.S. military personnel in administrative positions had remained in Vietnam after 1972, and although their departure from the American embassy roof is one of the popular images of the fall of Saigon, no significant number of U.S. combat troops had been in Vietnam for more than three years—and none were involved in combating the final North Vietnamese offensive.

peacetime forces. The army, which had never established an official sniper organization during the war, simply let the marksmen once again fade into obscurity. Their sniper schools in Vietnam had closed with the withdrawal of their senior headquarters and their sniper rifles had been placed in storage. The only semblance of a sniper legacy was the Marksmanship Training Unit at Fort Benning, which resumed its prewar marksmanship training and competitive shooting missions.

Initially, Marine Corps leaders, although satisfied with the concept and performance of their snipers in Vietnam, did not see a place for the infantry regiment and reconnaissance battalion scout-sniper platoons in the peacetime force organization. When the 3rd Marine Division began its withdrawal from Vietnam in August 1969, Marine Corps commandant General Leonard F. Chapman directed that the platoons be phased out by 1972.

While budget and political restraints ended the scout-sniper platoons that had evolved in Vietnam, Chapman and other Marine leaders intended to restructure the program so that the snipers did not completely disappear. In addition to proclaiming that snipers had a future in the Marine Corps, Chapman also directed that studies continue to determine their proper organization and to develop the most efficient weapon system.

Chapman detailed his directions in a letter to the Marine Corps Development and Education Command (MCDEC) on August 2, 1971, writing, "The capability will be maintained in the Marine division. It is envisioned that the sniper squads will be formed in infantry and reconnaissance battalions with Marines assigned on an additional-duty basis."

The commandant also directed that sniper training be conducted at the division level and stated that detailed training guidance would be forthcoming. More important, Chapman concluded, "It is deemed prudent at this time to continue evaluation of candidate sniper weapons systems and to develop a specific operational requirement for a sniper rifle and telescope."

Over the next five years various Marine commands conducted studies and tests to determine the most effective sniper organization, training, and weapons. That work produced an improved sniper rifle system, an updated sniper manual, an authorization for sniper units, and provisions for the reopening of a sniper-training school.

Experience in Vietnam had shown that the Marine Corps's M40, based on the Remington 700, and the army's M21, based on the M14, were the best available sniper rifles. After additional tests, Marine ordnance experts determined that the bolt-action M40, although needing improvements, continued to meet their requirements better than the gas-operated M21.

In 1976, the Marine Corps approved funding for improvements to the M40. The resulting M40A1 retained the Remington 700 receiver group but had a heavy twenty-six-inch-long barrel and a fiberglass/epoxy stock. Other modifications included the addition of a steel trigger guard and magazine cover to increase durability. By 1977 the Marines began delivering the rebuilt M40A1s to field units and training centers. The only other major modification to the M40A1 came in 1980, when the Unertl 10X telescope replaced the Redfield 3X-9X variable scopes. By 1983 all M40A1s were equipped with the Unertl 10X scope.

While the weapon studies continued, other sections of the MCDEC worked on updating sniper doctrine. On April 7, 1976, the Marine Corps issued FMFM 1-3B, "Sniping," replacing the 1969 edition used in Vietnam and laying out the techniques and procedures for selecting, training, and employing scout-snipers. With minor changes in 1981, the manual remains even today the primary Marine sniper document.

Other updates to Marine manuals of the period reconfirmed the military occupation specialty of scout-snipers and authorized their inclusion in infantry units. MCO P1200.7, "Military Occupational Specialties Manual," assigns MOS 8541 (military operational specialty, i.e., military for "job") to "Scout-Sniper." The manual's summary of the mission of scout-snipers differs little from that of Vietnam and previous conflicts. "Scout-snipers participate in activities designed to deny the enemy freedom of movement by shooting enemy leaders, crew-served weapons operators, radiomen, observers, messengers, and other key personnel with single, well-aimed shots. Scout-snipers also engage vital materiel targets such as command and control equipment, air defense radars, and missile launchers, which require precision fire to neutralize. Scout-snipers also provide close reconnaissance and surveillance to the infantry battalion."

Along with the 1976 FMFM and MOS assignments came changes in the division table of authorization and equipment, establishing an eight-man scout-sniper section in the infantry battalion's surveillance and target acquisition (STA) platoon. STAs had originally been established in 1973 with ground-surveillance radar, night observation devices, and scout sections. By 1977 the scouts had been replaced by eight-man scout-sniper sections.

That organizational structure remained until 1992, when the Marine Corps eliminated the maintenance-intensive and largely ineffective ground radar and night observation sections from the STA. It added four scout-sniper teams and relabeled the STA as the scout-sniper platoon. The platoon, with one officer and seventeen enlisted snipers, formally became part of the infantry battalion intelligence (S-2) section.

With a new sniper rifle system fielded, doctrine written, and personnel authorizations approved, all the Marine Corps sniping program lacked was a central training facility. On June 1, 1977, the USMC Scout-Sniper Instructor School opened at Quantico, Virginia. Veteran snipers of the Vietnam War, including Jim Land and Carlos Hathcock, took charge of establishing the school and conducting the training.

The Quantico Scout-Sniper Instructor School has, since its inception, served two purposes: to train infantrymen as snipers and to train qualified snipers as instructors. The trained instructors then return to their parent divisions to teach in additional sniper schools and to conduct refresher training. In 1979, trained instructors opened the 2nd Marine Division's Scout-Sniper School at Camp Lejeune, North Carolina, and the 1st Marine Division established its school at Camp Pendleton, California, a short time later.

The three schools operate to train new snipers to fill the 420 authorized scout-sniper positions in today's Marine Corps. The Quantico school also continues to train sniper instructors as well as being responsible for the development and testing of new sniper doctrine, equipment, and weapons.

In the years following Vietnam, the U.S. Navy recognized the value of snipers and added the specialty to its SEAL teams. The first SEAL snipers and sniper instructors attended the Marine scout-sniper schools before the SEALs developed a nine-week training course to hone individual marksmanship skills and train snipers as forward observers for naval gunfire, artillery, and air support.

Postwar, the U.S. Army, although satisfied with the performance of snipers in Vietnam, renewed its focus on mechanized, and possibly nuclear, warfare on the plains of Western Europe. Funding and priorities went to the development of a new main battle tank and an improved infantry tracked fighting vehicle. Developing handheld or crew-served weapons capable of destroying tanks and other mechanized vehicles of the Soviet Union was given a higher priority than small arms and long-range marksmanship.

During the final months of U.S. ground involvement in Vietnam and for several years afterward, the army conducted only a few staff studies on sniper capabilities and the possibility of authorizing positions for marksmen at battalion and division levels. None of the studies resulted in action. After limited investigation, the U.S. Army Infantry School announced that, on the future of snipers, it stood by its pre-Vietnam position: "A concept of small, hard-hitting units, moving almost continuously in armored personnel carriers throughout the extended distances envisioned for atomic-threatened battlefields, visualizes little use for the slow, patient, stealthy stalking tactics which are the trademark of the sniper."

In the post-Vietnam era, army personnel manning documents continued to exclude authorization for snipers, and the infantry school did not see the marksmen as having a role on the battlefield of the future. Yet both veteran snipers and sniper instructors were still on active duty, and many were serving in the Army Marksmanship Training Unit (AMTU). Major Willis Powell and the members of his staff, who had established sniper training in Vietnam, continued to assist in regular marksmanship training. They also resumed representing the army in marksmanship competition, using the M21 sniper rifle among other weapons.

The major mission of the AMTU in the early 1970s was not to train soldiers but to provide instruction and advice to civilian law enforcement officials in training their own snipers and SWAT teams. Fortunately, the veteran combat snipers maintained their personal efficiency and continued to record and disseminate their experiences and opinions on the need for specially trained, long-range marksmen.

The first substantial support for renewing sniper training in the post-Vietnam army came from Lieutenant General Hank Emerson, the commanding officer of the XVIII Airborne Corps at Fort Bragg, North Carolina, that included the 82nd Airborne and the 101st Air Assault divisions. Those two infantry divisions had parachutes and helicopters for their delivery but once on the battlefield would fight as conventional infantry.

Emerson, a former brigade commander in the 9th Infantry Division who had supported David Hackworth's formation of night hunter sniper teams, knew the advantages of long-range marksmen from firsthand combat experience. In early 1976, Emerson requested the AMTU to deliver 342 M21 sniper rifles to Fort Bragg and to train armorers in maintaining the weapon systems. By April the XVIII Airborne Sniper School was training future snipers from the two divisions as well as personnel from the John F. Kennedy Special Warfare Center.

For the next decade the army continued to leave the formation and training of snipers to individual commanders. A few, like Emerson, actively supported the inclusion of marksmen in their ranks, but most continued to ignore long-range shooting. As they implemented their own programs, new commanders often ceased sniper training established by their predecessors. Such was the case with Emerson's XVIII Airborne Corps sniper school, which operated only two years and closed when he departed the post.

The only significant contribution by the Department of the Army to the development of snipers in the late 1970s came from tests to determine the most efficient weapon system. From May through December 1977, the U.S. Army Test Evaluation Command at Aberdeen Proving Ground, Maryland, tested seven different rifles for suitability as sniper weapons. Included were the M21, the Remington 700, and the Winchester 70—all used in Vietnam—as well as French, Canadian, and other American rifles. The test report, issued in February 1978, supported the continued use of the M21 as the army's standard sniper weapon.

In 1983, the JFK Special Warfare Center and School (SWCS) attempted to renew sniper training at Fort Bragg. Although the center's leaders knew they wanted and needed snipers, they were unclear about the exact role the marksmen would play in their operations. As a result the school folded after only a few months.

Over the next year the SWCS staff studied the capabilities of snipers and developed doctrine for their use in special operations. Early in 1985 the SWCS initiated the Special Operations Target Interdiction Course (SOTIC) with sniper training as its core subject. In the July 1988 issue of SWCS's professional bulletin, *Special Warfare,* Captain John L. Stanley described the sniper training: "Today, the Special Warfare Center and School operates the SOTIC program with little flim-flam and with low visibility. The cadre members have put a lot of personal experience and knowledge into this course. Their ideas are not found in any army subject schedules, but they are garnered through experience and dedication. These instructors have met some very challenging tasks, developing ideas and techniques where none existed."

Many of the cadre members to whom Stanley referred were sniper veterans of Vietnam, and their experience in combat provided the information for the training. Stanley noted, "Little reference material exists on many of the subjects taught in the SOTIC program." In fact, the only available official doctrine continued to be Training Circular 23-14, "Sniper Training and Employment," which had not been updated since October 1969.

Other units also established limited sniper-training programs during the same general period. The 2nd Battalion, 325th Infantry, 82nd Airborne Division, briefly conducted unit sniper training in late 1985 and early 1986. In Korea, the U.S. 2nd Infantry Division also established a sniper school. Because of its isolation from the rest of the army and the constant threat from the North Koreans, the 2nd Division's sniper school remained active into the mid-1990s. Other, limited, army sniper courses were also offered during this period at Fort Sherman in the Canal Zone, and at Fort Ord, California.

Despite those widespread efforts to maintain some level of sniper training, the U.S. Army did not establish its official school until July 1987. With Department of the Army support, the Infantry School at Fort Benning assumed the directorship of the school, with operational responsibility assigned to the post's 29th Infantry Regiment. The three-week course included 54 hours of marksmanship instruction and 120 hours of fieldcraft classes to produce graduates who could successfully conduct sniper operations and engage targets out to 1,000 meters.*

While it had been slow to resume an official servicewide sniper school, once committed to that end the army made a concentrated effort to optimize its sniper capacity. In the January-February 1988 edition of *Infantry*, the chief of the infantry school, Major General Kenneth C. Leuer, explained, "Realizing that modern technology has not diminished the need for snipers, the army recently renewed its interest in them and is revitalizing its sniper program. The Infantry School has taken the lead in these efforts, and we are committed to providing the best sniper organization, equipment, doctrine, and training possible."

New weapons were an important part of the army's empha-

---

*In 1995, the army increased its sniper training to 332 hours.

sis on snipers. The army's marksmen were to be armed with the M24 modified bolt-action Remington Model 700s with a 10X fixed Leupold M3 Ultra telescope. Delivery of the weapons to the sniper school and to units began in April 1988. The army also provided updated sniper doctrine, releasing a revised version of TC 23-14, "Sniper Training and Employment," on June 14, 1989.

During the next few years the army continued to study and experiment with its sniper program and to make changes and adjustments in equipment, organization, and training. In 1989, the army awarded all graduates of the sniper school, retroactive to its opening in 1987, the additional skill identifier of "B4." On October 1, 1990, the army issued DA Pamphlet 351-4, "Army Formal Schools Catalog," which detailed the physical, mental, and other requirements for sniper school attendance.

On August 17, 1994, the Department of the Army published FM 23-10, "Sniping," which replaced early editions of TC 23-14 and provided the most detailed and official instructions and authorization for snipers in U.S. Army history. The introduction section of FM 23-10 described snipers as similar to marksmen of earlier wars but revealed the mission and profile of the modern long-range shooter: "The sniper has special abilities, training, and equipment. His job is to deliver discriminatory, highly accurate rifle fire against enemy targets, which cannot be engaged successfully by the riflemen because of range, size, location, fleeting nature, or visibility. Sniping requires the development of the basic infantry skills to a high degree of perfection. A sniper's training incorporates a wide variety of subjects designed to increase his value as a force multiplier and to ensure his survival on the battlefield. The art of sniping requires learning and repetitiously practicing these skills until mastered. A sniper must be highly trained in long-range rifle marksmanship and fieldcraft skills to ensure maximum effective engagements with minimum risks."

FM 23-10 also provided the first official authorization for snipers other than as an additional duty of an ordinary squad rifleman. According to the FM's paragraph 1-2, "In light infantry divisions, the sniper element is composed of six battalion personnel organized into three 2-man teams. The commander designates missions and priorities of targets for the team and may attach or place the team under the operational control of a company or platoon. In the mechanized infantry battalions, the sniper element is composed of two riflemen (one team) located in a rifle squad. In some special units,* snipers may be organized according to the needs of the tactical situation."

The Marine Corps's FMFM 1-3B and the army's FM 23-10 provided the basis of today's U.S. sniper organization, training, and equipment. A large part of those developments is a direct result of the lessons learned in combat against the Vietcong and North Vietnamese regulars in Southeast Asia.

However, not all of the advances in the army and Marine sniper programs in the 1980s and 1990s came as a result of the war in Vietnam. American snipers had several opportunities to practice their skills in live action during subsequent conflicts of various magnitude and length.

Both Marine and army snipers deployed with their units on October 25, 1983, as a part of Operation Urgent Fury to liberate the Caribbean island of Grenada from its Soviet- and Cuban-supported Communist government. Snipers from the army's Ranger battalions, trained in their own unit programs and at the USMC sniper school at Quantico, saw the most action during the brief operation. Shortly after their arrival by parachute on the island, the Rangers were threatened by a Cuban mortar crew. As the Cubans attempted to man their mortar tubes, the Ranger snipers began dropping them one by one. The survivors quickly surrendered.

Marine and army snipers also participated in Operation Just Cause to neutralize the Panamanian Defense Force (PDF) and to arrest Panamanian dictator Manuel Noriega, in December 1989. A sniper team in the Scout Platoon, Headquarters

---

*Such as Special Forces, Ranger, and Long-Range Surveillance Units (LRSUs).

Company, 3rd Battalion, 504th Parachute Infantry, 82nd Airborne Division, composed of a sniper sergeant and his observer, joined an infantry platoon to provide overwatching fires during an attack on a PDF-fortified building on the first night of the operation.

The sniper sergeant, a graduate of the Fort Benning 29th Infantry Regiment Sniper School, established a well-concealed position that provided a clear field of fire for the 500 meters to the objective. He assumed a prone position with his M24 sniper rifle braced on his rucksack. "A few minutes later," the sniper recalled, "the third platoon opened up on the back side of the building for about thirty seconds and then moved their clearing teams forward. Suddenly the front door of the building burst open and slammed against the opposite wall with a loud crack. Out ran a single soldier spraying the advancing platoon with Swedish-K 9-mm automatic gunfire.

" 'Eleven o'clock, four hundred and fifty meters, person running!' reported my observer. I knew it was hard for him not to just scream out the target location to me but he stayed cool. 'Got it,' I replied.

"This is it, I thought. This is the end of the road of all my training. I had a great bead on the target's stomach, and I knew at this range the bullet would strike high. *Crack!* I saw the round bulldoze right into the upper body of the target. It was just like all of the movies with the person falling back, arms flailing, with blood spraying out and behind. Then there was nothing; just the ringing in my ears, the sound of my breathing and my observer whispering, 'Holy shit, right in the chest . . . nice shot.' "

During the next few minutes two more PDF soldiers ran from the building firing at the advancing platoon. The sergeant fired two more rounds from his rifle. Three shots, three kills; more important, his marksmanship had protected his fellow soldiers. Similar scenes played out at other objectives across Panama to ensure the rapid success of the operation with minimal friendly casualties.

While the Marines were happy with the performance of the M40A1 rifle and the army was satisfied with the M24 system in Panama and other missions, operations in the late 1980s displayed the need for added range and penetrating power. To meet that requirement, the army, the Marine Corps, and the navy began purchasing a variety of .50-caliber rifles including the Barrett Model 82A1, the McMillan M1987R, and the RAI Model 500.*

These rifles were not intended to replace the M40A1 or the M24 but rather to add a secondary, special-purpose weapon to the sniper's arsenal. With the .50-caliber weapon, in addition to engaging enemy soldiers at ranges in excess of 1,000 meters, the sniper could also use the .50 calibers to fire through walls or light armor.

American snipers soon had the opportunity to use all of their weapon systems, when they assisted in liberating Kuwait from Iraqi invaders. On February 24, 1991, after forty-three days of air strikes on the Iraqi front lines and rear areas, the U.S.-led Coalition Forces began their ground attack. After only 100 hours of ground combat, Iraq surrendered and evacuated Kuwait.

The Gulf War, or Operation Desert Storm, has been portrayed by many historians as the turning point in modern warfare, where the sophisticated technology of smart bombs, long-range missiles, and fast-moving mechanized ground forces replaced the importance of the individual soldier, including the sniper. Nothing could be further from the truth. The individual foot soldier and Marine in the Gulf War once again proved that no territory is secure without the infantryman's boots firmly planted upon it. The vast, open spaces of the desert also provided a virtual shooting gallery for American snipers.

Figures for the number of successful engagements by American snipers in the Gulf War, as well as in Grenada and Panama, are extremely difficult to document. The U.S. military, avoiding the controversial "body count" policy of the Vietnam War, does not release specific claims of enemy casualties. The limited information available, however, confirms

*For additional information on these and other sniper rifles, see Appendix A.

that the "one-shot, one-kill" dogma of the Vietnam sniper has found a comfortable place in the ranks of today's snipers.

The American-led coalition victory in Desert Storm, combined with the fall of the Berlin Wall and the collapse of the Soviet Union, has left the United States as the single world power. No nation, or group of countries, offers a reasonable threat to U.S. national security and America's place as the world's dominant economic and military force.

A conflict of the magnitude of World War II is simply not visible in the foreseeable future. There also is no current threat of a guerrilla conflict on the scale of Vietnam or a conventional war to equal Operation Desert Storm. In this environment, the missions of the U.S. military become not fewer but more numerous and complex.

Since Desert Storm, the U.S. armed forces have deployed around the world in a multitude of missions in what have become known as "operations short of war." Those operations have been defined as "peace building," "peace keeping," "democracy reinforcing," "regional stability," and "stability." Some of the deployments were bloodless; others have pushed right up to the edge of "short of war."

All of the developments escalated the importance of trained long-range marksmen. Modern "operations short of war" call for snipers to neutralize opposing marksmen as well as to provide a deterrent to possible enemies by their presence.

While the United States still possesses large numbers of aircraft, helicopters, and artillery, many of the targets in today's limited engagements are in the middle of areas populated by noncombatants. The sniper, with his single well-aimed shot, engages only the intended target with minimal or no collateral damage. Instead of leveling a city block, killing innocent civilians, and destroying property, the sniper eliminates a target cleanly and efficiently.

In late 1993 and early 1994, Marine and army snipers provided covering fire to protect U.S. forces securing relief efforts in Somalia. When opposing bandit groups in the Somalian city of Mogadishu began sporadic fire at American troops, snipers became an important factor in restabilizing the

area. Performing mostly in a countersniper role, U.S. marksmen successfully neutralized more than 100 targets during the
operation.

The only two Medals of Honor, America's highest award
for combat valor, presented for actions in Somalia went to a
two-man sniper team assigned to the U.S. Army Special Operations Command's Task Force Ranger. On October 3, 1993,
Master Sergeant Gary I. Gordon of Lincoln, Maine, and
Sergeant First Class Randall D. Shughart of Newville, Pennsylvania, volunteered to be inserted by helicopter to secure the
crash site and survivors of another helicopter shot down by
enemy fire in the streets of Mogadishu.

Using their sniper rifles and side arms, and later other weapons taken from the downed helicopter, the two snipers secured
the crash site while fighting off intensifying attacks from automatic weapons and rocket-propelled grenade fire. Both snipers
continued their resistance after suffering fatal wounds and sac-
rificed themselves to save the helicopter pilot.

American snipers also played an important role in the more
recent stabilization efforts in Haiti and Bosnia. Army and Marine marksmen have been in the leading elements of those operations, providing observation and covering fire as needed for
the arriving forces, discouraging potential opposition by their
mere presence.

For nearly half a century after the end of World War II, nuclear weapons remained the focus of the Cold War between
East and West. With the threat of nuclear war greatly diminished and the United States occupying the position of single
world power, future military missions will likely continue to
fall in the category of "operations short of war." Just as the nuclear bomb characterized the Cold War, the sniper may very
well become the symbol of those future conflicts.

At the end of 1997, snipers in the Marine Corps total approximately 340, and the army has nearly 500. Many of those
young men, not born until after the Vietnam War, carry forward the concept honed during that conflict. Their rifles, training, operations—and, indeed, the very existence of their
specialty—can be largely attributed to the long conflict in

Southeast Asia. The legacy and the most important accomplishments of the Vietnam snipers are the marksmen behind the crosshairs who today stand as an integral part of the keepers of the peace and the guardians of freedom and democracy around the world.

✳✳✳✳✳✳✳

Sniper Rifle Systems Used in Vietnam (And More Recent Models Influenced by the War)

U.S. M1903 Springfield

Cartridge	.30 cal. (7.62 X 63 mm)
Operation	Manual, bolt action
Weight	8.75 pounds
Length	43.25 inches
Feeding Device	5-round integral with cutoff
Effective Range	500 meters
Muzzle Velocity	2,805 fps (feet per second)
Scope	A3 Model: 8X Unertl; A4 Model: 3.5X Weaver

Comments: Introduced in 1903 as the standard U.S. infantry weapon, its A3 and A4 Models served as sniper rifles in both world wars and in Korea. A few special operations and infantry units in Vietnam used the A4 Model prior to the official establishment of sniper schools and units.

U.S. M1C/D Garand

Cartridge	.30 cal. (7.62 X 63 mm)
Operation	Gas, semiautomatic
Weight	9.6 pounds
Length	43.5 inches
Feeding Device	8-round clip
Effective Range	500 meters
Muzzle Velocity	2,805 fps

Scope	M1C: M81 2.5X; M1D: M81
	2.5X or the M82 2.5X

Comments: The durable, easy to maintain M1 Garand greatly contributed to the U.S. victory in World War II. Its C and D sniper models, which differ only in the telescope mounts, were also used in Korea and in the early years of the Vietnam War. Although considered obsolete, it remained the only official sniper weapon in the U.S. inventory until the mid-1960s.

Winchester Model 70

Cartridge	.30-06 (7.62 X 63 mm)
Operation	Bolt action
Weight	9.5 to 13 pounds (depending on barrel type)
Length, Barrel	24, 26, and 28 inches
Feeding Device	5-round integral magazine
Effective Range	800 meters
Muzzle Velocity	2,640 fps
Scope	8X Unertl

Comments: First manufactured in 1937 as a sporting rifle, the Model 70 gained popularity in competition shooting because of its accuracy. Although never officially adopted by the military, the Winchesters saw service as sniper rifles in World War II and Korea as well as in Vietnam by the first Marine schools and shooters.

M40 Sniper Rifle

Cartridge	7.62 X 51 mm NATO (M118 match)
Operation	Bolt action
Weight	14.2 pounds
Length	41.6 inches

Feeding Device	5-round magazine
Effective Range	800 meters
Muzzle Velocity	2,790 fps
Scope	3X9 variable power Redfield Accu-Range

Comments: This military version of the Remington Model 700 commercial rifle replaced the Winchester Model 70 as the basic Marine sniper weapon in 1966.

M40A1 Sniper Rifle

Cartridge	7.62 X 51 mm NATO (M118 match)
Operation	Bolt action
Weight	14.5 pounds
Length	43.97 inches
Feeding Device	5-round magazine
Effective Range	1,000 meters
Muzzle Velocity	2,547 fps
Scope	Unertl 10X

Comments: The M40A1 combines the Remington 700 receiver group with the Winchester Model 70 floorplate and trigger guard and the McMillan fiberglass, epoxy-bedded stock. It became the primary USMC sniper rifle in 1977.

M21 Sniper Rifle

Cartridge	7.62 X 51 mm NATO (M118 match)
Operation	Gas, semiautomatic
Weight	12.25 pounds
Length	44.1 inches
Feeding Device	20-round detachable magazine
Effective Range	900 meters

Muzzle Velocity   2,805 fps
Scope   3X9 variable power Redfield

Comments: After testing in Vietnam, the U.S. Army approved the M14 National Match Accurized rifle and designated it the XM21, renaming it the M21 in 1972. It was the primary army sniper rifle of the war.

M24 Sniper Rifle

Cartridge   7.62 X 51 mm NATO (M118 match)
Operation   Bolt action
Weight   12.8 pounds
Length   43 inches
Feeding Device   5-round integral magazine
Effective Range   1,000 meters
Muzzle Velocity   2,805 fps
Scope   Leupold M3 Ultra 10X

Comments: The M24 replaced the M21 as the army's primary sniper rifle in 1988. It uses the Remington 700 receiver group with a Kevlar-graphite synthetic stock, an aluminum bedding block, and an adjustable butt plate.

Mosin-Nagant M1891/30 Rifle (K44)

Cartridge   7.62 X 54 rimmed
Operation   Bolt action
Weight   11.1 pounds
Length   49.3 inches
Feeding Device   5-round integral box magazine
Effective Range   800 meters
Muzzle Velocity   2,660 fps
Scope   3.5X PU or 4X PE

Comments: The K44 served as the principal sniper rifle of the Vietcong and the North Vietnamese regulars for the entire Vietnam conflict. Originally designed in 1891 and modified in 1930, the K44 was simple, durable, and reasonably accurate.

Dragunov SVD Sniper Rifle

Cartridge	7.62 X 54 mm rimmed
Operation	Gas, semiautomatic
Weight	9.64 pounds
Length	48.2 inches
Feeding Device	10-round magazine
Effective Range	800 meters
Muzzle Velocity	2,723 fps
Scope	PSO 4X

Comments: The Soviet Union began manufacture of the Dragunov SVD in the 1950s to replace the Mosin-Nagant. They provided the North Vietnamese with only a few of these rifles prior to the departure of American ground units from the war zone.

RAI Model 500

Cartridge	12.7 X 99 mm (.50-cal. Browning)
Operation	Bolt action
Weight	29.98 pounds
Length, Barrel	33.6 inches
Feeding Device	Single shot, no magazine
Effective Range	1,500 meters
Muzzle Velocity	2,913 fps
Scope	Ranging base provides mount for most modern scopes

Comments: Manufactured by Research Armament Industries in Rogers, Arkansas, the Model 500 is currently used by Marine and navy SEAL snipers.

Barrett Model 82

Cartridge	12.7 X 99 mm (.50-cal. Browning)
Operation	Recoil, semiautomatic
Weight	33 pounds
Length, Barrel	37.36 inches
Feeding Device	11-round detachable box magazine
Effective Range	1,500 meters
Muzzle Velocity	2,849 fps
Scope	Mount accepts any scope with one-inch rings

Comments: Manufactured by the Barrett Manufacturing Company of Murfreesboro, Tennessee, the Model 82 is the only semiautomatic .50-caliber sniper rifle.

McMillan M87R

Cartridge	12.7 X 99 mm (.50-cal Browning)
Operation	Bolt action
Weight	21 pounds
Length, Barrel	29.46 inches
Feeding Device	5-round box magazine
Effective Range	1,500 meters
Muzzle Velocity	2,840 fps
Scope	Any modern 10X or 16X

Comments: The M87R, manufactured by the McMillan Gun Works in Phoenix, Arizona, is the lightest of the .50 calibers.

APPENDIX B

✼✼✼✼✼✼✼✼

Syllabus, Sniper Training (From USMC FMFM 1-3B, "Sniping," dated August 5, 1969)

1. PURPOSE

The purpose of this syllabus is to provide uniform guidance in the conduct of sniper training in Marine Corps units.

2. OBJECTIVE

The objective of this syllabus is to instill in the individual sniper the military knowledge necessary for service with a Fleet Marine Force unit in the field.

3. GENERAL TRAINING NOTES

This syllabus is a guide for preparing training schedules. Training problems peculiar to a given unit or installation may necessitate modification or improvisation of some to the training outlined herein.

    a. The practical exercises should include a situation with several requirements involving individual and/or team actions covering the fundamentals of the subject being taught.

    b. When feasible, opposing forces' concept should be used for realism in training. Example: Train one or more sniper squads in defense while training others in offense.

    c. Separate exercises may be combined into a continuous tactical exercise where logical training situations can be portrayed. For example, combine night reconnaissance patrol with a dawn attack on an enemy outpost with long-range sniper fire.

d. A critique should be held after each phase or requirement of the problem to discuss good and bad points. A
general critique to emphasize the principles involved
should be held at the conclusion of each problem.

e. Hours of instruction allotted in this syllabus for each
subject are maximum, the total hours may be reduced
by concurrent training; however, THERE ARE NO
SHORTCUTS IN MARKSMANSHIP TRAINING.
Therefore, when additional training hours are available,
emphasis should be on the marksmanship phase of
sniper training.

4. SYLLABUS OF INSTRUCTION

Subject	Code*	Hours
Introduction to Sniper Training		
General	L	.25
Sniper Organization	L	.50
Selection of Personnel	L	.25
Total Hours		1.00
Sniper Equipment		
Rifles	L, D	.50
Telescopes	L, D	.50
Rifle and Telescope Assemblies	L, D	.25
Ammunition	L, D	.25
Special Equipment	L, D	.25
Total Hours		1.75
Care and Cleaning of Equipment		
Rifles	L, D	1.00
Optical	L, D	.25
Special Equipment	L, D	.25
Total Hours		1.50

* Code: L = Lecture, D = Demonstration, A = Application

Marksmanship Training
Sighting and Aiming	L, D	.50
Sling Adjustments and Positions	L, D, A	2.00
Trigger Control	L	.50
Sight Adjustments	L, D, A	2.00
Effects of the Weather	L	1.00
Zeroing	L	.50
Position Exercise	A	8.00
Range Practice Firing	A	40.00
Range Record Firing	A	8.00
Total Hours		62.50

Target Detection
	L, D	2.00
	L, A	8.00
Total Hours		10.00

Range Estimation
	L, D	1.00
	L, A	7.00
Total Hours		8.00

Holds and Leads
	L, D	1.00
	L, A	7.00
Total Hours		8.00

Intelligence Collecting and Reporting
	L	1.00
	L, A	2.00
Total Hours		3.00

Camouflage and Concealment
	L, D	4.00
	L, A	4.00
Total Hours		8.00

Individual Movement

	L, D	2.00
	L, A	6.00
Total Hours		8.00

Survival, Evasion, and Escape

	L, D	1.00
	L, A	7.00
Total Hours		8.00

Sniper Employment

Introduction of Employment	L	1.00
Offensive Operations	L, A	6.00
Defensive Operations	L, A	4.00
Special and Auxiliary Operations	L, A	2.00
Field Exercises	A	72.00
Total Hours		85.00

Recapitulation

Subject	Total Hours
Introduction to Sniper Training	1.00
Sniper Equipment	1.75
Care and Cleaning of Equipment	1.50
Marksmanship Training	62.50
Target Detection	10.00
Range Estimation	8.00
Holds and Leads	8.00
Intelligence Collection and Reporting	3.00
Camouflage and Concealment	8.00
Individual Movement	8.00
Survival, Evasion, and Escape	8.00
Sniper Employment	85.00
Total Hours	204.75

✳✳✳✳✳✳✳✳

3rd Marine Division Scout-Sniper Refresher Training Schedule (Division Order 1510.5 dated September 3, 1968)

Subject Title: Welcome, Orientation, Indoctrination
Hrs: (0.5)
Description: Welcomes the student aboard, orients him as to the location of facilities available to him and their hours of operation, and presents an overall view of the course to be presented.

Subject Title: Map Reading and Compass
Hrs: (7.5)
Description: Instructs the student on the use of maps and compass; covers legend, conventional and military signs and symbols, map scale distance, measurements, grid coordinates, basic direction, elevation and relief, inspection, orientation, intersection and resection, land navigation, thrust points and polar coordinates. Utilizes practical application.

Subject Title: Radio and Telephone Procedures
Hrs: (2)
Description: Sets forth the requirements and procedures for effective communications. Stresses communications security. In addition, the student is introduced to the AN/PRC-25 radio.

Subject Title: Air Support Procedures
Hrs: (1)
Description: Presents the procedures used to call close air support strikes and medevac missions.

Subject Title: Artillery/Mortar Forward Observer Procedures
Hrs: (3.5)
Description: Presents the methods to call for and adjust artillery and mortar fires. Utilizes practical problems in which each student acts as a forward observer.

Subject Title: Mental Conditioning
Hrs: (1)
Description: Presents the importance of concentration and necessity for mental control in order to achieve success as a sniper.

Subject Title: Nomenclature, Care and Cleaning of the M700
Hrs: (1)
Description: To refresh the student on the mechanics and proper care of the M700 rifle to ensure long life and proper functioning.

Subject Title: Redfield Telescope (3X9 variable)
Hrs: (2)
Description: Familiarizes the student with the nomenclature and operational use, through lecture and practical application, of the Redfield telescope.

Subject Title: Effects of Weather
Hrs: (.5)
Description: Points out the effects wind produces and the methods the sniper can use to determine wind velocities in order to compensate.

Subject Title: Holds and Leads
Hrs: (.5)
Description: Instructs the student on advanced techniques of marksmanship. Through lecture and demonstration the student is shown how to employ holds and leads when time does not permit a change to his sight setting.

Subject Title: Use of the 7X50 Binoculars
Hrs: (.5)
Description: Shows the student the proper procedures in using the M17A1 binoculars.

Subject Title: Review, Examination, and Critique
Hrs: (2)
Description: Previous information is reviewed and a fill-in examination is administered. Measures both the student's level of retention and effectiveness of the course.

Subject Title: Field Firing
Hrs: (18.5)
Description: Through practical application the student will fire for two days over the Dong Ha, 1,000 meter, Scout-Sniper Range. He will establish the zero for the Scout Sniper Team's M700 rifles for the 300 through 1,000 meter ranges at 100 meter increments. He will establish hold offs and sight settings as conditions exist at all ranges. The student will be required to fire on targets, both at slow and quick fire, at ranges announced by the instructor, thus conditioning the sniper to rapid response in sight setting changes or by employing hold offs. Teamwork is stressed as the Scout-Sniper Team will spot and call adjustments for each other.

Subject Title: Graduation
Hrs: (.5)
Description: Officer in Charge delivers graduation speech and presents certificates.

3rd Marine Division Order 3590.3B (June 9, 1968), Scout-Sniper Platoons*

References:

   (a) Commandant Marine Corps letter A03B2Z JEW of 29 December 1965

   (b) Personnel Allocation Change Number 753-65

   (c) Marine Corps Order 8110.1

   (d) Commandant Marine Corps letter A03CZ0 MEK of 16 February 1966

1. <u>Purpose.</u>

To promulgate policy, procedures, and administrative instructions concerning Sniper Platoons within the 3rd Marine Division.

2. <u>Cancellation.</u>

Division Order 3590.3A.**

3. <u>Background.</u>

   a. As a result of experience gained by the III Marine Amphibious Forces in the Republic of Vietnam, and on recommendations of the Commanding General, Fleet Marine Force, Pacific, and subsequent approval of the Commandant of the Marine Corps, reference (a)

---

*For the ease of readers, the format of the order is slightly changed and certain abbreviations have been spelled out. No changes have been made in content.
**Division Order 3590.3A, dated July 5, 1967, provided earlier, less detailed sniper platoon instructions.

approved the organization and formation of Sniper Platoons within each Regiment's Headquarters Company and the Headquarters and Service Company, Reconnaissance Battalion.

b. Reference (b) promulgated the Table of Organization increase for Scout-Sniper Platoons with the Marine Division.

c. Reference (c) promulgated Advanced Logistics Data for the Scout-Sniper Rifle.

d. Reference (d) promulgated the Standard Training Syllabus for Scout-Sniper Platoons.

4. Policy.

a. The unique capabilities of the Scout-Sniper Platoon are at the disposal of the regimental and/or battalion commanders. The platoon may be employed as a unit, or can be broken down into squads or teams which may be attached to any size tactical unit of the regiment/battalion.

b. Snipers should whenever possible be employed in pairs to minimize eye fatigue from incessant surveillance. The two members relieve each other in performing the duties of sniper and observer.

c. A squad (10–14 marines) built around a sniper team is generally considered as the smallest unit which should be employed on missions beyond the sight or direct communications from parent units. However, where the situation, terrain, and reaction capability permits the commander to reduce this force to exploit stealth and surprise, the calculated employment of smaller groups (4–8 marines) is authorized out to 2,000 meters from friendly positions. These forces may be made up primarily or even exclusively of scout-sniper personnel provided appropriate arms and equipment augmentation is provided. Again with appropriate situation, terrain, and reaction capability, commanders are also authorized to employ single scout-sniper teams out to 500 meters from friendly positions.

    d. Under all conditions of employment scout-sniper teams/ units will be provided with appropriate communications, artillery, and mortar fire support on an "on call" basis.

    e. Rifle Team Equipment (RTE) armorers, MOS 2112, will be the only armorers authorized to perform second echelon maintenance. Weapons and telescopes requiring third echelon maintenance will be evacuated to the Fleet Logistic Support Group.

5. Mission.

The mission of the Scout-Sniper Platoon is to support the Infantry/Reconnaissance Battalions by providing a specially trained and equipped unit capable of rendering sniper support in combat operations by providing personnel trained to kill individual enemy soldiers with single rifle shots from positions of concealment.

6. Organization.

Reference (b) promulgated detailed instructions concerning the organization of the Scout-Sniper Platoon within the Infantry Division.

    a. Infantry Regiment organization consists of 3 squads of 5 two-man teams and a squad leader each, a noncommissioned officer in charge (NCOIC), a Rifle Team Equipment (RTE) armorer, and an Officer-in-Charge with a total strength of 1 officer and 35 enlisted.

    b. The Reconnaissance Battalion organization consists of 4 squads of 3 two-man teams and a squad leader each, an NCOIC, and RTE armorer, and an Officer-in-Charge with a total strength of 1 officer and 30 enlisted.

7. Consideration for Employment.

    a. Conventional Offensive. The capability of snipers to support infantry offensive action by precision destructive/ neutralizing fires is invaluable. Snipers with telescopes have the distinct advantage of being able to see as much as nine times better (with 9X scope) than the infantry personnel being supported. Neutralization of enemy automatic weapons and defensive positions is facilitated by the utilization of optics. As advancing infantry elements continue in the advance, snipers must displace to forward echelon to effectively support the offense by fire. Depending upon the size of the objective, snipers may be massed to render proportionately more support. Upon seizure of the objective, pursuit by fire phase is enhanced by the presence of snipers.

b. Conventional Defensive. The effective range and optical advantage of sniper rifles used in defensive situations causes premature deployment of enemy elements and unquestionably creates a tremendous psychological demoralizing impact upon the enemy. Officers, NCOs, and crew-served weapons are likely targets. Variable telescopes with magnification at low power possess the capability of acquiring targets over rice paddies at ranges up to 600 meters when a full moon is evident. While the ability to penetrate heavy foliage and tree lines is limited, distinct objects such as monuments, pagodas, etc. may be identified. Conventional iron sights do not have this capability. With telescopic sights, an additional hour of effective shooting time, with accuracy, is possible. This capability denies the enemy movement during first light and at dusk.

c. Attachment to Patrols. Experience has shown that the VC/NVA invariably take patrols under small arms fire from concealment. Firing is sporadic, of short duration, and because of the dense foliage it is extremely difficult to detect the source. Snipers, attached to patrols, with telescopic sights have the capability of acquiring targets more readily than other patrol members without benefit of optics. Additionally, their long-range accuracy denies the enemy the ability to close and therefore minimizes the accuracy of their weapons. In built-up areas, targets frequently cannot be taken under fire by area-type weapons (mortars, artillery, and air strikes) because of the proximity of innocent civilians. The capability of the sniper in delivering precision, long-range fire is a tremendous asset to the patrol.

d. Daylight Ambush—Extended. This type employment is used in selected areas where there is likelihood of encountering VC/NVA. The concept of employment provides for the sniper team, with infantry protection, moving to a preselected ambush site under cover of darkness and being in position by first light. Surveillance is maintained throughout the day. Withdrawal is made after darkness. Snipers, with the dual capability of adjusting artillery fire, take identifiable targets under fire with artillery or sniper fire depending on the size of the target. Survivors of observed artillery fire are taken under fire by the sniper.

e. Daylight Ambush—Close. Close ambushes are those sniper team ambushes within approximately 300 meters of friendly positions. To avoid possible capture or destruction the sniper team is covered by friendly fires. The 300 meters, coupled with the 1,000-meter range of the weapon, theoretically denies the enemy movement within 1,300 meters of friendly positions and accordingly minimizes the effect of enemy sniper fire and surveillance. This type of employment also involves assumption of the preselected ambush site prior to daybreak and withdrawal after darkness has followed.

f. Countersniper. In situations wherein friendly positions receive small arms fire on successive days from the same general location, snipers are employed to decrease the enemy's effectiveness by delivering accurate countersniper fire. The distinct advantage lies in the sniper weapon's precision fire capability when firing into built-up areas, which normally preclude the utilization of automatic weapons or supporting arms.

g. Blocking Positions. Sniper teams attached to infantry elements in blocking positions have been used extensively and effectively in conjunction with search-and-destroy operations. The enemy is taken under fire when driven into the blocking positions or while attempting to evade capture. The sniper rifle's accuracy, range, and telescopic sights permit long-range fires at targets which normally are too far distant to allow positive identification. This capability, in effect, precludes indiscriminate firing at innocent indigenous who have inadvertently wandered into the area of operations.

8. Employment of Attached Snipers.

a. Employment of snipers in both an offensive and defensive role is generally limited only by the imagination. Types of employment for which snipers are suitably equipped and trained are as follows:

(1) Execution of long-range (500–1,000 meters) daylight ambushes.

    (a) To kill and harass the enemy by precision fire.

    (b) Striking fear in the enemy by the psychological aspects derived from long-range, accurate small arms fire.

(2) Daylight patrols—Providing the terrain is suited for long-range, accurate fire in support of patrol activities.

(3) Blocking forces—Cover likely avenues of approach.

(4) Offense

    (a) Provide accurate covering fire for advancing maneuver elements.

    (b) Attack prime targets such as: crew-served weapons, bunker apertures, and personnel in trench lines or fighting holes.

    (c) Pursue enemy by long-range fire.

(5) Defense

    (a) Take enemy under fire at distances up to 1,000 meters with accuracy.

    (b) Deny the enemy freedom of movement in approach to friendly positions.

    (c) Countersniper fire—decrease enemy effectiveness through accurate counterfire.

b. Supported Unit Requirements. Units employing sniper teams must insure that the following principles are adhered to in employing snipers:

   (1) Always employ in teams (pairs) to increase their capability.

   (2) Always cover by a security element (one fire team and a radio operator).

   (3) Do not employ as a security element to front, rear, or flanks in column movements.

   (4) Do not employ in ambushes, patrols, or listening posts during hours of darkness.

   (5) Always insure snipers are informed of any friendly forces within their operating area.

   (6) Always insure that units/teams departing on missions have good operable radio and compass, have maps oriented with local terrain, and know correct forward observer procedures.

c. Control of Teams

   (1) Units desiring sniper unit augmentation submit request to this headquarters. Request to include number of units/teams desired and estimated duration of utilization.

   (2) Sniper platoon personnel when deployed will be under the operational control of the supported unit and administrative control of Headquarters Company, Regiment. The supported unit will provide logistical support to sniper personnel under their operational command.

9. Reports.

a. Units participating in normal operations include the following information in 1800 hours Situation Report (SITREPS) to cover the period 0001–2400 hours that day.

b. Units submitting 24-hour SITREPS include the following information for consolidation into Division Daily SITREP.

c. Format and Example

Unit	No. of Teams	No. Deployed	Method of Employment	Results

d. A Sniper Incident Report will be forwarded to this head-
    quarters for each scout-sniper incident. These may be
    submitted as tactical operations permit.
e. A Monthly Sniper Platoon Report will be completed
    by individual infantry regiments and submitted to this
    headquarters by the 5th of the month following the
    month reported on.

                                        (signed)
                                        W. H. Cuenin
                                        Chief of Staff

APPENDIX E

✻✻✻✻✻✻✻✻

Sniper Training and Employment in the 9th Infantry Division*

1. Introduction.

This section describes the sniper-training program and methods of sniper employment developed by the 9th Infantry Division. Interested unit commanders may write the 9th Infantry Division for copies of the program of instruction for the division's eighteen-day sniper-training course. The division's APO is 96370.

2. Training.

    a. Sniper trainees are selected from a list of volunteers. Those selected must have 20/20 vision, have qualified as an expert rifleman, and be well motivated. Experience in competitive marksmanship is preferred but not mandatory.

    b. Trainees are trained in:

        (1) Basic firing positions and the integrated acts of shooting.

        (2) Methods of zeroing their weapons equipped with the adjustable ranging telescopic sight, Starlight scope, and the fixed-power M84 telescopic sight.

*Two versions of this document exist. The first, written by Major Robert G. Hilchey, Assistant Division Operations Officer, appeared in a division document dated July 15, 1969. A second, more organized version for distribution to other U.S. Army units, as well as USMC and the South Vietnamese army, was issued a few weeks later. The second version, reproduced here in its entirety, has been modified for this printing by spelling out abbreviations for ease of understanding. Paragraphs 4, 5, and 6 were originally classified as confidential; other paragraphs were not classified.

(3) Night firing: Each trainee learns to engage targets with his Starlight scope at ranges of 150, 300, and 600 meters.

(4) Adjustment of artillery fire.

(5) Day and night land navigation.

c. Qualification firing is conducted during the last two days of the course. Sixteen silhouette targets are engaged at 150, 300, 600, and 900 meters. Ten points are awarded for a first-round hit and 5 points for a second-round hit. The maximum score is 160 points, and the minimum for qualifying is 130. About 50 percent of the aspirants qualify.

3. Equipment.

The snipers of the 9th Division are equipped with 138 national-match-grade M14 rifles; 54 were accurized by the Army Marksmanship Training Unit (AMTU) at Fort Benning, Georgia. These rifles are glass bedded with impregnated stocks which are impervious to water. The remaining 74 rifles were prepared by the Army Weapons Command and are somewhat less accurate than the AMTU weapons.

a. The 54 AMTU accurized weapons are equipped with a 3X-9X variable-power adjustable ranging telescope sight. The telescope is mounted in conjunction with a ballistic cam. The sight reticle includes a pair of stadia lines. When the power of the telescope is varied to define a 30-inch area on the target with the stadia lines, the ballistic cam raises the sight to the proper elevation for that distance. Errors due to range estimation are almost eliminated.

b. The 74 weapons prepared by the Army Weapons Command are equipped with the M84 telescope. These sights are a fixed 2.2 power telescope with a post reticle. Using the M84, the sniper must accurately estimate the gun target range and either hold over the target or adjust the elevating mechanism on the sight to the estimated range.

c. The AN/PVS-2 Starlight scope has proven more effec-

tive for sniper use than the AN/PVS-1 because of better
focusing and more reliable windage/elevation controls.
Also the sight reticle in the AN/PVS-2 is better when
engaging long-range targets. Trainees bring a Starlight
scope and mount to the sniper school when they report
for training and that scope/rifle combination is retained
for subsequent operations.

d. Ammunition used in sniper training and combat is
7.62-mm national match grade.

4. Organization.

Six snipers are assigned to each battalion headquarters and
headquarters company and four to each brigade headquarters.
It is essential that sniper employment be planned at battalion
level to insure command interest and optimum utilization.
Sniper teams are normally composed of two snipers.

5. Methods of Employment.

a. Ambush Patrols

(1) When employed with a platoon ambush, the sniper
team remains close to the platoon command post.
When enemy activity is sighted, the sniper team is
alerted. Snipers engage at night with Starlight scope
or the telescopic sight in daylight. Individual targets
are taken under fire by a sniper to avoid compromising the ambush position and location of automatic
weapons. When a group of VC approach, the snipers engage leaders and radio operators while the
platoon fires into the general kill zone. Snipers may
fire tracers to mark the flanks of VC approaching
other than the specified kill zone. Snipers also engage VC probing the ambush site.

(2) A sniper team and a five-to-eight-man security element may be placed in a sniper/ambush position
just before dark. The location is selected to provide maximum range of fire and is located near a
friendly unit. The security element is equipped with

M16 rifles, an M79 grenade launcher, and an AN/PRC-25 radio. Eye fatigue is minimized by having the snipers alternate using the Starlight scope through the night. The M79 is useful when VC are observed in a tree line or vegetated area where low light levels impede aimed fire. The directing of M79 fire into the area can force the VC to move and expose themselves to sniper fire.

b. Stay Behinds: A sniper team with a five-to-eight-man security element is selected to provide long-range observations of the route over which the unit has traveled. Snipers with telescopic sights are able to engage the enemy at ranges up to 900 meters. At extreme ranges the enemy is not cautious about cover and concealment.

c. Offset: The Starlight scope is sensitive to a portion of the infrared band that is pink and near the visible light portion of the spectrum. An area can be illuminated with invisible light that registers in the Starlight scopes by using a pink filter on a xenon searchlight.

   (1) Successful ambushes have been conducted by placing a filtered searchlight on a one-quarter-ton vehicle 1,200 to 1,500 meters from a road intersection. Snipers with Starlight scopes were placed 300 meters from the intersection. By maintaining radio contact with the searchlight operator, the snipers controlled the covert illumination of the intersection and the surrounding areas. By offsetting the sniper teams from the searchlight and placing the searchlight and vehicle in a position remote from the ambush site, the enemy in the kill zone were not alerted by vehicle engine noise.

   (2) In base camp security operations, the searchlight responds to radio-equipped sniper teams either on the berm or in ambush positions outside the berm. Background noise of the fixed base camp conceals the noise of the engine and activity of the searchlight crew. In forward base camps the searchlight

> remains in the center of the camp. By swinging its beam through 360 degrees, it covertly illuminates avenues of approach into the position.

d. Countersniper: Sniper teams, equipped with telescopic sights and M49 spotting scopes, search the areas of suspected VC sniper activity. The optical equipment permits a detailed search of distant areas.

e. Night Hunter Operations: A sniper team in the lead helicopter observes the ground with Starlight scope-mounted rifles. When the enemy is sighted the snipers mark the targets with tracers. Gunships following at a high altitude then engage the targets.

6. Problem Areas.

a. Sniper teams employed for prolonged periods with units other than units of assignment may be overlooked when promotions, R&R, and other personnel matters are considered.

b. Battalion and company commanders should participate in selecting sniper candidates. Selection and training of only well-motivated men with a reasonable amount of in-country time remaining is essential.

c. When the commander imaginatively employs his snipers the results have been better than in units where the commanders were less interested. There are examples of snipers positioned in dense vegetation with limited fields of fire while riflemen in the same unit were located with wide fields of fire.

d. Unknown to the commander, a sniper who has been well motivated may suddenly lose interest in sniping after witnessing a kill with his optical equipment. This can be detected by careful, regular debriefing of both members of the sniper team.

7. Statistical Data.

The snipers were assigned to maneuver battalions on 7 November 1968 and obtained their first kill on 10 November

1968. During the period from November 1968 to April 1969 seventy snipers were employed in the division. They had 286 contacts and accumulated a total of 475 confirmed enemy kills, or 1.67 kills per contact.

✳✳✳✳✳✳✳✳

MACV Order of Battle Study ST 67-029 (January 6, 1967), VC/NVA Employment of Snipers*

I. Introduction.

This is a study of VC/NVA employment of snipers in South Vietnam. It encompasses the training, unit organization, tactical employment, and mission of snipers.

II. Discussion.

A. Training.

1. Known sniper training has been restricted to North Vietnam. Snipers are trained in the unit with which they will deploy. The training is three months long and includes instruction in the care, cleaning, assembly, and disassembly of the K44 rifle and mounted scope. Live firing is practiced with silhouettes at ranges up to 1,000 meters. Additional training is given in camouflage, movement, and selection of sniper positions.

2. Captured documents indicate that snipers use explosive devices such as mines and booby traps in their operations. However, interrogations of captives

---

*Prepared by the MACV Combined Intelligence Center with a cover letter signed by Brigadier General J. A. McChristian, U.S. Army, Assistant Chief of Staff, J2. Information is based on documents and reports from the MACV Combined Military Intelligence Center, MACV Combined Documents Exploitation Center, I Corps Advisory Group, 196th Light Infantry Brigade, 25th Infantry Division, the Coa Xa and Ben Soi Special Forces Camps, and the Republic of South Vietnam. Original report included annexes with pictures of the K44 (Soviet 7.62-mm Mosin-Nagant M1891/30) sniper rifle, the 3.5 power telescope, and an organizational diagram of the NVA Sniper Battalion.

disclose that they received no training in the use of explosives. This could mean that further training is given the individual after he has reached his final destination in South Vietnam.

3. Returnee Nguyen Van Sinh states that local guerrillas in South Vietnam are being instructed by NVA snipers in the use of the K44 sniper rifle. It is possible that training courses for snipers are being conducted in South Vietnam. Recently found caches of undistributed K44 sniper rifles and friendly encounters with accurate sniper fire in areas where VC units are located indicate the presence of trained snipers. The K44 rifle with scope is the 7.62-mm Mosin Nagant Model 1891/30 with scope. Its characteristics are:

Magazine capacity—5 rounds
Maximum effective range with scope—1,400 meters*
Maximum horizontal range—3,500 meters

B. Organization. Snipers are grouped into independent training units in North Vietnam. The only known sniper units are the 700th Battalion and C.100 Sniper Company, both trained by the 32nd Regiment. The 700th Battalion is composed of five companies, each consisting of a headquarters element and three platoons. The platoons are composed of three squads each containing three cells. Once each unit reached its final destination in South Vietnam it was broken down into cells, which operated independently of each other. Ideally, one sniper platoon would support about five battalions.

C. Employment:
1. Although snipers are deployed to support main force units, they operate within an area and do not maneuver with main force units. In the course of their missions, snipers employ guerrillas as guides and

*This is either an error or a misprint in the original study; 800 meters is more correct.

reconnaissance agents. Most of these trained snipers are encountered when entering strategic VC areas. Their mission is to wear down Allied morale and limit troop activity in these areas.

2. The snipers operate in three-man cells or five-man squads and use mines and booby traps. The mines and booby traps are used to channel friendly troop movements, to increase the number of casualties, and to allow the snipers time to withdraw. Allied troops advancing on snipers have encountered mines between them and the snipers. By the time they cleared the area the snipers have withdrawn to another position.

3. Although snipers are taught to take advantage of all existing nonprominent terrain features, they usually restrict their operations to trench networks and trees that are found in VC base areas. Other favorite positions are both sides of jungle clearings and roads. The positions are chosen to give maximum range and fields of fire plus mutual support of cell members. The positioning of the cell and its plans of attack and withdrawal are determined by the cell leader. He plans positions along his enemy's probable route of advance. The cell's withdrawal route coincides with the enemy's route of advance.

4. Engagement is usually initiated at ranges from 50 to 500 meters, depending on the terrain. The lead element is engaged first by a sniper. This fire slows the enemy's forward advance and draws the unit toward the sniper cell. The remaining members of the cell fire at the column from the flanks and rear. The snipers on the flanks and rear aim primarily for the unit commander, radio operator, and heavy weapons men. They expend no more than five rounds each, with a kill resulting on the first or second shot. Once the snipers are in contact with the opposing force, they continue to follow its movement while proceeding

along their withdrawal route and shooting from predetermined positions.

5. A large portion of fire reported by Allied troops has
   been erroneously labeled sniper fire. It would be
   more accurate to call this "harassing" fire rather than
   "sniper" fire. Harassing fire can be distinguished
   from true sniper fire because it is less accurate and is
   characterized by a larger ammunition expenditure.
   Harassing fire is usually directed by an individual local force guerrilla, who is given a sector of responsibility. This man operates as an individual rather than
   as a member of a cell.

III. Conclusions.

Based on past reports, organized sniper resistance has been experienced only in areas the VC consider valuable. This would
indicate that sniper units are employed mainly in a defensive
role. There is no evidence that snipers are used in any other
combat role or that they will be used as such in the future.

APPENDIX G

✳✳✳✳✳✳✳✳

Information Request

1. Name: _____
   Unit(s) in Vietnam: _____
   Dates of Service in Vietnam: _____

2. Address:
   Street _____
   City/State _____
   Zip _____

3. Your experiences. Please send copies of any official or unofficial reports or correspondence.

Forward to:
   Michael Lee Lanning
   Inside the Crosshairs
   c/o Ivy Books
   201 E. 50th Street
   New York, NY 10022

Or e-mail to:
   Mlann1037@aol.com

****

Annotated Bibliography

Books

Armstrong, N. A. *Fieldcraft, Sniping, and Intelligence*. Aldershot, England: Gale & Polden, 1943. An overview of British sniper activities.

Askins, Charles. *Unrepentant Sinner: The Autobiography of Charles Askins, U.S. Army Colonel*. San Antonio, Tex.: Tejano Publications, 1985. Includes a section on the author's experience as an unofficial sniper in the European Theater in World War II.

Bishop, Chris, and Ian Drury, eds. *The Encyclopedia of World Military Weapons: The World's Armies and Their Equipment*. New York: Crescent Books, 1989. Includes a chapter that illustrates and describes the sniper weapons of the world's leading military forces.

Brophy, William S. *The Springfield 1903 Rifles*. Harrisburg, Pa.: Stackpole Books, 1991. Includes sections on the use of the '03 Springfield in World Wars I and II.

Butler, David F. *United States Firearms, the First Century, 1776–1875*. New York: Winchester, 1971. Details the advancement of firearms in the United States in the stated period.

Chandler, Roy F., and N. A. Chandler. *Death From Afar*. Volumes I–IV. St. Mary's City, Md.: Iron Brigade Press, 1992–1997. Magazine format published as books; includes sniper history, mostly USMC, from Vietnam to present.

Culbertson, John J. *Operation Tuscaloosa*. New York: Ivy Books, 1997. Includes description of VC/NVA snipers.

Dupuy, Trevor N. *The Evolution of Weapons and Warfare*. New York: Bobbs-Merrill Company, 1980. Includes advances in guns and ammunition from their invention to the modern era.

Ewell, Julian J., and Ira A. Hunt Jr. *Sharpening the Combat Edge: The Use of Analysis to Reinforce Military Judgment*. Washington, D.C.: Department of the Army, 1974. Contains several sections on Ewell's establishment of the 9th Infantry Division Sniper School and some of its results.

Ezell, Edward C. *Personal Firepower: The Vietnam War*. New York: Bantam Books, 1988. Includes two chapters on sniper weapons and equipment of both sides in Vietnam.

Gilbert, Adrian. *Sniper.* New York: St. Martin's Press, 1995. A history of snipers around the world; includes a chapter on the Vietnam War.

Greener, W. W. *Sharpshooting for Sport and War.* London: Everett & Company, 1900. A gun maker and marksman's early account of precision shooting in peace and war.

George, John B. *Shots Fired in Anger.* Washington, D. C.: National Rifle Association, 1981. (Originally privately published in 1947.) Discusses American and Japanese snipers and their equipment in the Pacific Theater during World War II.

Grossman, Dave. *On Killing: The Psychological Cost of Learning to Kill in War and Society.* New York: Little, Brown, and Company, 1995. Brief mention of snipers in Vietnam and their reactions to long-range killing.

Hackworth, David H., and Julie Sherman. *About Face.* New York: Simon & Schuster, 1989. Contains several pages on the development of sniper operations in the 9th Infantry Division.

Hasket-Prichard, H. *Sniping in France.* Mount Ida, Ark.: Lancer Militaria, 1993. (Originally published by Hutchinson & Company in London in 1920.) A British officer's classic account of sniping in World War I.

Hay, John H., Jr. *Tactical and Material Innovations.* Washington, D.C.: Department of the Army, 1975. Contains a brief analysis of the effectiveness of army snipers in Vietnam.

Held, Robert. *The Age of Firearms.* New York: Harper Brothers, 1957. A pictorial history of firearms from their beginnings to the end of the nineteenth century.

Henderson, Charles. *Marine Sniper: 93 Confirmed Kills.* New York: Berkley Books, 1988. (Originally published in Briarcliff Manor, New York, by Stein and Day in 1986.) The story of Carlos Hathcock, one of the most successful snipers in USMC history.

Hunter, Stephen. *Black Light.* New York: Doubleday, 1996. Novel about a Vietnam Marine sniper veteran's fight against current enemies at home.

———. *The Master Hunter.* New York: William Morrow, 1980. Novel about a World War II German sniper.

———. *Point of Impact.* New York: Bantam Books, 1993. Fiction adventures of a Vietnam Marine sniper two decades after the war.

Kugler, Ed. *A Dozen Things I Learned About Life as a Marine Sniper in Vietnam.* Spring, Tex.: Dozen Group, 1996. A former 4th Marine Regiment sniper's advice on learning, health, and happiness based on his Vietnam experiences.

Larsen, Stanley R., and James Lawton Collins Jr. *Allied Participation in Vietnam.* Washington, D.C.: Department of the Army, 1975. Includes information on weapons used by the allies of the South Vietnamese and United States.

Law, Richard D. *Backbone of the Wehrmacht: The German K98k Rifle, 1934–1945.* Ontario, Canada: Cobourg, 1993. Information on the use of K98k as a sniper rifle by the Germans in World War II.

Long, Duncan. *Modern Sniper Rifles.* Boulder, Colo.: Paladin Press, 1988. Photos and descriptions of long-range rifles.

McBride, Herbert W. *A Rifleman Went to War.* Mount Ida, Ark.: Lancer Militaria, 1987. (Originally published in 1935 by Samworth Books of Plantersville, South Carolina.) A Canadian army veteran's account of sniping in World War I.

Melville, Michael Leslie. *The Story of the Lovat Scouts.* Edinburgh, Scotland: Saint Andrews Press, 1981. The story of the regiment that originated Great Britain's sniper training.

Nolan, Keith William. *The Magnificent Bastards.* Novato, Calif.: Presidio Press, 1994. Includes information on actions of Marine sniper James L. O'Neill during the 1968 defense of Dong Ha.

Page, Warren. *The Accurate Rifle.* South Hackensack, N.J.: Stoeger Publishing Company, 1978. Mostly about bench-rest shooting but contains information on adjusting rifle systems to increase accuracy.

Plaster, John L. *The Ultimate Sniper.* Boulder, Colo.: Paladin Press, 1993. Contains training guidance for military and police marksmen.

Rosser-Owen, David. *Vietnam Weapons Handbook.* Wellingborough, England: Patrick Stephens Limited, 1986. Includes a chapter on rifles and carbines with a brief mention of sniper weapons.

Sasser, Charles W., and Craig Roberts. *One Shot—One Kill.* New York: Pocket Books, 1990. Personal narratives of American combat snipers in World War II, Korea, Vietnam,and Beirut.

Senich, Peter R. *Limited War Sniping.* Boulder, Colo.: Paladin Press, 1977. Includes information on sniping in Korea and Vietnam.

———. *The Complete Book of U.S. Sniping.* Boulder, Colo.: Paladin Press, 1988. U.S. military snipers from the Civil War to the present—extensive illustrations of weapons.

———. *The German Sniper 1914–1945.* Boulder, Colo.: Paladin Press, 1982. History, especially of weapons, of German snipers in World Wars I and II.

———. *The Long-Range War: Sniping in Vietnam.* Boulder, Colo.: Paladin Press, 1994. History, including exceptional pictures, of army and Marine snipers in Vietnam.

———. *The One-Round War: USMC Scout-Snipers in Vietnam.* Boulder, Colo.: Paladin Press, 1996. History, including exceptional pictures, of Marine snipers in Vietnam.

———. *The Pictorial History of U.S. Sniping.* Boulder, Colo.: Paladin Press, 1980. Covers long-range shooters throughout U.S. history by illustrations.

———. *U.S. Marine Corps Scout-Sniper: World War II and Korea.* Boulder, Colo.: Paladin Press, 1993. Excellent pictures and some documents on Marine snipers in the two major wars preceding Vietnam.

———, and Howard Kyle. *The German Sniper: The Man and His Weapons.* Wickenburg, Ariz.: Normount Technical Publications, 1974. German snipers and their rifles in World War II.

Shore, C. *With British Snipers to the Reich.* Mount Ida, Ark.: Lancer Militaria, 1988. (Originally published by Small Arms Publishing Company of

Georgetown, South Carolina, in 1948.) Classic study of British and German World War II snipers by a British army sniper instructor.

Shulimson, Jack, and Charles M. Johnson. *U.S. Marine Corps in Vietnam: The Landing and the Buildup, 1965.* Washington, D.C.: History and Museums Division, USMC, 1978. Includes a brief mention of early Marine sniper operations.

Skennerton, Ian D. *The British Sniper and Commonwealth Sniping and Equipment.* Margate, Australia: Ian D. Skennerton, 1984. Covers British Commonwealth sniping from 1915 through 1983.

————. *The Lee-Enfield Story.* London: Greenhill Books, 1993. Contains information on the use of various models of Lee-Enfield rifles during World Wars I and II.

Sleath, Frederick. *Sniper Jackson.* London: Herbert Jenkins, 1919. The fictionalized version of a British officer's sniping adventures in World War I.

Stanton, Shelby L. *Vietnam Order of Battle.* New York: Galahad Books, 1986. (Originally published in Washington, D.C., by *U.S. News & World Report,* Inc., in 1981.) A complete reference of U.S. Army and Allied ground forces in Vietnam; also includes two pictures and brief descriptions of the XM21 sniper rifle system.

Tantum, William H., IV. *Sniper Rifles of Two World Wars.* Ottawa, Ontario: Museum Restoration Service, 1967. A pictorial history of sniper rifles used in World Wars I and II.

Taylor, F. A. J. *The Bottom of the Barrel.* London: Regency Press, 1978. The story of a enlisted British sniper in World War I.

Telfer, Gary L., Lane Rogers, and V. Keith Fleming Jr. *U.S. Marine Corps in Vietnam: Fighting the North Vietnamese, 1967.* Washington, D.C.: History and Museums Division, USMC, 1984. Includes a paragraph about snipers in the 3rd Marine Regiment.

Trench, Charles C. *A History of Marksmanship.* Chicago: Follett Publishing Company, 1972. A history of marksmanship in both war and peace from earliest recorded history to the modern era.

Truby, J. David. *Silencers, Snipers, and Assassins.* Boulder, Colo.: Paladin Press, 1972. The use of silencers from World War I through Vietnam.

————. *Silencers in the 1980s: Great Designs, Great Designers.* Boulder, Colo.: Paladin Press, 1983. Includes sections on modern silencer technology for snipers.

Ward, Joseph T. *Dear Mom: A Sniper's Vietnam.* New York: Ivy Books, 1991. Personal narrative of Ward's experiences as a 1st Marine Division sniper in Vietnam during 1969 and 1970.

Whelen, Townsend. *Telescopic Rifle Sights.* Onslow County, N.C.: Small-Arms Technical Publishing Co., 1936. Early general study of available rifle telescopes.

————. *Telescopic Rifle Sights.* Plantersville, S.C.: Samworth Books, 1944. A revised and updated version of the 1936 edition; includes World War II sniper scopes.

————. *Fundamentals of Scope Sights.* Washington, D.C.: National Rifle Association, 1952. Contains information on more advancements in telescopes.

Wilber, Martin. *The History of the Crossbow.* Seattle: Shorey Book Store, 1982. Reprint of a 1936 Smithsonian Institution report on the invention and evolution of the crossbow.

Wynne, Barry. *The Sniper.* London: Macdonald & Company, 1968. The story of a British enlisted sniper in Europe during World War II.

Young, Darryl. *The Element of Surprise.* New York: Ivy Books, 1990. A navy SEAL's narrative of his Vietnam tour.

Periodicals

Abbott, Philip K. "Snipers: A Neglected Combat Multiplier." *Infantry,* November–December 1991. Outlines weapons and personnel requirements for snipers.

Allen, Henry. "Squinting at Death: The Desert Snipers." *Washington Post,* December 28, 1990. Marine snipers in Saudi Arabia prepare for Operation Desert Storm.

Amos, Albert R., Jr. ".50 Caliber Sniper." *Infantry,* September–October 1970. Adaptation by the army's 25th Infantry Division of .50-caliber machine guns as sniper weapons in Vietnam.

Bierman, Harris. "State of the Art Sniper Rifles." *Guns & Ammo Annual,* 1988. A survey of the world's best sniper rifles.

Bacon, Lance M. "Goodbye to Romance." *Marines,* June 1996. Explains that real Marine sniper training is different from movie versions.

Borsdorf, Captain. "The Sniper." *Military Review,* September 1944. A translation of a brief article by a German army officer that appeared in the *Hamburger Fremdenblatt* on May 9, 1944; discusses German and Soviet snipers in World War II.

Bowen, James W. "Sniper-Observer Teams." *Infantry,* March–April 1986. Describes the initial post-Vietnam formation of sniper teams in the army's 82nd Airborne Division.

Brantley, Robert M. "Sniper." *Marines,* August 1995. Marine sniper training at Camp Lejeune, North Carolina.

Bull, Stephen. "British Army Snipers, 1914–1918." *Military Illustrated,* September 1992. In-depth account of British snipers in World War I.

Burks, Arthur J. "The Sniper." *Leatherneck,* August 1926. Fictionalized account of a World War I German sniper and the Canadians who neutralized him.

Carman, W. Y. "The Burial of General Fraser, Saratoga, 1777." *Journal of the Society for Army Historical Research,* Summer 1970. Details the death of a British general by an American marksman in the Revolutionary War.

Carter, Ernie. "Snipers Train to Stalk." *Marines,* November 1988. Snipers of the 6th Marine Regiment train on Okinawa.

Childs, Jack. "Sniping in Vietnam." *American Rifleman,* June 1966. Detailed account of the establishment of the first sniper training in Vietnam.

————. "VC Defector Unveils Elite Sniper Company." *Sea Tiger,* July 19, 1966. One of the few accounts of North Vietnamese sniper training and operations.

————, and Bruce Martin. "Sniper." *Leatherneck,* January 1967. Discusses early Vietcong snipers in Vietnam and records history of the establishment of the 3rd Marine Division Scout-Sniper School.

Clapham, Richard. "Sniping and Observing in War Time." *Cavalry Journal,* January-October 1940. Former British sniper discusses long-range shooting in World War I and supports the concept for World War II; the article concludes with a drawing, "A Sniper's Dream," of a telescope's crosshairs centered on the head of Adolf Hitler.

Coleman, John. "One Shot, One Kill: Army Sniper School Is Dead on Target." *Soldier of Fortune,* December 1986. Notes the status of army sniper training of the period.

Collins, Edward J. "Wanted: A Killer." *Infantry,* January-March 1959. Supports peacetime sniper training.

Creighton, Linda. "School for Snipers." *U.S. News & World Report,* April 21, 1986. A look at Marine post-Vietnam sniper training.

Crupi, A. J., and William F. Odom. "A Warning." *Infantry School Quarterly,* October 1951. Brief history of sniping and unofficial opinion survey by soldiers during the Korean War about snipers.

Daniel, Edward D. "USMC Scout Snipers: Issues and Answers." *Marine Corps Gazette,* July 1990. Detailed summary of post-Vietnam Marine sniper developments.

Dearolph, Jeffery E. "The Infantry Battalion Scout/Snipers: Scouts or Snipers?" *Marine Corps Gazette,* November 1994. Includes a history of post-Vietnam sniper training and recommends improvements in scout-sniper platoon organization.

Dragnett, Kevin P. "Light Infantry Snipers." *Infantry,* January-February 1993. Recommends standardization of sniper personnel and equipment authorizations for light infantry units.

Dunnigan, James A. "The American Sniper." *Guns & Ammo Annual,* 1981. General history of U.S. military snipers.

Ellis, Earl S. "The U.S. Army Sniper School." *Infantry,* November-December 1991. Criteria for selecting sniper students.

Enoch, Leslie B. "Sniper—Sayonara." *Infantry,* January-March 1959. Provides pros and cons on sniper training and recommends renewed studies of the concept.

Foley, John E. "Scouts, Snipers, and Designated Riflemen." *Infantry,* September-October 1990. Supports increased marksmanship training and describes the M24 sniper rifle system.

Garavaglia, Louis A. "Snipers in Vietnam Also Need Firepower." *American Rifleman,* January 1968. A discussion of the need for adequate sniper rifles in Vietnam by a veteran of the army's 4th Infantry Division.

Graves, Patrick H. "Observations of a Platoon Leader." *Infantry,* May-June 1967. A veteran of the army's 101st Airborne Division gives his ideas on how to counter enemy snipers.

Greaves, Fielding L. "A Single Well-Aimed Shot." *Army,* September 1987. The brief story of American marksman Timothy Murphy and British gun maker Patrick Ferguson in the Revolutionary War.

Grigg, Weldon M. "One Shot—One Kill." *Infantry,* November-December 1979. A report on the status of army sniper training.

Hargreaves, Richard. "The Lonely Art." *Marine Corps Gazette,* December 1954. A brief history of sniping, mostly British, from the Napoleonic Era through World War I.

Harrison, E. H. "Why U.S. Match Ammunition Ranks High." *American Rifleman,* July 1967. A look at the Lake City, Missouri, ammunition plant that manufactured match-quality ammunition for army and Marine snipers in Vietnam.

Hedges, Chris. "War Is Vivid in Gun Sights of Sniper." *New York Times,* February 3, 1991. Marine snipers in Operation Desert Storm.

Hicks, Norman W. "Team Shots Can Kill." *Marine Corps Gazette,* December 1963. Discusses sniping during the Korean War.

Hofues, John L. "Modernize the Sniper Rifle." *Army,* June 1957. Recommends that the post–Korean War army acquire a rifle and scope specifically made for long-range precision shooting.

"How the Japs Train Snipers." *Military Review,* October 1945. Japanese sniper training during World War II.

Howell, Phil. "New Sniper Rifle." *Army Times,* May 23, 1988. Contains a picture and a brief description of the M24 sniper rifle system.

Jenkins, B. Wheeler. "The Shots That Saved Baltimore." *Maryland History Magazine,* December 1982. The author credits American marksmen with preventing the British capture of the city in 1814.

Johnson, David A. "At 13 Cents Per Round, Army and Marine Snipers Were Among the Most Cost-Effective Weapons Systems of the War." *Vietnam,* December 1989. A brief history of army and Marine snipers in Vietnam; the title summarizes well.

Kersey, Bob. "Turkey Shoot at 1,000 Meters." *Pacific Stars and Stripes,* November 12, 1967. Sniper school and operations of the 1st Marine Division.

Kriventsov, M. "Soviet Snipers." *Infantry Journal,* October 1942. A Soviet army officer's view of early sniper operations on the Eastern Front during World War II.

Lawson, Chris. "Sniper." *Navy Times,* April 15, 1996. A brief history of Marine snipers; includes Somalia.

"Let's Get the Most From Our Shooters." *Army,* February 1957. Advocates sniper training in the peacetime army.

Leuer, Kenneth C. "Sniper Training Program." *Infantry,* January-February 1988. The commandant of the infantry school describes efforts to renew the army's sniper-training course.

Lewis, Jack. "A Matter of Accuracy." *Leatherneck,* May 1996. A detailed article on post-Vietnam Marine sniper training and the M40A1 sniper rifle.

Lister, C. B. "The Sniper." *American Rifleman,* September 1942. Supports sniper training for operations in World War II.

Little, Steward. "Sniper School Aims to Create Elite Units." *Cleveland Press,* November 26, 1980. Training at Quantico's scout-sniper school.

Lubell, Dan. "3dMarDiv Develops Counter-Sniper Plan." *Sea Tiger,* February 1, 1967. The employment of Marine snipers against enemy marksmen.

"Marine Snipers Pick Off VC." *Saigon Observer,* April 16, 1966. An account of the first sniping missions conducted by Marine captain Robert Russell and his NCOs.

Martin, Bruce. "4th Marines Snipe at 1,000 Yards Range." *Sea Tiger,* July 26, 1966. A brief article on 4th Marine Regiment snipers in Vietnam.

Martin, Glen E. "They Call Their Shots." *Marine Corps Gazette,* April 1953. Discusses Marine snipers in the Korean War.

Mason, James D. "The U.S.M.C. Specialized 'Varminters' Are Now Beating the Viet Cong at Their Own Game." *Guns and Ammo,* January 1968. Early account of Marine snipers in Vietnam.

McGuire, Frank G. "Snipers—Specialists in Warfare." *American Rifleman,* June 1967. Overall history of sniping, including early Marine efforts in Vietnam.

Miller, Henry. "Interview: American Pointman." *Vietnam,* April 1997. Includes a brief mention of snipers in Miller's army unit.

"Modernize the Sniper Rifle." *Army,* June 1957. Calls for a replacement rifle for the C- and D-Model M1.

Morozov, G. "Sniper Tactics." *Marine Corps Gazette,* August 1943. A Soviet army officer's view of sniping against the Germans on the Eastern Front in early World War II.

Murphy, Jack. "Lejeune Marines Learn to Save Hides in Sniper Class." *Wilmington (NC) Morning Star,* July 15, 1985. Sniper training in the 2nd Marine Division.

———. "Marine Snipers Learn Skill, Discipline at Special School." *Wilmington (NC) Sunday Star News,* June 30, 1985. More on 2nd Marine Division sniper training at Camp Lejeune.

———. "Snipers Learn a Deadly Art." *Wilmington (NC) Morning Star,* July 8, 1985. More on sniper training at Camp Lejeune.

Neumann, George C. "Firearms of the American Revolution, Part I." *American Rifleman,* July 1967. (Parts II, III, and IV appeared in the August, September, and October 1967 editions.) Pictures and descriptions of the Revolutionary War rifles and pistols of both sides.

Nichols, Timothy W. "Building a Scout/Sniper Platoon." *Marine Corps Gazette,* June 1996. Ideas on increasing platoon proficiency.

Odom, William F. "The Case of the U.S. Sniper." *Infantry School Quarterly,* April 1954. Supports the authorization for snipers in the post–Korean War army; includes recommendations for their training, organization, and arms.

Ogle, Clarence O. "Let's Get the Most From Our Shooters." *Army,* February

1957. Recommends the permanent assignment of dedicated snipers in each infantry company in the post–Korean War army.

"The Proper Way to Kill." *San Francisco Chronicle,* July 18, 1968. An Associated Press article on the initial draft of the Marine Corps Sniper Manual; it also appeared in other newspapers across the country under various headlines.

Ricks, Thomas E. "Sniper." *Marine Corps Gazette,* October 1995. Emphasizes the importance of snipers in post–Cold War actions such as Haiti in 1995.

Roberts, Craig. "At Stalingrad in 1942, the Great Battle Focused for One Deadly Moment on Sniper Versus Sniper." *World War II,* September 1989. Soviet sniper Vassili Zaitsev stalks and kills a German sniper during the Battle of Stalingrad in World War II.

Rogers, Glenn F., and Michael S. Hackney. "MILES Sniper Training." *Infantry,* March-April 1983. Describes a scenario for sniper and countersniper training using the Multiple Integrated Laser Engagement System (MILES).

Rozycki, Mark L. "U.S. Army Sniper School." *Infantry,* May-June 1989. Describes the army's post-Vietnam sniper school at Fort Benning, Georgia.

Senich, Peter R. "The Shooter: Scout-Sniper Chuck Mawhinney, 103 Confirmed Kills." *Precision Shooter,* December 1996. The story of Chuck Mawhinney, the most successful Marine sniper in Vietnam.

Silkett, Wayne A. "Urban Snipers." *Infantry,* September-October 1982. Techniques for sniper use in cities and towns.

Simpson, Ross W. "One Shot, One Kill." *Leatherneck,* January 1991. Marine snipers in Saudi Arabia prepare for Operation Desert Storm.

————. "Crosshairs on Baghdad." *Soldier of Fortune,* March 1991. Expanded version of Simpson's January 1991 *Leatherneck* article.

Sines, Kenneth A. "What's in the Future for the Sniper?" *Infantry,* May-June 1972. Recommends that the army maintain snipers and the M21 sniper rifle system in the post–Vietnam War era.

"Sniping—a Neglected Art." *Army Ordnance,* January-February 1946. Supports the army's postwar retention of snipers.

Smith, Philip W. "Marine Snipers' Credo: One Shot—One Kill." *Washington Post,* February 9, 1986. Sniper training at Quantico, with some background on Vietnam operations.

————. "Snipers Learn to Kill at a Distance." *Los Angeles Times,* December 5, 1980. Marine sniper training at Quantico.

Spencer, Jim. "The Sniper." *Chicago Tribune,* September 7, 1986. Covers Marine sniper training of the period; includes background from Vietnam.

Spiller, Ruth J. "Find It, Sight It, Shoot It!" *Soldiers,* January 1995. A brief overview of sniper training, weapons, and operations.

Stanley, John L. "Beyond the Sniper: Special Operations Target Interdiction." *Special Warfare,* July 1988. Describes post-Vietnam employment and training of snipers in Special Forces and Ranger battalions.

————. "New Sniper Weapon System Designed to be Rugged, Dependable and Accurate." *Special Warfare,* July 1988. Describes the M24 sniper rifle system.

Starch, Stephen G. "A Memoir of the Exploits of Captain Alexander Fraser and the Company of British Marksmen, 1776–1777." *Journal of the Society for Army Historical Research,* parts I and II, Summer 1985; part III, Autumn 1985. The story of leading British organizer of marksmen in the Revolutionary War.

Stein, Jeff. "Stealth Warriors." *Washington Post Magazine,* March 9, 1997. A detailed look at current Marine snipers and their training.

Tantum, William H., IV. "Sniping Rifles of the First World War." *Guns Review,* July 1963. A survey of sniper rifles used by both sides during World War I.

———. "Sniping Rifles of the Second World War." *Guns Review,* September 1963. A survey of sniper rifles used by both sides during World War II.

Teegerstrom, Eric J. "Scout-Snipers: One Shot, One Kill." *Armor,* July-August 1994. Recommendations on how to employ the armor and cavalry unit sniper sections.

Thompson, P. L. "Scout-Sniper School." *Leatherneck,* March 1985. A description of post-Vietnam Marine sniper training.

Tolbert, Frank X. "Deadly Teams Emerge From This Academy." *Leatherneck,* October 1943. USMC sniper training at Green's Farm, California, during World War II.

Trussell, John B., Jr. "He Never Missed His Aim," *Parameters* 1, 1976. The story of American marksman Timothy Murphy in the Revolutionary War.

Ukeiley, Scott E. "Reconnaissance and Surveillance: Combined Arms for the BLT." *Marine Corps Gazette,* September 1996. Recommends combining the Marine Battalion Landing Team's reconnaissance and scout sniper platoons.

Walsh, Steven L. "Reorganizing Scout Sniper Training." *Marine Corps Gazette,* July 1990. Recommends changes in Marine sniper training.

West, Mike. "Sniper!" *Octofoil,* January-March 1969. A brief history of the army's 9th Infantry Division's sniper school in Vietnam.

Wilson, G. E. "1st Div Scout-Snipers Killing Two VC a Day." *Sea Tiger,* February 1, 1967. Contains a brief history of Captain Jim Land's scout-sniper school.

Wright, D. L. "Training the Scout Sniper." *Marine Corps Gazette,* October 1985. Discusses use of day and night observation devices.

Official Records/Documents/Manuals

Army Headquarters, Canada

Directorate of Military Intelligence. "Snipers in Action" (a translation of a USSR Ministry of War publication on the history of Soviet snipers.) September 10, 1952.

U.S. Army

DOCUMENTS

U.S. Army Center for Lessons Learned. "Bulletin No. 1-88," April 1988.

U.S. Army Combat Developments Command. "Trip Report (33-69), Sniper Program," April 28, 1969.

U.S. Army Concept Team in Vietnam. "Final Report—Sniper Operations and Equipment," February 23, 1968.

U.S. Army 41st Division Training Note No. 3. "163 Infantry: Counter-Sniping from Musket Perimeter," 1943.

U.S. Army Ground Forces, Pacific. "Report Number 183: Training and Use of Snipers," January 5, 1945.

U.S. Army Infantry School. "Snipers," student paper by John W. Pinkston, August 1971.

U.S. Army Marksmanship Training Unit. "Accurized National Match M14 Rifle," June 23, 1968.

———. "Sniper Firing Data Book," May 13, 1968.

U.S. Army 9th Infantry Division, "Operational Report—Lessons Learned," July 1967–September 1970.

———. "Sniper Training and Employment in the 9th Infantry Division," July 15, 1967.

U.S. Army 25th Infantry Division. "Operational Report—Lessons Learned," January 1969–October 1970.

FIELD MANUALS

FM 21-27. "Combat Training of the Individual Soldier and Patrolling," October 1950.

FM 21-75. "Combat Training of the Individual Soldier and Patrolling," January 19, 1962.

FM 23-5. "U.S. Rifle, Caliber .30, M1," September 26, 1958.

FM 23-5. "U.S. Rifle, Caliber .30, M1," May 17, 1965.

FM 23-10. "Sniper Training," August 17, 1994.

TRAINING CIRCULARS

TC 23-11. "Starlight Scope, Small Hand-Held or Individual Weapons Mounted Model No. 6060," November 1966.

TC 23-14. "Sniper Training and Employment," October 1969.

TECHNICAL MANUALS

TM 5-9341. "Operation and Maintenance Instructions for Sniperscopes Models M1 and M2," August 1951.

TM 5-9342A. "Repair Instructions for Sniperscope, Infrared Set No. 1," April 1952.

TM 9-270. "U.S. Rifle, Cal. .30, M1903A4 (Sniper's) Characteristics and Operation; and Use of Telescopic Sight," September 28, 1943.

TM 9-1005-205-12. "Operator's and Organizational Maintenance Manual Including Repair Parts and Special Tool Lists: Rifle, Cal. 30 M1903A4 (Sniper's)," December 1970.

TM 9-1005-221-10 (draft). "Operator's Manual: Rifle, 7.62 mm, XM21, Sniper W/Adjusting Ranging Telescope and Mount With Equipment," November 1969.

U.S. Department of Defense

Weapons and Equipment—Southeast Asia. 1965.

U.S. General Accounting Office

"Army's Civilian Marksmanship Program Is of Limited Value," May 23, 1990.

U.S. Marine Corps

DOCUMENTS

Equipment for the American Sniper by George O. Van Orden and Calvin A. Lloyd, 1942.

Marine Corps Competitive Shooting by Robert E. Barde, 1961.

U.S. Marine Corps Development and Education Command, Public Affairs Office, Quantico, Virginia. Release No. 004-86, "Scout-Sniper's Ghillie Suit," January 27, 1986.

U.S. Marine Corps Equipment Board, Quantico, Virginia. "Project No. A9-757: Sniper Rifles, Telescopes, and Mount Study," 1951.

U.S. Marine Corps 1st Marine Brigade, FMF. News Release No.: 16-62, "This Is a Sniper," January 26, 1962.

U.S. Marine Corps 3rd Marine Division. "Division Order 3590.3B, Scout-Sniper Platoons," June 9, 1968.

U.S. Marine Corps 3rd Marine Division. "Division Order 1510.5, Scout-Sniper Refresher Training Course," September 3, 1968.

MANUALS

FMFM 1-3B. "Sniping," August 5, 1969.

FMFM 1-3B. "Sniping," April 7, 1976.

FMFM 1-3B. "Sniping," January 28, 1981.

SL-3-05539A. "Components List for Rifle, 7.62 mm: M40," August 1970.

SL-3-05539B. "Components List for Rifle, Sniper, 7.62 mm M40A1," May 1978.

SL-4-05539A. "Repair Parts List for Rifle, 7.62 mm: M700," November 1966.

TM 00539-13/1. "Operation and Maintenance, Rifle, Sniper, M40A1 and Related Optical Equipment," November 1981.

U.S. Military Assistance Command, Vietnam

U.S. Military Assistance Command, Vietnam, Headquarters. "Combat Experiences: Sniper Training and Employment in the 9th Infantry Division," 1969.

U.S. Military Assistance Command, Vietnam, Office of the Assistant Chief of Staff Intelligence. "Order of Battle Study ST 67-029: VC/NVA Employment of Snipers," January 6, 1967.

U.S. Navy

NAVMC 2614. "Professional Knowledge Gained From Operational Experience in Vietnam," 1967.

U.S. War Department

MANUALS
FM 21-75. "Infantry Scouting, Patrolling, and Sniping," February 6, 1944.
TM 5-9340. "Sniperscope and Snooperscope," September 1944.
TM 9-1275. "U.S. Rifles, Cal. .30 M1, M1C, and M1D," 1947.
TM 9-270. "U.S. Rifle, Cal. .30 M1903A4 (Sniper's)," September 1943.
TM 5-9341. "Sniperscope M2," June 1945.

Correspondence and Interviews

The following individuals gave freely of their knowledge, experience, recollections, personal papers, and research time. Without their support, candor, and hard work, this book would not have been possible.

INDIVIDUALS
Lee V. Abbott, Queensland, Australia
Stephen E. Atkins, College Station, Texas
Bob Aylward, Fort Benning, Georgia
Colonel Roger H. Barnard, USMC (Ret.), Quantico, Virginia
General George S. Blanchard, USA (Ret.), McLean, Virginia
Major General A. R. Bolling Jr., USA (Ret.), Dallas, Texas
Frank J. Camper, Dolomite, Alabama
David K. Canfil, Oxford, England
Master Sergeant Roy F. Chandler, USA (Ret.), St. Mary's City, Maryland

Sergeant Major Dan Cragg, USA (Ret.), Springfield, Virginia
John J. Culbertson, Oklahoma City, Oklahoma
General Raymond G. Davis, USMC (Ret.), Stockbridge, Georgia
General Michael S. Davison, USA (Ret.), Arlington, Virginia
Richard P. DeMarco, North Royalton, Ohio
Colonel James A. Donovan, USMC (Ret.), Atlanta, Georgia
Ed W. Eaton, Walla Walla, Washington
Lieutenant General Julian J. Ewell, USA (Ret.), Fort Belvoir, Virginia
Lieutenant Colonel James Fitter, USA (Ret.), Fairfax, Virginia
Thomas R. Hargrove, Galveston, Texas
William J. Houser, Hinsdale, Illinois
Major General Kenneth J. Houghton, USMC (Ret.), La Jolla, California
First Lieutenant Peter Joannides, USA (Ret.), McLean, Virginia
Lieutenant General William K. Jones, USMC (Ret.), Alexandria, Virginia
Brigadier General Frederick J. Karch, USMC (Ret.), Arlington, Virginia
First Lieutenant David Kasten, USA, Glendale, Arizona
General P. X. Kelley, USMC (Ret.), Arlington, Virginia
General Walter T. Kerwin Jr., USA (Ret.), Alexandria, Virginia
General Frederick J. Kroesen, USA (Ret.), Falls Church, Virginia
Ed Kugler, Spring, Texas
Major Jim Land, USMC (Ret.), Woodbridge, Virginia
Lieutenant Colonel James W. Lanning, USA (Ret.), San Marcos, Texas
Bill Laurie, Mesa, Arizona
H. R. (Lefty) Luster, Naturita, California
Major General S. H. Matheson, USA (Ret.), Carmel, California
Lieutenant General William J. McCaffrey, USA (Ret.), Alexandria, Virginia
JoAnna M. McDonald, Carlisle, Pennsylvania
Mike Monfrooe, Bemidji, New Mexico
Jack Murphy, Croydon, Pennsylvania
Lieutenant General Herman Nickerson Jr., USMC (Ret.), Jacksonville, North
    Carolina
Major Willis L. Powell, USA (Ret.), Columbus, Georgia
Donn R. Proven, Glenview, Illinois
Lieutenant Colonel Jim Reid, USMC (Ret.), Fallbrook, California
Rick Reynolds, Albuquerque, New Mexico
Lieutenant General Elvy B. Roberts, USA (Ret.), San Francisco, California
Terry B. Roderick, Cocoa, Florida
General W. B. Rosson, USA (Ret.), Salem, Virginia
Ray Sautter, Long Beach, California
Captain Scott R. Schoner, USA, Fort Campbell, Kentucky
Lieutenant General Ormond R. Simpson, USMC (Ret.), Bryan, Texas
Gary Smith, Perrin, Texas
James W. Sotherland, Glen Allen, Virginia
Major General Paul F. Smith, USA (Ret.), Melbourne, Florida
Lawrence W. Tahler, Whitefish, Montana
Brigadier General Joseph R. Ulatoski, USA (Ret.), Bellevue, Washington

Joseph T. Ward, Lafayette, Colorado
Ray Weiner, Roselle, Illinois
General William C. Westmoreland, USA (Ret.), Charleston, South Carolina
General Fred C. Weyand, USA (Ret.), Honolulu, Hawaii
Gary M. White, Phoenix, Arizona
Colonel Nevin Williams, USA (Ret.), Carmichael, California
Major General Ellis W. Williamson, USA (Ret.), Arlington, Virginia
Darryl Young, Carmel, California

Archives, Museums, Libraries, Installations

The staffs of the following assisted in the search for documents and provided papers and other information that contributed to this study:

Don R. Pratt Museum, Fort Campbell, Kentucky
Department of the Army, General Officer Management Office,
    Washington, D.C.
Department of the Navy, Office of Information, Washington, D.C.
Library of Congress, Washington, D.C.
Los Angeles Public Library, Los Angeles, California
Pentagon Library, Washington, D.C.
Phoenix Public Library, Phoenix, Arizona
Public Affairs Office, Fort Campbell, Kentucky
Public Affairs Office, Fort Benning, Georgia
Public Affairs Office, NAB Coronado, California
Public Affairs Office, Quantico, Virginia
Public Affairs Office, Schofield Barracks, Hawaii
Redcatcher, Inc., McLean, Virginia
Scottsdale Public Library, Scottsdale, Arizona
Southwest Business, Industry, and Rehabilitation Association, Phoenix,
    Arizona
U.S. Army Marksmanship Unit, Fort Benning, Georgia
U.S. Army Military History Institute, Carlisle Barracks, Pennsylvania
U.S. Army Public Affairs Office, Washington, D.C.
U.S. Army Recruiting Command, Phoenix, Arizona
U.S. Marine Corps Public Affairs, Washington, D.C.
U.S. Marine Corps Museum and Library, Washington, D.C.
U.S. Marine Corps Recruiting Station, Phoenix, Arizona
U.S. Marine Corps University, Quantico, Virginia
U.S. Naval Institute, Annapolis, Maryland

✳✳✳✳✳✳✳✳

Index